The Borough Park Papers

SYMPOSIUM I

The Gospel and the Jewish People

The Borough Park Papers

SYMPOSIUM I
The Gospel and the Jewish People

October 8 – 10, 2007

Borough Park Symposium
An imprint of
Messianic Jewish Publishers
Clarksville, MD 21029

2020 7

Library of Congress Control Number: 2012951378

ISBN 978-1-936716-59-3

The Borough Park Papers, Symposium 1

The Gospel and the Jewish People

Printed in the United States of America

Published by

Borough Park Symposium

An imprint of

Messianic Jewish Publishers

6120 Day Long Lane

Clarksville, Maryland 21029

Distributed by

Messianic Jewish Resources Int'l.

www.messianicjewish.net

Individual and Trade Order line: 800-410-7367

Email: lederer@messianicjewish.net

******

COVER DESCRIPTION:

"Brooklyn Bridge with Manhattan buildings in background by night" (purchased from istockphotos.com)

The Brooklyn Bridge connects Brooklyn, New York with downtown Manhattan. Brooklyn is home to many Orthodox Jews who have not recognized Yeshua as their promised Messiah … yet.

******

TABLE OF CONTENTS

HOW THE BOROUGH PARK SYMPOSIUM CAME TO BE AND WHAT IT IS

The Borough Park Steering Committee

The time had come for leaders across the organizational spectrum of the Messianic Jewish/Jewish Missions world to unite as members of the Jewish community, leaders of a Remnant, with a responsibility to the God who called us his chosen people. On October 19-20, 2006 ten Messianic Jewish colleagues met in Brooklyn, New York. We agreed on a direction, a Steering Committee, and shared convictions that would determine who should actively participate:

> *We are Jews who believe in Yeshua and in God's covenant with Israel, and as members of the Jewish community, are committed to the welfare of our people.*
>
> *We feel compelled by the spirit of God to advance the good news of Yeshua among our people.*
>
> *We desire to preserve the unity and secure the future of the Messianic Jewish movement and our common mission through respectful dialogue, without acrimony, even in the face of critical disagreements.*
>
> *We believe in the authority of Scripture and the deity of Yeshua, and that eternal life is the gift of God in Messiah Yeshua our Lord.*

Since we held our planning meeting in an Orthodox Jewish hotel in the Borough Park neighborhood of Brooklyn, our setting provided a great name for this consultation—"the Borough Park Symposium." We scheduled it for a year later, October 2007, and chose a topic that we knew would be controversial, but which seemed like a logical starting point for our dialogue: *The Gospel and the Jewish People*.

When the symposium arrived, we discussed the nature of the gospel itself, how it applies specifically to Jewish people, and what outreach should look like in light of all this. Participants were impassioned, and not afraid of ideological clash or of expressing agreement when it was there. Leaders who had staked out opposite ends of the Messianic Jewish spectrum years earlier now sat down together and talked. Indeed, several leaders reconnected with colleagues with whom they hadn't spoken, for one reason or another, for twenty or thirty years.

When the Steering Committee evaluated the Symposium, we determined that it was a big success, not only in discussing the issues, but also in helping to "preserve the unity and secure the future of the Messianic Jewish movement and our common mission through respectful dialogue." Although we didn't want the Symposium to become institutionalized into an annual event, we started to think about a second one. The Steering Committee met in May 2008 and chose a topic that we imagined to be less controversial among us, *The Deity of Messiah and the Mystery of God.*

Paradoxically, this is the issue most controversial in the wider Jewish community, the boundary-marker that the Jewish community has set for centuries to define itself. No matter how Jewish in all other ways a person might be, a Jewish gatekeeper might say, belief in the deity of Yeshua, by itself, drives him or her out of Judaism into Christianity. And Messianic Jews are problematic (and even to be feared) because they refuse to accept that they've crossed this line.

From this perspective, all of us who gathered for BPS II, as diverse as we might have been, were on the same side of the divide, despite our differences, and even despite our lack of precise definition of the deity of Messiah. Our goal in meeting was not to produce a precise theological definition, but to discuss how we can embrace and share the truth of the deity of Messiah specifically as Jews. How do we respond to questions we often hear from non-Messianic Jewish friends? "Are you telling us to worship a man as God?" "Can it possibly be right for a Jew to acknowledge a Messiah who claims (or whose followers claim for him) to somehow be God?" "Why are you trying to bring such a non-Jewish idea into Judaism?" Much was accomplished by hearing the thoughts of others in our Community.

A clear benefit of the Symposium was the heightened sense of unity that came out of this event. Some of the panels included speakers who had been in robust debates with each other in recent years, who had widely different perspectives, and yet, at the Symposium, communicated with the greatest respect and deference. There were disagreements on many specific points, but an underlying sense prevailed that we are all in this together—marking out new territory as Jews who recognize the unique nature of the Messiah of Israel. It is our hope that this renewed awareness of our underlying unity will help the entire Messianic Jewish community to move forward. As one of the Steering Committee members remarked afterwards, "I guess this BPS Symposium was about more than our theology!"

With that irenic spirit, a third symposium was set for October 22-24, 2012 in which the Steering Committee decided to tackle the subject: How Jewish Should Messianic Judaism Be?" This may seem like a question with an obvious answer, but when you look at the topics in BPS III, you'll see that there are varied views. Talks are underway to hold future symposiums, perhaps on Israel and other topics that are vital to our people.

No one expected that we'd ever have total agreement, but in the larger scope of things, we have more in common with each other than many other people in the world. We are Jews who all agree that Yeshua is the Messiah. We all believe that our people are the chosen people. We all hold that the Land of Israel was uniquely given, and still belongs to, the Jewish people. We all accept the Torah, and its obligations upon us as Jews, to one degree or another. Compared to the entire 6.6 billion people in the world, we have more in common with each other than many other groups in the world.

That's why these symposiums are so important. Our numbers are small, but great things can happen as we learn how to listen and work together. There's strength in unity. That's why we agreed that:

> The purpose of the Symposiums is to provide a forum for members of the broader Messianic Jewish community to articulate their beliefs with an expectation that they will receive a respectful hearing, but without the expectation that agreement concerning these beliefs will be achieved. The Symposium is designed to provide an internal platform for leaders to

better understand each another and the various positions held within the Messianic movement.

So, as you read one or more of the papers in the Borough Park Symposiums, you may be challenged. You may read papers that present both sides of an argument, with few, if any, conclusions drawn. This is the way of the Jewish people.

In the Second Temple era, the time of Yeshua, there were quite a few sects of Judaism—Pharisees, Sadducees, Essenes, Zealots, Herodians, and more, but they were all considered, and considered themselves, to be Jews. Judaism then was like Judaism today—pluralistic. Orthodox, Conservative, Reform, Reconstructionist, Hasidic, Zionistic branches may disagree today on many matters, but all see themselves as part of the same people—the nation of Israel, the Jewish people.

That's the way we in the Borough Park Symposiums see ourselves—Jews, albeit Messianic Jews. We are getting more comfortable talking about serious issues, in the hope of understanding God and his revelation better. You are invited to "read over our shoulders" as we have these discussions, much like when you read the New Testament, which also records discussions Jews had about critical issues. Please just remember that you are "listening in" and our discussions may not fit into your previously held pre-suppositions. You may need some paradigm shifting in your thinking.

There were response papers given to most of the papers in this volume. They can be read, as can the papers, on line at:

http://www.boroughparksymposium.com
or
http://www.boroparksymposium.com

We're pleased you are interested in the discussions we in the Messianic Jewish community are having. We believe that you will be challenged to think about these issues alongside us.

For more information, email info@boroughparksymposium.com.

The Borough Park Symposium Steering Committee

WELCOME AND INTRODUCTION

Barry Rubin, M.A., CPA
Rabbi of Emmanuel Messianic Jewish Congregation, Clarksville, Md.
President and CEO of The Lederer Foundation,
Messianic Jewish Publishers and Resources

Shalom and welcome to the Borough Park Symposium, right here in Queens, New York. No, this is not Borough Park. That story will be told to you shortly. You'll find it interesting.

So, here we are, not far from Shea Stadium, the home of the New York Mets, one of the two professional baseball teams in this city. Sadly for Mets fans, they aren't in the post-season playoffs. That doesn't bother me, much, since I've been a fan of the other team, the New York Yankees, since I was born, having spent my formative month in the Bronx. As a Yankee fan, I must say that I'm glad that the Bronx Bombers made it into the post season again. It's just how it ought to be, don't you think?

With the theme of baseball in mind, I want to suggest something. At a baseball game, there are two competing teams on the field, around 100 players, coaches, umpires, batboys, etc., being watched by millions and millions of people. While the fans watch, the teams go at it. But, in a sense, the players are on the same side. Why do I say this?

As long as the games stay interesting—as long as baseball attracts fans and support, these ball players are fulfilling their childhood fantasies. Nearly every boy imagines playing pro baseball at one time in his life. So, as long as they get to play on some team, they're happy. Yes, the ball clubs compete, but it's even more important to make sure that the game itself remains popular. That's why ball players are usually very friendly with one another, even in the middle of an intense game. It looks like they're asking each other if they have plans after the game. You see, they know that, win or lose, they all win in the long run. They get to play baseball. Although they may be on different teams, they are really on the same one—baseball.

In a way, our symposium is a little like that. We may be on different theological teams, we may have different ways of operating, but we're all in the same "game," the effort to promote the Kingdom of God among our people. We're really on the same team.

Some of us call ourselves Messianic Jews, others, Hebrew Christians. Some of us are missionaries, some rabbis. Some are dispensational; others lean toward covenant theology. Still others would classify themselves differently.

Yet, no matter what we call ourselves, no matter how many ways we find ourselves to be different from others in this group, the Jewish community and the Church see us pretty much as members of "the Jews that follow Jesus (or Yeshua if they've been clued in to the way many of us talk) team." To outsiders, we're all pretty much the same. To the spectators, our differences don't matter much. In fact, one might say that to the outside world, we barely qualify to play in the major leagues.

According to the latest census, there are approximately 6.6 billion people in the world today. Of that number, only around 13 million are Jews, that's only two tenths of one percent of the world's population (.002). For the sake of discussion, if we assume that Jews in Messianic congregations and churches total 100,000, we're only .007 of the Jewish people, or .000015 of the world's population. We are minor leaguers, no matter how major we think we, our organizations, our missions are.

I'm not saying this to be discouraging or disparaging. In fact, Messianic Jews haven't been so noticed by our people since the first centuries of the Common Era. The word is out—there are Jewish people who follow Yeshua, believing him to be the Messiah. In the Christian world, Messianic Jews are having major successes: God is bringing us into positions of influence—seminary professors, TV and radio show hosts, speakers to huge international conferences, authors, etc. I don't have to tell you how amazing our success stories have been, but that's in our eyes. Even with our successes, to the non-Messianic Jews, as well as the vast majority of those who call themselves Christians, we're still only in the minor leagues. That's why this symposium is so important. As we learn how to listen and work together, we will accomplish much more than the sum total of what we're all doing separately. We all know how easy it is to break a small stick. Yet, when enough sticks are put together, the task becomes more and more difficult. There's strength in unity.

The primary purpose of the Borough Park Symposium is to provide a forum for members of the broader Messianic Jewish community to articulate their beliefs with an expectation that they will receive a respectful hearing, but without the expectation that agreement concerning these beliefs will be achieved. The Symposium is designed to provide an *internal* platform for leaders to better understand one another and the various positions held within the Messianic movement.

The Borough Park Steering Committee thought that if we can help us all listen to each other we might build more cooperation and understanding to help us accomplish our shared goal. Many brilliant minds have devoted countless numbers of hours to reading, to studying, to researching, to thinking and to writing their views on issues that concern us all. A lot goes into our desire to express what we believe to be true, but where we sometimes go wrong is to behave as though we "own" *the* Truth and others are just plain wrong. This causes division in our small community, something that we cannot afford and something that goes against the instructions of the team's manager. Yeshua haMashiach challenges us to be unified and loving toward one another, to the glory of God. What a statement that would be to our people and the Church!

Isn't it amazing how many disagreements we can have? These are ultimately important for us as individual leaders because they help us refine our thinking, as "iron sharpens iron." They matter since sometimes they serve as correctives if we're somewhat, or a lot, off track. But, our differences shouldn't separate us, which too often they do. We are a miniscule movement, and because we are small, we need to be unified.

We may be comfortably ensconced in our respective organizations, whether they are schools, missions, congregations, etc., but we are connected (whether we like it or not) to one another. We are connected even though we may seriously disagree with each other, but is that so unique among our people? If we didn't disagree, one might ask if we really are Jews. It's just how we Jews are. Through respectful dialogue, even disagreement, we can all think more clearly and understand each other more fully.

The Steering Committee of the BPS organized this event to help us get past our disunity and move more toward unity, not uniformity, if not in our theology, then in our relationships.

A few years ago, I was talking with my good friend, Mitch Glaser, about the struggle between the mission and congregation worlds. This conflict didn't seem necessary or useful. In fact, it was counterproductive. More can be done through cooperation than competition. Since CPM was involved in both missionary and congregation planting work, I thought this idea would resonate with him. I'm very glad that Mitch and David Sedaca and their staff, invited a bunch of us to meet in Borough Park last fall to discuss the viability of such a symposium. And now, we're all here. You might say it's a minor miracle that we're all sitting down and talking together. Wouldn't you agree?

In baseball, the leadoff hitter's job is to get on base so other batters can move him around the bases to score. I am honored to get our conference on base. Let me tell you who's on deck. David Rudolph has prepared a well thought out paper that will help guide our discussions. We might call them our "rules of the game." Let's face it: There are no slouches among this group. Each one of us could hold his or her own in any theological ball game. But, that's not what we're trying to do. If any one of us tries to win at the expense of others, we all lose. We don't need to prove how right our theological points of views are; we all *know* that each one of us is right or we wouldn't be who we are. What we need to do is hear each other, understand each other, and respect each other. David's paper will help us do just that.

Following David in the lineup will be Mitch Glaser, who has written a challenging paper that we will all identify with, in one way or another. Mitch's paper offers some provocative points for us to consider, not the least of which is the amazing growth of the Messianic Jewish community. We may still be small, but Mitch will remind us of just how small we once were so we can thank God for so how far we've come. We'll also be challenged to seek ways to enlarge the tent pegs of our movement through his words.

Each of the three sessions, tomorrow morning, tomorrow afternoon, and Wednesday morning, will have a moderator, or should I say, an umpire. Knowing that there might be some controversial presentations made, the moderator is to call balls and strikes, and determine if someone is safe and out. Remember there is no arguing with the umpire, no kicking dirt on his feet, no throwing of objects … or you may be ejected and have to watch the rest of the conference from the locker room.

Actually, we need to start praying for these moderators now since we know how we can be, sometimes. I believe that if we let them guide our conversation, we'll have some excellent, productive discussions.

To clarify, each presentation should be no more than twenty minutes long. Then there'll be a five-minute clarification period. After all the papers for any one session are given, there'll be a fifteen-minute break and then an hour to an hour and a half discussion about the papers.

We are asking everyone to raise their hands and get called on so we can keep things running smoothly. We also don't want to have any interruptions of the speakers. We will make a list of those people who want to speak and will call on each of them in turn. Once we get through about five or so questions, we'll call for other questions and make a new list. We will favor those people who haven't spoken, in calling on people. All questions and discussions should be only 2-3 minutes long.

So, tomorrow morning's session will be "The Gospel Message" and we'll hear from Rachel Wolf, Stuart Dauermann, and Arnold Fruchtenbaum. The afternoon session will be about "Salvation and the Jewish People" and our speakers will be John Fischer, Michael Rydelnik, and Mark Kinzer. Then, on Wednesday morning, "Presenting the Gospel to our Jewish People" will be the theme, with papers presented by Tsvi Sadan, Sam Nadler, Susan Perlman, and Vladimir Pikman. After our lunch break, Jason Sobel and Joel Chernoff will offer some thoughts about "The Future of our Movement." Then, David Sedaca will be the closer, wrapping everything up with some comments and an evaluation form for you to fill out.

I don't know about you, but I think we're going to have an awesome series, uh, symposium. Let's appreciate the intellectual stimulation that comes from these papers, enjoy the fellowship with fellow ballplayers, seek the spiritual growth that might come from our time together. Who knows, we might even change our minds a little about some of these issues, but, even if we don't, it's truly worth getting together to listen to each other with an open mind and heart. After all, we are a unique community of brothers and sisters.

May we be like those Jews of the Jerusalem Council who met so many centuries ago to deliberate about some controversial matters. They were all pretty intense about their convictions, perhaps wondering if the others were really true followers of Yeshua. "After all," they might have thought, "how can they be since they disagree with *me*?" But, the Ruach HaKodesh overruled their differences and they were able to continue in fellowship together and launch the Gospel throughout the world. May God help us do the same and be pleased with us as we talk about the Gospel. Now, let's "Play ball."

GUIDELINES FOR HEALTHY THEOLOGICAL DISCUSSION

David Rudolph, Ph.D.
Assistant Professor of Bible and Theology at
Messianic Jewish Theological Institute,
Chair of the Theology Committee of the
Union of Messianic Jewish Congregations.

When I learned that this session was entitled "Guidelines for Healthy Theological Discussion," the story of Michael Wyschogrod's meeting with Karl Barth came to mind. As a little background, Michael Wyschogrod is an Orthodox Jewish theologian who lives in New York City. Karl Barth was a Swiss Reformed theologian and one of the most influential Christian thinkers of the 20th century. Michael Wyschogrod writes of his meeting with Barth:

> On a sunny morning in August 1966 I visited Barth in his modest home on the Bruderholzallee in Basel. He had been told that I was a "Jewish Barthian," and this amused him to no end. We spoke about various things and at one point he said: "You Jews have the promise but not the fulfillment; we Christians have both promise and fulfillment." Influenced by the banking atmosphere of Basel, I replied: "With human promises, one can have the promise but not the fulfillment. The one who promises can die, or change his mind, or not fulfill his promise for any number of reasons. But a promise of God is like money in the bank. If we have his promise, we have its fulfillment and if we do not have the fulfillment we do not have the promise." There was a period of silence and then he said, "You know, I never thought of it that way."[1]

This is a very inspiring story to me because here one of the most distinguished Christian theologians of the 20th century says, "You know, I never thought of it that way." My hope for this symposium is that we would all leave here on Wednesday having said at least once, "You know, I never thought of it that way." The ability to say these words is a sign of healthy theological discussion.

This evening, with your permission, I would like to address the subject—guidelines for healthy theological discussion. In Part One, we will focus on the power of our words and the importance of using our tongues to impart life and not death. In Part II, we will discuss how we can move toward "thinking together" as leaders (and away from merely talking to each other *or at each other*) in theological discussion.

Part I. The Power of Our Words In *Leviticus Rabbah*, the Midrash states:

One of the ancient rabbis sent his servant to the market with the general instruction, "Buy the best thing there that one can eat!" The servant returned with a tongue. Later, the rabbi asked him to go back to the market to buy the worst thing that one could eat. The servant again came back with a tongue. "What is with you?" asked the rabbi. "Here, I've asked you to buy both the best and the worst, and you come back with a couple of tongues." "That's true," responded the servant. "After all, cannot a tongue be one of the best things in the world and an evil tongue be one of the worst?" (*Lev. Rab.* 33).

What is the biblical principle behind the servant's perspective?

Proverbs 12:18 says, "Reckless words pierce like a sword, but the tongue of the wise brings מַרְפֵּא (healing or health)."

Proverbs 18:21 puts it this way, "מָוֶת וְחַיִּים בְּיַד־לָשׁוֹן (Death and life are in the power of the tongue)."

In every theological discussion, there is the potential to speak words that build up and words that tear down. Contrary to the view of some, theological discussion cannot be academically partitioned off from spiritual life in the name of "symposium" or "Jewish debate." We need to ask ourselves the question every time we open our mouths publicly (and privately), "Is there death or life in what I am about to say?" To underscore this point (and I am speaking especially to myself), I would like to pass on an observation that Rabbi Joseph Telushkin makes in his book *Words That Hurt, Words That Heal*. In his Introduction, he writes:

> Think about your own life: Unless you, or someone dear to you, have been the victim of terrible, physical violence, chances are the worst pains you have suffered in life have come from words used cruelly—from ego-destroying criticism, excessive anger, sarcasm, public and private humiliation, hurtful nicknames, betrayal of secrets, rumors and malicious gossip … We choose our clothes more carefully than we choose our words, though what we say *about* and *to* others can define them indelibly. That is why ethical speech—speaking fairly of others, honestly about others, and carefully to everyone—is so important. If we keep the power of words in the foreground of our consciousness, we will handle them as carefully as we would a loaded gun.[2]

At this symposium, some will give papers. Others will be moderators. Others will participate in the discussion times. All of us will talk at break times. This symposium is an extraordinary opportunity for dialogue that cuts across the spectrum of the broader Messianic Jewish community.

We share a lot in common, more than we realize. We can build something here that is of lasting value for the Lord, something we can leave for the next generation. Let's not blow it. Let's remember that words (*devarim*) are things. They can create, as in Genesis 1, or they can destroy as in Revelation 22. We need to be careful what we say and how we say it (not to be politically correct but to honor Yeshua who bought us at a price; we are not our own).

Once I publicly and needlessly embarrassed a friend of mine, what our sages call *halvanat panim* (turning someone's face white). I repented after my friend pointed out my sin but there was no way to nullify the soul-piercing impact of my words and the temporal damage done to our relationship. Once arrows are shot, they cannot be called off. May none of us commit the sin of *halvanat panim* at this symposium.

Having said this, most of the theological discussion that will take place over the next two days will not be in this hall. It will be in more private settings: at restaurants, in our hotel rooms, in the car, at the airport. In these one-on-one settings, when we are with trusted friends and no one else, let us commit ourselves not to speak words that are "derogatory or potentially harmful" to others (Finkelman and Berkowitz, 50), even if they are true, even if they are said discreetly. Let us also commit ourselves not to listen to such words. As the Talmud says, "Why do human fingers resemble pegs? So that if one hears something unseemly, one can plug one's fingers in one's ears" (*b. Ketubot* 5b). If we do this, our friends will understand. That is what being a good friend is all about.

Rabbi Telushkin reminds us:

> In a dispute with someone, you have the right to state your case, express your opinion, explain why you think the other party is wrong, and even make clear how passionately you feel about the subject at hand. But these are the only rights you have. You do not have amoral right to undercut your adversary's position by invalidating him or her personally.[3]

Let us remember the power of our words and ask the critical question, "Is there life or death in what I am about to say?" This brings us to—

Part II. "Thinking Together" in Theological Discussion

We have come from all over the world to talk about the בְּשׂוֹרָה (the good news, the gospel) and how we should present it to our people. It is easy to think of the בְּשׂוֹרָה as only a spoken message, but I would like to put forward for your consideration the possibility that **the spoken message of the** בְּשׂוֹרָה should be a natural extension of **the crucified** **בָּשָׂר (the crucified flesh) that proclaims it and embodies it.**[4] We testify to the truth of the gospel message by being men and women who live crucified and resurrected lives in Messiah. And we invalidate the gospel message when we do not.

We are to be imitators of Paul who said, "I have been crucified with Messiah; and it is no longer I who live, but it is Messiah who lives in me. And the life I now live in the flesh (בָּשָׂר/σάρξ) I live by faith in the Son of God, who loved me and gave himself for me" (Gal 2:19-20). Paul was a living expression of the gospel message that he proclaimed. And like Paul, we are called to be living expressions of the gospel message that we proclaim.

What are the implications of this for healthy theological discussion? If it is correct that the spoken message of the בְּשׂוֹרָה should be a natural extension of the crucified בָּשָׂר **(the crucified flesh) that proclaims it and embodies it**, then it is the height of hypocrisy for us to talk about the gospel for two days and not seek to live out the gospel in our relationships with one another. Lord, help us to live out your בְּשׂוֹרָה among us.

How do we live out the gospel practically in our symposium context? I would like to suggest that we do so by adopting a humble stance toward one another, seeing our relationship with each person here as one characterized by interdependence. We practically live out the gospel when we are "thinking together," for this leads, as Paul puts it in Philippians 1:27, to "standing firm in one spirit, striving side by side with one mind for the faith of the gospel."

What do I mean by "thinking together"? I would like to suggest a number of ways that we can conscientiously move in the direction of thinking together:

First, we can listen before speaking. We can try to fully understand the other person's point of view.

Second, we can view ourselves as students, even if others think of us as teachers. Thinking together about the gospel and so teriology begins with the humble acknowledgement that we do not know everything about this subject. We all have a lot to learn and we can learn from each other. This is what interdependence is all about. Remember, one of the most renowned theologians of the 20th century could say, "You know, I never thought of it that way."

Third, we can adopt a holistic approach to truth. A holistic approach to truth avoids one-sided statements and concerns itself with the whole, including limitations and factors that affect implementation. As Klyne Snodgrass writes in his book *Between Two Truths*:

> Truth is like a flower with deep roots. To enjoy it very long, we must take it all. If we take only the top part, it will wither in our hands … Holistic thinking will cause us to look for tensions. *When we know that a statement is true, we ought to ask what its limitations are, what other statements need to be made to prevent misunderstanding or extremism, and how circumstances might affect the implementation of the statement.* (Italics mine)[5]

Fourth, we can choose not to rehearse old thoughts and feelings. Thinking together involves *thinking* and not simply rehearsing what we have long believed and taught. In theological discussions, we can fall into the habit of playing old tape recordings back and forth to each other. We may be talking but not really thinking. William Isaacs, in his book *Dialogue and the Art of Thinking Together*, writes:

> What is true thinking? To think truly is to say things that may surprise us—things we have not said before—that are not in our memory … To think is also to listen to our own automatic reactions and gain perspective on them. It is to ask, Now, why did I do that? … What we usually call thinking is often merely the reporting or acting out of patterns already in our memory. Like a prerecorded tape, these thoughts (and feelings) are instantly ready for playback … True thinking moves more slowly, more gently than this … Thinking has a freshness to it, like a flow of water softly moving through the mind, and requires space. The fruit of thinking is sometimes a seemingly simple, quiet idea that stands out among a crowd of passing thoughts. It arrives unannounced.[6]

Here is a good question to ask yourself: "How much of my 'thinking' comes from memory and is an automatic response? How much is based on original thinking about the present circumstances?"

Fifth, we can contribute questions. One of the best ways to stimulate thinking together is to ask questions. Rather than making statements, we can raise questions that spark all parties in the conversation to think more deeply. For example, one of the important questions we can ask in a group is, "Whose perspective are we disregarding or not paying proper attention to in this discussion?"

Sixth, we can acknowledge our vulnerability. We are sometimes tempted to emphasize the strength of our position and the weakness of the other's position while deep down knowing that there is weakness in our own position. We do not acknowledge our own position's weakness because we do not want the other party to exploit it. "Thinking together" involves each party in the conversation being willing to express the strengths, weaknesses and underlying presuppositions of their own case. This involves a measure of trust. We should avoid withholding information relevant to the discussion. When each party can honestly articulate the potential vulnerability and imbalance in his or her own position, the situation is ripe for new and creative ideas to be generated through thinking together.

Seventh, we can follow the disturbance. When our listening is being colored by a disturbance (perhaps something the other person has said that rubs us the wrong way or a negative memory), it is helpful to follow the disturbance and ask why we are bothered. This often leads to true thinking. By considering the source of the disturbance—whether it is in us, from them, or both—and why it irritates us, we become more keenly aware of what the person is actually saying. We may also recognize a tendency in us to respond to the disturbance by listening in a selective way—we may find ourselves instinctively sifting what they have said for evidence that we are right and they are wrong. Sometimes reframing helps. We can choose to see the person who disturbs us as a protector of important values within our movement rather than a nuisance. Following the disturbance may lead us to see our own inconsistency—we may realize that we have the same problem as the person whose words disturb us.

Eighth, we can avoid abstraction wars. Abstract points often elicit abstract counterpoints. Thinking together requires resisting the temptation to speak or write in generalizations. This means thinking about what we want to say before we say it. It means asking the question, "Is this too abstract? What is my real point?"

Ninth, we can view each other as team members. "Thinking together" in our symposium context involves viewing the other parties in the conversation as teammates. We are working together for the Lord. We are all part of the body of Messiah with Yeshua as the head. God has designed us to complement each other with our different gifts and perspectives. We fit together and need each other. Let me say that again, "We need each other." When we think by ourselves, and find little to no value in the contributions of others, we fragment the team. When we think together, we contribute to the unity of the team, and this pleases the Lord.

These are all suggested guidelines for healthy theological discussion at the symposium. In a nutshell, remember the power of words. Ask yourself the critical question, "Is there life or death in what I am about to say?" Live out the *besorah* (the gospel) you proclaim in the way you relate to other members of the symposium. Adopt a humble stance characterized by interdependence. Move in the direction of "thinking together." And belike Karl Barth in your willingness to step back and say, "You know, I never thought of it that way."

Endnotes

1. Michael Wyschogrod, *Abraham's Promise: Judaism and Jewish-Christian Relations* (ed. R. Kendall Soulen; Grand Rapids: Eerdmans, 2004), 211.
2. Joseph Telushkin, *Words That Hurt, Words That Heal: How to Choose Words Wisely and Well* (New York: Harper, 1996), xviii, 4-5.
3. Telushkin, 89.
4. The word for "messenger" in Hebrew is מְבַשֵּׂר.
5. Klyne Snodgrass, *Between Two Truths: Living with Biblical Tensions* (Grand Rapids: Zondervan, 1990), 180-84.
6. William Isaacs, Dialogue and the Art of Thinking Together: A Pioneering Approach to Communicating in Business and in Life (New York: Currency, 1999), 59-60.

BOROUGH PARK SYMPOSIUM OPENER TO THE FIRST SYMPOSIUM

Mitch Glaser, Ph.D.
President of Chosen People Ministries,
co-recipient of *Christianity Today* magazine's 2009 Award of Merit in the Apologetics/Evangelism category for the book
To The Jew First: The Case for Jewish Evangelism in Scripture and History

How many of you remember the days when you felt like you were the only Jewish believer in Yeshua in the world? It feels like yesterday! Isn't it wonderful to know that our children will not feel the same way? We have come along way *Bubby*! The Messianic movement has a bright and promising future.

And yet, I believe this Symposium comes at a critical juncture in time and that some of what happens here will help chart the future course of our Messianic movement.

I pray that our discussions will help clarify our various positions, build better personal relationships between us and take some of the tension out of the air. I do not want to minimize or simplify our differences and the deep concerns we have with one another both theologically and in the ways we express ourselves as Jewish followers of Yeshua.

But, when you think about it, if we called for a conference of this nature years ago, we would have had very few people show up. Instead, our planning committee has gone through a very difficult process of deciding whom we would invite to this event! We have so many gifted, mature and thoughtful Messianic leaders among us today. It is just too bad that you all do not perfectly agree with me!

Brothers and sisters, we live in a very different time than we did a few decades ago. There are now many of us who are Jewish and believe in Yeshua. We are in the midst of raising a new generation of sons and daughters who affirm their Jewish-ness and also follow Yeshua as Messiah. Some of us even have grandchildren who know they are Jewish and believe in Yeshua!

Because of the contributions of many in this room tonight, we know we are not alone and that God is still committed to His covenant promises. So from my perspective—no matter what happens at this Borough Park Symposium—I stand overwhelmed by God's grace and mercy simply because we all are here tonight.

The Messianic Jewish movement is alive! We even have Messianic versions of the Bible and commentaries thanks to David Stern, Arnold Fruchtenbaum and others. We have Siddurs, Machzors thanks to John Fischer, Stuart Dauermann, Barry Budoff and others who I do not have time to mention. We have ongoing alliances, multinational fellowships, conferences, camps, publishing houses and so much more because of the Chernoff family, David Sedaca, Barry Rubin and many others who have contributed so much to our growth. And we have great Messianic music reflecting the contributions of Stuart Dauermann, Marty Goetz, Joel Chernoff, Mark Chopinsky and so many others.

When I became a Jewish believer at age 19 there were less than a half dozen Messianic congregations in the world—and now there are hundreds. I remember when we were accused of various forms of heresy because we believed you could be Jewish and believe in Yeshua and lived in a way where we identified as Jews. Many Christians ask me if I still embrace Jewish traditions and celebrate the Jewish holidays and even if we as a ministry start Messianic congregations. When I say yes, instead of getting a theological third degree I get a smile and am asked if there was some way they could attend a service too.

Last September we held a conference in Germany where we invited Russian Jewish believers who were planting congregations to come and meet one another and participate in what turned out to be an excellent training program. Dear friends, we had almost 90 congregations where Russian was the primary language—and they came from Russia, the Ukraine, Israel, Canada, Australia, the United States and many other countries. What was most remarkable was that not one of these congregations began before 1989.

In Israel we have seen a moving of the Holy Spirit in bringing many Messianic believers back to the Land and now to our delight we are witnesses to the doubling and tripling of the Messianic Jewish community within the Land. Today there are more than a hundred congregations in Israel of every stripe: Hebrew-speaking, Amharic-speaking, Russian-speaking and French- and Spanish-speaking as well. And one day they will all be speaking and conducting their services in

Hebrew as their children assimilate to Israeli culture and become full members of Israeli national life.

We have so much to be thankful for, and certainly the Lord has brought our movement a long way over the last three decades. We are alive as a movement!

Still, we must ask our selves the question: *Are we alive AND well*? I think so. Sort of … somewhat! It depends on your perspective, so allow me to give you my opinion. I want to share my thoughts by means of a chart that might give us all a different look at where we have come from as a movement and help us to know where we are going. I prepared this chart for the LCJE meeting held in Hungary this summer:

Contemporary Jewish Mission and Messianic Jewish History

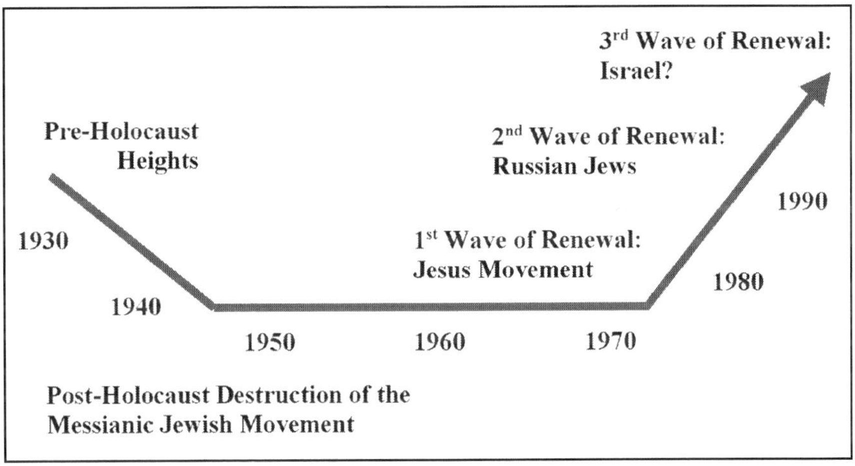

As you can see, we are living in a new day and in my estimation we are at the dawn of a movement, which will one day find its fulfillment as described by Rav Shaul:

> *For I do not desire, brethren, that you should be ignorant of this mystery, lest you should be wise in your own opinion, that blindness in part has happened to Israel until the fullness of the Gentiles has come in. And so all Israel will be saved, as it is written: "The Deliverer will come out of Zion, And He will turn away ungodliness from Jacob; For this is My covenant*

with them, When I take away their sins." (Rom 11:25-27)

From my perspective, we are doing pretty well—as well as can be expected—because we are young. And we are growing—in numbers, in understanding, ability, scholarship, wisdom and in almost every conceivable area where new and dynamic movements tend to and need to grow. Reflect for a moment upon the chart I just showed you. Who would have ever thought the Lord would be working in such power in the modern state of Israel? Sixty years ago, the modern state of Israel did not even exist.

And so, we have much to be thankful for and of course many serious concerns to handle as our worldwide, multi-lingual, multi-cultural movement propels forward on its course to the fulfillment described in Romans 11.

The Holocaust decimated our movement as our leaders were murdered, our congregations and properties brought to ruin. The Holocaust silenced the voices of a generation of young Messianic leaders and nailed the coffins on our more immediate European Messianic future. Hitler snuffed out our schools, congregations, mission stations, libraries and even our corporate sense of Messianic Jewish-ness. A deep chasm resulted, cutting us off from our rich Messianic heritage, which only today is being recreated and renewed to some degree.

Some of you have asked why we wanted to have this conference. May I say it simply? Those of us who planned this event believe we have a duty to repair our Messianic past and to step forward in redeeming the future of our movement. This conference is essentially an act of Tikkun Olam!

We are a vibrant witness—to the Jewish community, the Church and even to those who still seek the destruction of the Jewish people—that we are Jews who love Yeshua, and we are now growing more rapidly than ever before. And if we do not repair the past by accepting our losses and moving forward, we will never be able to assure our Messianic children—our offspring by both natural and spiritual birth—of their divine destiny as the remnant of Israel.

This is why a diverse group of Messianic leaders; including Russ Resnik, Michael Wolf, Barry Rubin, Akiva Cohen, Dave Rosenberg, Mark Kinzer, Stuart Dauermann, Jason Sobel, Andrew Sparks, David Sedaca and myself met in a meeting chaired by a righteous Gentile,

John Holbrook, in an Orthodox Jewish hotel in Borough Park, Brooklyn to see if there was any possibility of organizing a small theological symposium to discuss our very different viewpoints on the issues that are so important to many of us. We agreed that we would not seek to unite, but instead to listen to each other with deference and respect, without acrimony.

We invited others from varying perspectives and eventually reduced our group to a smaller planning team that met a number of times in Borough Park to make this evening become a reality. What a beautiful thing it is to see so many of our Messianic leaders gathered together in one room (sound familiar), because each of us loves Yeshua and cares so deeply about our Jewish people.

I am sorry we could not actually meet in Borough Park, but first of all the hotel was too small and secondly they finally figured us out!! But, we will keep the name!

Brothers and sisters, so many of you have been enthusiastic about coming together because I believe we all understand that we need this meeting at this time—and that what happens here will impact the future of our Messianic movement. We understand, do we not, that any movement that is growing will have growth-related problems. Much of what we have understood as *disunity* during the past few years is in reality signs of life and vigorous spiritual growth. If we were dead, we would not have any problems.

The 21st century Messianic movement is seeking to define itself and you and I are part of this great defining process. We know we are Jews. We know we love Yeshua. We know He is the promised Messiah of Israel, but how we put this all together is a perplexing pilgrimage for each one of us.

I hope this Symposium will go a long way towards helping us get to know one another—both as theological thinkers and as brothers and sisters in the Messiah. I am sure that some of our misunderstandings about one another will be clarified over the next few days. Some of us will come to understand that our differences are smaller than we thought before we came to this gathering. I am also certain that some of us will conclude that our theological differences are far greater than we previously thought. It is the hope of the planning committee that our discussions will produce more light than heat and that in general we will leave having a better understanding of one another at this critical time in the history of our movement. More than anything, we believe a new generation of Messianic Jews are observing us and are not only interested in what we believe but also want to see if knowing Yeshua makes a difference in how we disagree with one another. They want to know if we are capable of contending for truth while at the same time treating one another with both grace and respect.

Brothers and sisters in our beloved Messiah Yeshua, we are moving rapidly towards the culmination of world history when an *end time* Jewish remnant cries out to Yeshua and confesses Him to be Lord of Israel and Lord of all. In the meantime, thousands of Jewish people are coming to know Yeshua as their Messiah. These new believers speak English, Russian, Hebrew, and a host of other languages, and as leaders we need to be part of encouraging and nurturing their spiritual growth. We must provide the next generation with a role model for this Messianic faith and life that is relevant, flexible, encouraging of new ideas, joy-filled and marked by grace yet true to our growing understanding of what it means to be faithful to the living and written Word and as Jews.

Personally, I have already found it a joy just to be in the same room with so many other Jewish people, and especially leaders who love Yeshua. All I can say is Baruch Hashem, times have changed since the day I accepted Yeshua as my Messiah in November of 1970. I don't feel alone any more. It is good to know that He is faithful to His promises and that our Remnant and Messianic community is growing.

A Final Story

Allow me to conclude with a brief story. Earlier, I mentioned a conference for Russian Jewish believers who were planting Messianic congregations, which was held last September in Germany. We have about 100 representatives of more than 85 congregations—all of which had been planted since Perestroika in 1989. The leaders of these congregations came from the Former Soviet Union, Israel, the United States and places with the particle "stan" attached to it that I had never heard of before! We had a wonderful time enjoying one another's fellowship and good teaching—all by Russian Jews—though of course I did not understand more than a word or two. The conference in itself was one of the sure signs that our movement is growing!

But perhaps nothing compared to what took place on Friday afternoon of the conference. We decided to do what every conference does and take a group picture. But, our German director Vladimir Pikman decided that the best place to take the picture would be standing on the steps of the Reichstag! Can you imagine more than a hundred Messianic Jews standing on the stairs of a building that promoted policies of hatred that almost destroyed the our Jewish people.

Not only did we gather for a picture, but we began spontaneously singing Hebrew songs as well. One of them was Hiney Ma Tov, from Psalm 133:1, "How good and pleasant it is for brothers to dwell together in unity." And then we sang another Jewish folk song that is somewhat of a "secondary" national anthem … the words simply say, Am Yisrael, Am Yisrael Chai: The people of Israel will live … the people of Israel will live. It is sung as a chant and in reality is a Jewish rallying cry that testifies to God's faithfulness in not allowing His Chosen People to be destroyed. And we sang that song on the very steps that were walked daily by those planning our destruction.

The entire conference was a powerful testimony to our God who keeps His word and promises. Singing with my brothers and sisters on these steps was a witness for the Lord. In fact, there were a number of people who asked us what we were doing including a number of Israeli tourists and one Jewish couple from New York City. I suppose they did not expect to see 100 Messianic Jews singing Hebrew songs on the steps of the Reichstag!

The Gospel and the Jewish People

The genesis for the current topic, **The Gospel and the Jewish People** was formulated by the committee in response to growing and intensifying conversations related to Messianic soteriology rising within our movement. As a result of various books and conferences the question of whether or not a Jewish person could go to heaven without accepting Yeshua as their personal Messiah was or expressed differently, is it possible for a Jewish people who either had not heard the Gospel or because of circumstances "could not understand" the Gospel but lived a righteous life find a place in heaven? We had found that in our growing movement we did not really know how to discuss this emotionally charged issues in an irenic manner.

Our movement seemed to be producing more heat than light through various on line community discussions and our broad based committee felt there was a great need to understand one another's positions on these more controversial subjects. We did not expect all of our Messianic leaders to agree with one another, but we hoped to reduce the tensions within our growing movement and understood the dire need for face to face to discussion so that the discussions could be held within the framework of closer personal relationships. Additionally, various other issues deemed less controversial, but not less important, begged for further discussion such as; the role of Messianic congregations, public Gospel proclamation, the image of Messianic believers in the Jewish community and other concerns related to Jewish people and the Gospel. It was our hope that the Symposium would be the one place where leaders on every side of these issues, especially those who were Jewish, could come together for honest discussion and either better understand what they agreed with or continue to disagree, but to do so knowledgably and without being contentious.

In retrospect, these goals have been wonderfully accomplished and our movement continues to grow in theological and spiritual maturity. Our relationships have improved and this has been good for the Gospel and especially for our next generation of Messianic leaders, as they have witnessed an example of leaders who are willing to listen to and love one another in spite of some remaining deep and heartfelt disagreements.

WHAT IS OUR MESSAGE?

Rachel Wolf

> *"I have been occupied for some time past with a work which is of immeasurable greatness. I cannot tell today whether I shall bring it to a close. It has the appearance of a gigantic dream."*
>
> —From Theodor Herzl's first entry in his diary, Shavuot 1895, a year before writing his treatise on Zionism

Messianic Judaism is a movement with a message

The Messianic Movement was born of God's spirit, a miraculous birth. Because of the radical life-change most of us experienced, and because of our sense of destiny, our message is intimately connected with how we understand ourselves. Our identity and our message are intertwined. The clarity and content of our message depends on the clarity and content of our identity.

This paper is a bit like origami. It appears to have many angles and sides, but when it is opened up, we find that it is all of one piece. There are three main points. One, we need a message that speaks to the community of Israel, not just to Jewish individuals. Two, we ARE our message; as our identity as Yeshua-followers is more clearly integrated into our Jewish souls, our message will be more authentic and have more authority. Three, our message has to, not only integrate with the Jewish past and present, but communicate a compelling vision, even a gigantic dream, of the crucial calling of the people of Israel in the ongoing story of humanity.

We need to speak, and live, a message that is both relevant and challenging, not only to certain individuals who happen to be Jewish, but to the Jewish community as a whole. This means that our message must address issues of *Jewish community* and Jewish history that are often overlooked—or at best only vaguely considered.

A MESSAGE FOR THE JEWISH COMMUNITY

There are both biblical and cultural reasons to develop a Jewish community gospel—a gospel for the Jewish nation.

Biblical Reasons

First, the original biblical message is one that addresses the Jewish nation. Restoring this biblical message will restore the essential good news to the Good News. What is the good news? "Extra, extra, read all about it!" The headline news is that God has visited us (the Jewish people) as the first "installment" in the restoration of all things! (See, for example, Luke 1:68-75). The enduring hope of Israel—enduring in its modern form even to this day—the hope of justice and peace on earth, is near! "The kingdom of God (the restored kingdom of David) is near!" That is the news—and news of renewal, peace and justice is always good news!

Within this headline story is related good news that many have mistaken for the main story. That is the news that even sinners (those that repent) can participate in this kingdom, or government, of justice and holiness due to the boundless mercy of God, who has provided for us (the nation of Israel) an even better atonement for sin than the method previously provided. In fact, he will transform us on the inside with the creative power of his own spirit. ("I will put my spirit in you and move you to follow my decrees" Ezekiel 36:27).

Without the context of the restoration of the Kingdom of David, of God's government come to earth,[1] of the lion lying down with the lamb, of nations turning their swords into plowshares, the individualistic gospel of forgiveness and going to heaven floats aimlessly in a sea of religious currents. Without the biblical context of the restoration of God's creation with Israel at the center (see Rom 8:19-23), the doctrines of personal forgiveness and justification have come to mean salvation FROM this world, instead of participation in the salvation OF this world. And salvation from this world (to heaven) developed in Christian thought to mean salvation from the carnal practices of the Jews.

Cultural Reasons

Getting the message right in biblical terms is important, but it only gives us a place to begin. Our message is not a mathematical theorem or philosophy that finds its perfection in abstract form. Our message is only successful if it communicates to those for whom it is intended.

If someone asked you, 'What message do you want to leave your children?' how would you answer? Perhaps you would find a scripture like "Trust in the Lord with all your heart, lean not on your own understanding, in all your ways acknowledge him and he will direct your ways" (Prov. 3: 5-7). This gives an excellent life principle that can be put to use in any situation. But the fact is, no matter what message any of us would leave, the words will only be as good as our relationship with that child.

There is a social reality that I believe to be God-given. I call it the "Arm in Arm Principle." Jews stand (metaphorically) linked arm in arm. The Jewish community forms a nearly impenetrable circle as individual Jews stand together with arms linked. Jewish individual have an innate resistance to breaking the communal circle. The last thing we Jews will give up, after we have given up any shred of religious practice or affiliation, is our Jewish identity, our sense of being connected to the historic and present people of Israel.[2]

So far, largely because of sociological and historical factors beyond our control, in order for Jewish people to come to Yeshua, we have had to pull them out of the circle, even while we tell them and generally believe they are still part of the circle. At this point in time, even belonging to a Messianic Jewish synagogue is outside of the circle.

Jewish individuals will never receive the message of Yeshua the Messiah in any significant numbers until that message speaks to the Jewish community as a whole—addresses the issues of *Jewish community, and Jewish identity*—the question of the ongoing and eternal significance of the Jewish people.

"The Jewish view of redemption begins with the assumption that the renewal of all things begins with God and Israel, not with God and the individual Jew … I suggest that our *Besorah* needs to emphasize that the Messiah is essential to individual Jews precisely because he is the Messiah/Redeemer of *all* Israel … While the place of personal response to the gospel should not be ignored, it is a significant loss to reduce Yeshua to the savior of individuals while barely mentioning that *Yeshua is central to the accomplishment of redemption for Israel, all humanity, and the cosmic order*"[3] (emphasis in original).

INTEGRATING OUR IDENTITY

When I came to believe in Yeshua in 1971, the message we heard, and then preached ourselves, was "You can be Jewish and believe in Jesus" or "You don't have to give up your Jewishness to believe in

Jesus." This of course was based on the facts that Yeshua spoke only to Jews, that all of his first century followers were Jews, and that the "gospel" message was straight out of the Jewish scriptures and tradition. It was offered first to Jews, who then spread it to the rest of the Mediterranean world. We relished pointing out the irony, when seen in the light of history, of the apostles' deliberations over whether gentiles could believe in Yeshua without becoming Jews.

Why, then, did the gospel message, even as the Messianic Movement preached it—the basic message of Yeshua's atonement for the forgiveness of one's sins and the promise of eternal life—never seem Jewish to me?

Why, no matter how we tweaked and Yiddishized it, did it seem like a Christian message made kosher-style—the spiritual equivalent of turkey ham? How could I share this message with my friends and family when it caused so much unrest in my own heart?

For decades I labored in a profound struggle to understand my identity as a Jew who believes in Yeshua, and to find articulation for the message I wanted to share with my beloved family and community. Even as an active *rebbetzin*, teacher and leader in the Messianic movement, inside I felt terribly lost. "I was found and then I became lost." Yes, I was still Jewish and always would be, but what did that mean? I knew in my heart that Yeshua was indeed the Jewish Messiah—why could I not find rest in Him? For many years a cloud of melancholy—hopelessness of ever integrating my heart with my mind, my spirit with my soul—hovered over me.

Though my crisis of identity was probably more persistent than most, I am far from unique. The identity conflicts of Messianic Jews have been documented by a number of researchers including Natalia Yangarber-Hicks[4] and Carol Harris-Shapiro.[5]

Yangarber-Hicks demonstrates, through written surveys filled out by Messianic Jews, that significant populations of Jewish believers in Yeshua feel uncomfortable and unsure about their identity in relation to the larger Jewish and Christian cultures. She also notes, "The importance of being grounded in one's ethnic identity and its positive impact on emotional well-being has been emphasized by a number of social scientists."[6]

Harris-Shapiro sees similar identity conflicts among the Messianic Jews she interviewed. She summarizes: "Thus the Jewish self is a site of ambivalence and continual 'working out' of one's Jewish identity. … This love-hate relationship with Jewishness does seem to appear and reappear as a pattern of discourse. The struggle to affirm Jewishness and yet separate from Jewishness ranges over the whole life experience of the Messianic Jew."[7]

These identity issues are not primarily the result of personal or organizational weakness in our movement. They are the result of the fact that our beliefs about the world and about ourselves are in direct conflict with the schema the rest of the world, including our own family and community, accepts as reality.

SCHEMA, NARRATIVE AND OUR MESSAGE

Why do we have to ask the question, 'What is our Message'?

It is because we have found the gospel message that we hear and have heard from the churches, one that we ourselves have presented, albeit with changes in language, does not speak to us and our people.

An answer, to be meaningful, must meet a fitting question. Just as "a curse without cause does not alight," an answer without a question does not find a home.

"The most serious obstacle which modern men encounter in entering a discussion about revelation does not arise from their doubts as to whether the accounts of the prophets about their experiences are authentic. The most critical vindication of these accounts, even if it were possible, would be of little relevance. The most serious problem is *the absence of the problem.* An answer, to be meaningful, presupposes the awareness of a question, but the climate in which we live today is not congenial to the continued growth of questions that have taken centuries to cultivate. The Bible is an answer to the supreme question: *what does God demand of us*? Yet the question has gone out of the world. … [The Bible] is a sublime answer, but we do not know the question any more. Unless we recover the question, there is no hope of understanding the Bible."[8]

We preach that Yeshua is the Jewish Messiah, but none but a small group in Brooklyn is asking who the messiah is.

Schema

Another way to look at the problem of an answer without a question is the idea of *schema.* A schema is an organizational or conceptual pattern in the mind. In order to incorporate new facts or ideas into our thinking, these have to fit into existing mental structures.[9] A schema is like a diagram or a map of one's world. It is through our various schemata that we make sense of the greater world. If an incoming fact or concept does not fit our schema we will normally do one of three things: we will ignore it, forget it, or we will alter it to fit our existing schema.

The traditional gospel message is some form of the following: Everyone has sinned and come short of the glory of God. Sin must be punished and Jesus/Yeshua took the punishment for us on the cross/tree. Confess that you have sinned, believe that Jesus/Yeshua took your punishment, repent and ask God to be in charge of your life. Be baptized/immersed and receive the Holy Spirit/Ruach HaKodesh.

Everything in the above gospel message is derived from Jewish scriptures. It is not *wrong*, so what's wrong with it?

It does not fit a modern Jewish schema. It exists totally apart from our mental framework as Jews.

Intellectually, it does not answer our deepest questions. It refers to a schema that is not our own, that we don't understand or accept as true.

Emotionally, it doesn't hit the "pocket." It doesn't deal with questions of immediate concern for most Jewish people.

Culturally it feels alien, and, in some circumstances, hostile.

Spiritually, and eschatologically, it lacks the central focus of the "gospel" preached by Yeshua and his disciples: the coming kingdom.

Evidentially, It has not been historically effective. Plain and simple it has not produced much in the way of results.

What is missing? Any hint of how this salvation, this forgiveness, this eternal life, has anything to do with being Jewish, i.e. how does it inform and affect the purpose of the Jewish people, and our personal lives as Jews? It is entirely mute on the subject.

The Messianic Jewish subjects of Harris-Shapiro's study are reportedly not able to resolve the conflict they experience between these two schemata. They cannot mesh the *Jewish* and the *Messianic* into one framework of understanding. Generally they feel obligated to end up on the Christian side when it comes to theology and questions of eternity, while maintaining an emotional connection to their Jewish heritage.[10]

I could not incorporate the inherited Christian schema. It rattled around in my mind and soul, like a loose part, causing pain and irritation that presented itself as a chronic state of mild depression. How could something that clearly sprouted from Jewish soil have become so alien to the Jewish soul?

Insights into a Messianic Jewish Message

One of my first clear insights into a resolution to this identity crisis came while I was driving alone to Nashville, TN. This drive became an unusual time of worship and communion with God. I wanted to save some of my thoughts so I stopped off at a Circuit City and purchased a hand-held mini-cassette recorder. Just about an hour or two north of Nashville I recorded the following thoughts, transcribed here verbatim:

I just saw a license plate that said, "forgiven." And it made me think about the fact that that's the gospel message that most people think about—to talk about being forgiven, to express to other people that Jesus died on the cross that they might be forgiven. And I was thinking about the fact that what drew me, and what touched me, as I was becoming a believer back in 1971 was not that message at all, which even, as essential as it is, does not hit me in my center.

But the message that drew me was the message that Derek Prince preached, which was in essence, looking back on it, the message of the restoration of the kingdom. Prince taught that the coming back to the Land, that the resurrection of the land of Israel, the state of Israel, was indeed God's hand—that it was GOD'S HAND. *This is what drew me*—the fact that God was still actively involved in the lives of his people. That God was still actively involved with our people, with Israel and that my longings as a Jew, everything that I had grown up with, were not simply religious tradition, were not simply something to keep us alive, to keep us together as a people, but were even *from the hand of God*.

This is what drew me to the Lord. And this is the gospel of the kingdom. I don't understand it fully. But I believe that is what we need to preach. Our gospel, our good news, for Jewish people is not necessarily, firstly, the message of forgiveness, but it is the message of the Messiah, which is the message of the resurrection, the restoration, of the Kingdom of David.

And to the ever-popular Jewish question: "If we have God why do we need Jesus?" maybe this is part of the answer: that we need him because he is the herald who is to usher in the kingdom of God. He is our prince. He is the L-rd of Hosts who will enter the gates (Ps. 24). He is our prince, our king, who will bring in, and sit on, the throne of David. And without him the purposes of God will not be fulfilled in this world, *and the purposes of God for Israel and our purpose as a people will not be fulfilled*—that without the messiah we have no prince, we have no king, we don't have anyone to usher in the kingdom that God has planned, and that was part of his plan *for us* from the beginning.

The King of Glory—He is the mysterious King of Glory (Psalm 24). He brings the Glory of God. He is the Glory of God and he causes us—the people of Israel, the Jewish people—to dwell in the glory of God.

Now, there was an answer to a real question! All my life I had heard in synagogue "Lift up your heads O ye gates that the king of glory may come in." The question always followed, "Who is this King of Glory?" I kept looking around hoping someone would answer, but nobody ever did.

The traditional gospel message does not stand on neutral ground. It exists as part of a wider context that is commonly known to be Christian (non-Jewish). It does not speak to the Jewish mind, heart or culture; neither does it fully represent the message Yeshua brought. Let's look at a related idea: the essential nature of narrative.

THE "GOSPEL" IS PART OF A STORY

The Good News is not a novel message from God dropped into the Earth in the first century, along with a mystical "Son of God." It is part of a story. In fact, the message that Yeshua brought—in his person and on his lips—is not a *new* story (as many tell it) but, rather, the turning point of an ongoing story. A turning point is "an event marking a unique or important historical change of course, or one on which important developments depend."

The Power of Narrative

All human beings relate to a good story because it touches something essential about being human.

Narrative has been credited with being a "fundamental structure of human experience," a "solution to a fundamental problem in life … creating understandable order in human affairs," "the most fundamental way of grappling with new experience," and a "primary act of mind."[11]

We each live within a story, in fact, a set of stories. We act in our life alone, and we play a particular role within the story of our family, and we act within the story of our culture. Within each of these stories there are subplots in which we may play different roles and affect different outcomes. We may also understand ourselves as a player in the larger story of our contemporary world. Beyond that, we live and act in God's complete story of the history of all humanity.

How we understand ourselves within these stories shapes our identity and shapes how we see ourselves in relation to others. How we tell a particular story—what we decide to leave in and what we decide to take out, as well as how we order the selected events—is crucial to the meaning that the story conveys.

The Jewish people are unique in that part of our story—the beginning, as well as prophetic utterances about our future—is recorded in a sacred book. The book we, and many others, consider to be the Word of God contains mostly the story of God in relation to the people of Israel.

We Jews have told our own story for generations. There are many variations, of course, but there are some events that are consistently part of the story, and some that are consistently left out of the story.

Christians tell their story as well, and, like the Jews, have variants, yet the essential framework of the story remains the same. The two stories are said to arise from the same texts, yet they are very different.

How we Messianic Jews understand and frame our narrative, will determine whether we will land within the context of the ongoing Jewish story or the Christian story. And this context will determine who will hear, understand and receive our message.

The Flow of History

Picture if you will a large organic timeline of space and time merged into one broad sweep of the tedious and wayward journey of history. Imagine the members of this symposium standing around on our span of the timeline. Only it is not a line, it is a river perhaps, in a sweeping aerial shot that spans over 5000 years of Jewish history and the geography of the entire world. Along this river, this timeline, are our people milling about throughout history: in Jerusalem in every era, in Babylonia, in Rome and the cities of the Mediterranean, In towns up the Rhine river and into northern Europe, in the Spain of Yehuda HaLevi and Maimonides, in the shtetls of the Pale of Settlement, in ships bound for America, in gas chambers and hiding in forests, in synagogues in Brooklyn, fighting in the Sinai and on the Golan, and even living in mansions in Hollywood.

We stand at one particular place with the expanse before us yet out of focus. We stand among our people who have also been brought to this place by this cascading river. We, with the others, look back over who we have been and where we have come from.

How do we tell our Messianic Jewish story? What are the needs formed out of our history, and our thinking about our history? How do we understand our common heritage, particularly the centuries of exile and suffering, and even this strange modern invention of secular godliness? How is our post-biblical history part of the plan of God? What are the cries of the hearts of the Jewish people around you? What is God's heart crying for them? Where is Yeshua as we look back over the river of Jewish lives that brought us to this place?

We have a message, but how does that message tell the story of the past and write the story of the future? We have rightly proclaimed the Jewishness of the new covenant and of the collection of literature erroneously, but conventionally, known as the New Testament. But the trajectory of that story, the way it has been told for centuries, has caused it to diverge by a vast distance from the Jewish story, a story that continued in another direction. My personal identity, as well as that of other Jews, is derived, in large part, from my understanding of myself as an ongoing part of the Jewish story. A meaningful message must share DNA with that story.

How do we retell the story of Yeshua, of the new covenant, of our own history, with a trajectory that runs straight through Jewish history of the last 2000 years and finds us smack in the middle of the Jewish community today?

Two Stories We Must Overcome

First, the bad news is we are not starting with a blank page. Before our story can be believable we have to confront two stories that stand as formidable barriers, in contradiction to the story we want to tell. These two stories are The Story of Exile and the Story of Christian Theology.

Strangely, the two stories look curiously alike—like looking at the same phenomenon from two sides of the looking glass. In the Story of Exile, God sent us from the land of promise, the land of our inheritance, causing us, for age upon age, to wander, homeless, over the face of the earth, seemingly abandoned by the One who called us in the first place.

> *How long O Lord? Will you forget me forever? How long will you hide your face from me? How long must I wrestle with my thoughts and every day have sorrow in my heart? How long will my enemy triumph over me?*
>
> Psalm 13

The second is like the first, but from the hand of man, rather than the hand of God. It is the story of expulsion. The expulsion of the Jews from the narrative of The Story of Christian Theology was played out many times over in history by the physical expulsion of the Jews from just about every country in Christendom. Most believed they were doing God's will because of their flawed theology.[12]

The Story of Exile

Exile is a physical state and a spiritual state. Though we as a people have returned from exile physically, we have not yet returned, as a people, spiritually. In a way, Jewish self-understanding has never fully recovered from the destruction of the second temple and the subsequent genocide/expulsion of the Jews of Jerusalem and Judea. Though your average Jewish person today does not walk around in mourning over the destruction of the Temple, it remains the "background radiation" of all religious thinking that came after. Inasmuch as Judaism is shaped by the Talmud, it is largely shaped by the dilemma of the Exile.[13] We are the chosen people who spent the last 2000 years wondering when God would remember.

Echoing many Jewish humorists, Michael Wex calls this "the fundamental absurdity of Jewish existence … We are God's chosen people; it says so over and over in the Bible, His favorites. And how does He show it? Just look at Jewish history: persecution and pariah-hood are both tributaries of the one big river of *goles*—exile-the fundamental fact of Jewish life for the last couple of thousand years"[14]

Centuries of exile have produced, according to Wex, the culture that produced the Yiddish language, which is characterized by the *kvetch*. He explains, "If we stop kvetching, how will we know that life isn't supposed to be like this? If we don't keep kvetching we'll forget who we really are … Kvetching lets us know that we're in exile, that the Jew and hence the 'Jewish,' is out of place everywhere, all the time."[15] Though the new Israelis banished Yiddish as the language of exile, they imported Yiddish inflection and attitude directly into Israeli Hebrew.

"Disappointment—awareness of the difference between things as they are and things as they're supposed to be—is the basis of kvetching."[16]

Edward Feld, in exploring the faith consequences of the Holocaust, says:

> We are past waiting for intervention from outside, for a glorious endtime that will transform existence. Our disappointment will no longer bear such a leap of faith. If the God we wanted so much did not appear when our need was so desperate, what use would that God be to us now?[17]

With the humiliations and tragedies of exile, comes the sense of abandonment, a diminished hope in the power of God to act on our behalf. For many the Holocaust killed this hope entirely.

"No divine intervention will come from the outside to make history right again, just as there was no resounding miracle to save millions of innocent people from death … Traditional theologies that find an ultimate meaning displayed by history make no sense in light of the gas chambers and the rod of Dr. Mengele choosing who shall live and who shall die. The Messiah was buried at Auschwitz."[18]

As holocaust survivor Elie Wiesel once noted, what we say about God, we must be able to say over the darkest pits of life. What we know about God, we must be able to profess in the midst of brokenness, in the middle of a very dark world, in the midst of disorienting pain, and the angst of "Why?"[19]

In order to overcome The Story of Exile, a story of endless disappointment resulting in lost hope, our message needs to sprout from the ground of the kind of faith Wiesel describes. This kind of faith does not come automatically with a simple prayer, or a good teaching. It is fought for in the dark places of the spirit. Have we truly asked ourselves "Where was God at Auschwitz?" We must face our deepest doubts and fears and find God there. We must wrestle until the dawn breaks, and then not let Him go until He blesses us with Life we can share. We wrestle to find faith in the dark places of lost hope, not merely for ourselves, but for our people. Our message depends on it.

Feld asks, "Do we not need a theological matrix to begin to understand and to articulate our own history? Do we not need to recover a sense of the holy?"[20]

The Story of Christian Theology

"Not one major creed of the Church even identifies "Christ" in any way as a Jew, much less the King of the Jews. Not as Messiah, not as the son of David, not as the Lion of Judah. Instead of restoring the kingdom of David, the "Christ" of the creeds declares that the kingdom will never again exist."[21]

The Christian Narrative

The following radio essay succinctly and eloquently tells the classic Christian narrative that explains how the Bible holds together as one story. This story is the Christian schema, the interpretive framework through which the whole Bible is understood:[22]

> There are five crucial moments in Scripture's definition of humanity. The first comes in Genesis when God said, "Let us make man in our image." Every human is a bearer of the likeness of God. Each of us is impressed with His mark. This is how and why we love and relate and reason and choose. This is the source of our mysterious and wonderful personhood.
>
> The second moment comes quickly on the heels of the first: the Fall. In the garden God pronounced that we were good, but our choosing to rebel against Him resulted in our deformation. Yet though, marked by sin, we retain the image of God. This ambiguity is why humans are at times angelic and at times demonic. Our estate is a mixed heritage: we were created good, so we show glimmers of the divine; but our sinful flesh is also in effect, so we cast the shadows of the demonic.
>
> The third moment is the crucifixion. Here God unequivocally states that we are utterly sinful, and yet utterly loved. Our sin is so great that only the crucifixion of the Son of God could deal with it. Yet, God's love for us is so great, that He would not let us go. At once, it is the divine proclamation of our debasement and our worth.
>
> Fourth, the resurrection. Christ rose, and offers us the same opportunity: resurrection. Victorious over death, He offers us victory over the flesh and entrance into

> His Kingdom. This is the ultimate definition of human possibility. Fifth and finally, the promised re-creation of earth where the Kingdom of God will rule in full power and glory. As Christians, we ought to be defined by these five moments. They tell of our past, empower our present, and orient us towards our glorious future.[23]

This teaching offers important, even vital, insights into biblical truths, but like the traditional gospel message, the Christian biblical narrative has no place for the Jewish people, their history and their relationship with God. If the mind of God is to be understood as moving seamlessly from the Fall to the Crucifixion, why, then, the peculiar—and very lengthy—biblical story of the people of Israel, one filled with all manner of intimate pathos from the heart of Almighty God?

We cannot overcome the story of Christian theology alone. Thankfully there is a strong movement today among Christians that seeks to overcome this grievous error in Christian theology. For our part, we need to clearly distinguish ourselves from institutional Christianity and Christian theology, while acknowledging its contributions and embracing those who truly embrace Yeshua.

Forays into Telling a Yeshua-narrative for the Jewish Community

We as a movement agree that God has not abandoned, has not forsaken Israel. But where was God over the last 2000 years? Where was Yeshua? Our message, our story, is not complete without coming to terms with this difficult question. Without it, our narrative has lost its audience for lack of continuity.

The Mystery of his Hiddenness

In our Messianic Jewish story, we must find the Messiah the central (though often hidden and mysterious) figure in the long continuous story of the intimate and intense relationship of the God of Israel with the people whom he chose to bear his name—the people of Israel. Unraveling the mystery of his hiddenness, both in the biblical account and in our subsequent history, to reveal his true identity, like that of Joseph to his brothers, is one task before us.

Joel Marcus' extraordinary little book, Jesus and the Holocaust: Reflections on Suffering and Hope explores Marcus' "intuition of an identification between Christ's suffering and that of the martyrs of the Holocaust."[24]

In Julia Blum's beautiful telling of the Akeda story she sees "the father-son relationship, gradually displayed more and more fully ... a path down which the father leads his son, a path on which the son starts out as just a son but ... in walking down it, the son becomes the *lamb*, with none other than the father himself leading him to be sacrificed ... In this is the mystery and secret of the Father's plan, the Father's love, and the Father's election: the Mystery of Sonship."[25] (p. 29)

She is referring, not to Yeshua here, but to Israel. Blum asserts that the ram in the thicket, not Isaac, represents Yeshua. Isaac, with Israel in his loins, represents the people of Israel. Isaac/Israel remains bound on the altar even as this story ends. Blum paints a tender picture of how both Israel's election and chosen-ness can be seen in the nation's historical suffering.

"Out of Egypt I called My Son" (Hosea 11:1). Matthew applies this verse to Yeshua, though it refers to Israel in the original text. There is a mysterious parallel and identification between the son-ship of Israel and the son-ship of Messiah that runs throughout scripture. It begins to make sense of our national suffering. It helps us identify with the Messiah. It speaks both of our chosen-ness and of our need to rely solely on God. This is a deep and sensitive question to explore with a lot of creative spiritual potential to uncover.

WHAT ARE THE ESSENTIAL FEATURES OF A MESSAGE FOR THE JEWISH COMMUNITY?

As a trained artist, I understand that a painted object will only appear real to a viewer's eye if it is in harmony with the foreground, middle ground and background, in shape, size, tonal value, lighting and color. Likewise, our message, no matter how "true" needs to be part of a harmonious unified picture. The foreground, middle ground and background of our picture is the Jewish CONTEXT that will give our message reality and beauty.

Overall, our message must have authentic Jewish CONTEXT. It must have CONTINUITY with Jewish culture. It must affirm and confirm God's special COVENANT with Israel. It must have meaning for the Jewish COMMUNITY. It must communicate a clear vision of the CALLING of the nation of Israel. It must have CURRENCY. It must have COMPASSION. It must CHALLENGE our people. It must also AMAZE and ASTOUND and give our people a vision for their prophetic destiny. Finally, it will take COMMITMENT AND COURAGE on our part to see it through.

There is not space to look at each of these in detail, but following are some examples of how to flesh out these principles.

CONTEXT

In the biblical text, the people of God is the people of Israel; God has set up no other people, no other kingdom, and no other "Israel" than the one he called into being from the time of Abraham or David. Yeshua broke down the wall of partition (that God had previously erected) so that God could bring in the "other sheep that are not of this sheep pen," but the pen is Israel's.[26]

CONTINUITY

Our message must have continuity with the Jewish past (both biblical and postbiblical), real consequence for the Jewish present, and build connection to the Jewish future.

I will put my dwelling place among you and I will not reject you, I will walk among you and be your God, and you will be my people (Lev. 26: 11-12).

God's desire and intent from the beginning was that he would dwell with mankind, and that his human creation would dwell in his presence. This is clearly seen from Genesis 2 through Revelation. These words from Leviticus are repeated throughout Torah and appear again in Revelation 21:3.[27]

When sin caused God to send the first humans out from his presence, his intent did not change. He set out to bring all of humanity back to relationship with himself by calling out a "peculiar" nation in which he would dwell, first in a limited and conditional way, and finally in all of His Glory.

God's indwelling presence is not a "New Testament concept." God's indwelling presence rested on the *mishkan* (tabernacle) in the wilderness and in the Temple in Jerusalem, This is the place that the Lord chose for his divine presence to pitch its tent in the world. The nation of Israel was, in essence, the incarnation of the Spirit of God, the body in which God dwelled. In this manner, the more concentrated and compact incarnation of the spirit of God in the

Memra, the Messiah, exists in continuity with God's habitation in Israel.[28]

Orthodox Jewish scholar Michael Wyschogrod sees this connection. "The covenant between God and Israel] depicts a drawing together of God and Israel. In some sense … it can also be said to involve a certain indwelling of God in the people of Israel whose status as a holy people may be said to derive from this indwelling. Understood in this sense, the divinity of Jesus is not radically different—though perhaps more concentrated—than the holiness of the Jewish people."[29]

Though we know that Messiah, being deity, is worthy of our worship, whereas Israel is not, the continuity of God's indwelling presence reveals much about God's character and his purpose for Israel and all of mankind.

COVENANT

Our message must foundationally affirm and confirm God's special covenant with the Jewish people in a way that is both faithful to the scriptures and makes sense to today's Jews.

First, we need to affirm that God has not rescinded any of the special covenants He has made with the Jewish people, particularly the Sinai covenant. Yeshua himself said, "I have not come to abolish the Torah and the Prophets; I have not come to abolish, but to fulfill them" (Matt. 5:17).

For much of Christian theology "fulfill" became a synonym for "abolish." If it is 'fulfilled,' it is finished and so it can be discarded. We have to actively counteract this pervasive view about Torah. Mark Kinzer is very helpful in looking at difficult passages regarding Jews and Torah.[30]

Second, it needs to be made clear that the new covenant is made with the House of Israel and the House of Judah (Jer. 31). There is no Biblical covenant made with the Church. There is no New Covenant made with individuals who "get saved." The only covenant that brings eternal life and citizenship in the coming Kingdom of God is God's covenant made with the House of Israel.

Third, God has chosen to cut an eternal covenant with the Jewish people, not based on merit, but based purely on his grace. Jeremiah 32: 40 says, "V'karati lahem brit olam" (I will make an everlasting covenant with them). The faithfulness is all on God's side.

COMMUNITY

Our message must be directed to, and relevant to, the whole Jewish community *as a community*, while it is also a message to individuals within that community. One way to do this is to understand the communal nature of Yeshua's atonement.

Leviticus 16 gives the ordinances for Yom Kippur. It is clear that this once-a-year special atonement is meant to be atonement for the whole house of Israel as a community. It is to be a lasting ordinance "for the priests and all the people of the community" (v. 33).

This Yom Kippur offering is the model for the Messiah offering up himself, "once for all." In a sense, the comforting message evangelicals are fond of is not true: "If you were the only person in the world, Jesus would have died for you." Perhaps he would have; I can't say. But that is not the way his atonement is presented in the scriptures. He dies for a nation, for the nation of Israel. Yes, individuals, Jew or Gentile, have to turn from their own way, and turn to God to receive the benefit of that national atonement, but the atonement is made for the nation of Israel.

The communal nature of the atonement gives the Jewish people as a nation the ability to live up to its calling as a people to be a light to the nations. The Jewish community already knows its calling. We call it Tikkun Olam, and many Jews see this as the heart of Judaism. We need to affirm this calling, while challenging our people to work for Tikkun Olam in partnership with the One who destroyed the power of evil.

History has shown that we cannot overcome the vast evil in the world solely by our natural gifts and generosity.

CURRENCY

Our message must have currency—we must be able to trade our ideas in today's marketplace. Both usages of *currency* (the other meaning 'money') come from the noun, current. Both come from the idea of being "in the current" or "in circulation." If sharing our message is like trying to spend outdated coins, we will only be received with blank stares. Nothing will be bought or exchanged.

"'Many people … insist on a single self-consistent verbal scheme into which they try to force all experience. In doing this they create a purely verbal world in which they can live a pretty autonomous existence.' This of course is what makes a cult—a group of people who thus isolate themselves from the evolving mainstream. *By staying within their own closed verbal world they forfeit the opportunity to lead others*"[32] (emphasis mine).

Among the unending din of information and messages coming at us today, there is no shortage of messages aimed specifically at our people. In addition to the hundreds of excellent books, there are many websites and magazines devoted to Jewish thought and the Jewish seeker. Just a few of these are zeek.net, *Moment Magazine*, *Mishpacha Magazine*, books and articles by Jubus (Jewish Buddhists), popular articles and classes on kabala, conferences to bring the secular back into the fold, etc.

How do we fit into this picture? What do the answers provided by these groups say about what today's Jewish people are seeking? Can we enter into intelligent compassionate discourse about these subjects?

To further complicate the picture we live in a postmodern, not a biblical, world. The subject of postmodernism is beyond the scope of this paper, but it is interesting to note that the concept of story and narrative finds a natural home here. Postmodernism is fueled by authenticity, acceptance, love, emotional health, pragmatism (whatever works), novelty (new is better than true), feeling/experiencing, and believing the journey is better than the destination.

Using these values we can challenge people with story. Inside, we all want to make a difference. Stories can fire up our God-given longing to be brave and meet adversity head-on for a higher purpose.

CHALLENGE: AMAZE AND ASTOUND

Our message must make sense to our people, but it must also amaze and astound them, while communicating an exciting vision of our purpose as a people. In Acts 2:5&12, the "God-fearing Jews" were "amazed and perplexed, they asked one another, 'What does this mean?'" In Acts 4:13 the people were "astonished" when they saw the courage of Kefa and Yochanan. In Acts 8:13, Simon the (former) sorcerer was "astonished by the great signs and miracles he saw." In Acts 9:21 "all those who heard him were amazed" at the preaching of Saul of Tarsus.

Yeshua "went through Galilee teaching in their synagogues, preaching the good news of the kingdom, and healing every disease and sickness among the people" (Matt. 4:23). He was preaching the kingdom, and he was demonstrating the kingdom. Large crowds of Jews began to follow him wherever he went.

Healing and miracles were quite clearly part of the message. Yeshua gave his Jewish disciples this charge: As you go, preach this message: The kingdom of heaven is near. Heal the sick, raise the dead, cleanse those who have leprosy, drive out demons" (Matt. 10: 7-8).

The message had two parts: the announcement of the kingdom, and the demonstration of the kingdom. God's realm, his kingdom, overcomes the sickness and death of this world. That is the good news, and it is amazing and astounding news. It is God dwelling with us. It is the Spirit of God dwelling in Israel, in Jewish flesh, breaking out of the boundaries of the Mishkan and the Temple, and, eventually, even out of Jerusalem—beyond the courts of the gentiles. It is our calling as Jews to bring this restoration to the nations.

Yeshua amazed the people, not only by his miracles, but also by his teaching. "They were amazed at His teaching; for He was teaching them as one having authority, and not as the scribes" (Mark 1:22). He taught the people about the kingdom without concern as to whether they were officially "believers." He preached to them "where they're at." We see Yeshua teaching about the kingdom, living the kingdom, demonstrating the kingdom, and he is amazing the people.

Outgoing Holiness

In the Sinai covenant the holiness of the altar was protected by many safeguards; it was constantly threatened by the defilement of this world. Conversely, the people were threatened by the holiness in their midst—one false move and judgment followed.

But God had always intended to dwell in Israel, among the people. Because Yeshua was not a stone altar, but God in the flesh, he did not need to carefully guard his holiness, lest it be defiled. Yeshua brought a prophetic outgoing holiness[33] right to the people.

That is the kingdom of God coming NEAR. The kingdom of God was always present in Israel in a limited sense—dwelling in the Mishkan, in the pillar of fire, speaking through the prophets—but it was fenced off, both from impurity and from the gentile nations. It had to be kept separate.

Yeshua broke through these boundaries to bring the holiness of God, the kingdom of God, to Israel in a way that was beyond expectations. It was prophetic because it revealed the truth of God's ways to the people. It was outgoing and invasive because it actively invaded the realm of evil. It was not defiled by the unclean, but rather cleansed the defiled. In the same prophetic way, we are to speak and demonstrate our message in the Jewish community, so that the community of Israel can fulfill its work to bring the message and power of the kingdom of God to the world.

"The kingdom of heaven is near" doesn't mean, "you'll die soon and heaven is near (if you believe)." It means the presence of God is near; the holiness of God has come to this earth in an invasive way to scatter the forces of darkness. And while you are preaching it (says Yeshua), DO it too. Scatter the forces of darkness, demonstrate the power of God, bring the kingdom of heaven near. This is the heritage of the sons of Jacob. Raise the gauntlet of the prophetic destiny to which he has called our people. This is Tikkun olam with power.

COMMITMENT AND COURAGE

If we are not demonstrating the kingdom now in a way that astounds, amazes and challenges our people, we need to pray until this happens. Our message is incomplete without it.

Above and beyond the "rightness" of our message, is the utmost importance of our commitment to prayer—not just as individuals, but also as *klal yisrael b'yeshua*, the People of Israel standing in Yeshua. We are called, together, to endure in faith and endure in prayer, which is the place we reveal what we really care about. "For the revelation awaits an appointed time; it speaks of the end and will not prove false. Though it linger, wait for it; it will certainly come and will not delay" (Hab. 2:3). This is God's work. It is all predicated on God's promise and on His character alone. Our message is only as effective as the Spirit of God makes it, and that through the prayer of our community.

Difficult times are here. It seems evident that it will soon get worse. We need to persevere in prayer and faithfulness, and prepare to be people of hope in hopeless times. We need to be tough compassionate leaders that can stand with courage and faith in times of war and extreme hardship. We need to stand in stern and serious unity before God for the redemption of Israel. We are our message.

> *"Im tirtzu, ayn zo agada"*
> *If you want it, it is not a dream.*
>
> — Theodor Herzl

ENDNOTES

1. "Yeshua did not need to come into this world to reign in heaven. He was already reigning in heaven … Yeshua was born as the son of David so that he can rule from David's throne in Jerusalem." Daniel Gruber, *The Separation of Church & Faith, Vol. 1, Copernicus and the Jews* (Elijah Publishing, 2005), 216. See also all of chapters 16 and 21.
2. "[Mordechai] Kaplan used to teach that there are three possible ways of identifying with a religious community: by behaving, by believing, or by belonging. Kaplan himself insisted that the primary form of *Jewish* identification is belonging—that intuitive sense of kinship that binds a Jew to every other Jew in history and in the contemporary world. Whatever Jews believe, and however they behave as Jews, serves to shape and concretize that underlying sense of being bound to a people with a shared history and destiny. When that connection disappears, Judaism too will disappear." Neil Gillman, *Sacred Fragments: Recovering Theology for the Modern Jew* (Jewish Publication Society, 1990), xvii.
3. Carl Kinbar, "Communal Aspects of the Besorah," *Hashivenu Forum* (2004), 15 and 28.
4. Natalia Yangarber-Hicks, "Messianic Believers: Reflections on Identity of a largely misunderstood group" *Journal of Psychology and Theology 33* (2005): 127-139.
5. Carol Harris-Shapiro, Messianic Judaism: A Rabbi's Journey through Religious Change in America (Boston: Beacon Press, 1999).
6. Yangarber-Hicks, 140 (14).
7. Harris-Shapiro, 61.
8. Abraham Joshua Heschel, *God in Search of Man* (New York: The Noonday Press, 1976; first published by Farrar, Strauss and Giroux, 1955), 168-69
9. "A view of mind predicated on an information-processing model is critically at odds with sociocultural perspectives that assert that the genesis of thought, language, and, therefore, development lies in social and cultural activity. " Mary B, McVee et al., "Schema Theory Revisited," *Review of Educational Research, Vol. 75, No. 4* (Winter 2005), 541. This article reviews schema theory in relation to learning and literacy in children but there are many applicable findings. The authors feel that learning is dependent on sociocultural factors.
10. Harris-Shapiro, 86.
11. Jerome Bruner.
12. It is important to recognize that though, historically, the majority of Christian theologies have been anti-Judaic, there is, in our time, a large and growing, very vibrant, movement of Christians who are eager to understand the place of the Jewish people in God's plan. Most of these are faithful and generous supporters of Israel, and see their support of Israel as their spiritual duty. This move of God's spirit parallels the move of God among the Jewish people of the last generation, of which the members of this symposium are a part. We gratefully welcome the heartfelt support and prayers of these Christians. We are delighted to consider them part of the family.

13. Edward Feld, *The Spirit of Renewal: Finding Faith After the Holocaust* (Woodstock, Vermont: Jewish Lights, 1994) This idea that Rabbinic Judaism is shaped by the dilemma of exile is explored in chapters 1 through 9.
14. Michael Wex, Born to Kvetch: Yiddish language and culture in all its moods (New York: Harper Collins, 2005), 6.
15. Wex, 6.
16. Wex, 7.
17. Feld, 138.
18. Feld, 139.
19. Wiesel quotation.
20. Feld, xvi.
21. Gruber, 221.
22. This is a transcription of a portion of "A Slice of Infinity" from Ravi Zacharias Ministries (RZIM). It is important to note that I highly respect this ministry and have supported it in a variety of ways. I have gained innumerable insights from RZIM that have proved very useful for spiritual growth. My objective is not to berate this ministry but to understand that the theology that leaves out Israel is so entrenched in Christian thought that even an excellent ministry like RZIM, one that offers many unusually deep insights into the Bible and into life in general, can still miss this part of the picture.
23. Keith Cox, *Who Defines the Word 'Humanity?'* A Slice of Infinity, A Ministry of RZIM (March 14, 2003) Copyright (c) 2003 Ravi Zacharias International Ministries (RZIM) The quotation represents over two-thirds of the short radio essay. Reprinted with permission.
24. "Might one not suggest that there is an analogy, a likeness, a mysterious identification between the redemptive suffering of Jesus and the sufferings of other innocent victims, including Holocaust victims? After all, Paul himself says in Colossians 1:24 that he makes up what is lacking in Christ's sufferings. And even some Jewish writers and artists have expressed a similar sort of intuition of identification between Christ's sufferings and that of the martyrs of the Holocaust. One thinks, for example, of the crucifixion scenes painted by Marc Chagall in the late thirties and early forties — scenes in which the crucified one is always an identifiably Jewish figure, and the background is usually a burning Jewish settlement or shtetl of Eastern Europe." Joel Marcus, *Jesus and the Holocaust: Reflections on Suffering and Hope* (New York: Doubleday, 1997), 28-29.
25. Julia Blum, *If You Be the Son of God Come Down From the Cross* (Chichester, U.K.: New Wine Press, 2006), 29-31.
26. "The Biblical *ekklesia* [usually translated 'church'] is the *kahal* [community] of Israel." Gruber, 62.
27. "And I heard a loud voice from the throne, saying, "Behold, the tabernacle of God is among men, and He shall dwell among them, and they shall be His people, and God Himself shall be among them." Revelation 21:3, NASB.
28. Mark S. Kinzer, "Beginning with the End: The Place of Eschatology in the Messianic Jewish Canonical Narrative," *Pasadena Hashivenu Forum* (2002), 12-15.

29. R. Kendall Soulen, *The God of Israel and Christian Theology* (Minneapolis: Augsburg Fortress, 1996), 9. Soulen is quoting from: Michael Wyschogrod, "Christology: The Immovable Object," *Religion and Intellectual Life 3* (1986), 79.
30. Mark S. Kinzer, Post-Missionary Messianic Judaism: Redefining Christian Engagement with the Jewish People (Grand Rapids: Brazos Press, 2005), particularly chapters 2 and 3.
31. Gruber, chapter 19.
32. Robert K. Greenleaf, *Servant Leadership: A Journey into the Nature of Legitimate Power and Greatness* (New York: Paulist Press, 1977), 32. Greenleaf is quoting and commenting on the words of physicist and philosopher Percy Bridgman.
33. Kinzer, "Beginning with the End," 14.

Scriptures References:

Luke 1:68-75 NASB "Blessed *be* the Lord God of Israel, For He has visited us and accomplished redemption for His people, and has raised up a horn of salvation for us In the house of David His servant — As He spoke by the mouth of His holy prophets from of old-Salvation from our enemies, and from the hand of all who hate us; To show mercy toward our fathers, And to remember His holy covenant, The oath which He swore to Abraham our father, To grant us that we, being delivered from the hand of our enemies, Might serve Him without fear, In holiness and righteousness before Him all our days."

Romans 8:19-23 NASB "For the anxious longing of the creation waits eagerly for the revealing of the sons of God. For the creation was subjected to futility, not of its own will, but because of Him who subjected it, in hope that the creation itself also will be set free from its slavery to corruption into the freedom of the glory of the children of God. For we know that the whole creation groans and suffers the pains of childbirth together until now. And not only this, but also we ourselves, having the first fruits of the Spirit, even we ourselves groan within ourselves, waiting eagerly for *our* adoption as sons, the redemption of our body."

WHAT IS THE GOSPEL WE SHOULD BE COMMENDING TO ALL ISRAEL IN THESE TIMES OF TRANSITION?

Stuart Dauermann, Ph.D.
Senior Scholar of Messianic Jewish Theological Institute,
Founder and President of Hashivenu

Introduction

I was about ten years old the first time somebody called me a Christ-killer.

I had just come out of Morris Schaeffer's candy store, on the corner of Winthrop Street and Nostrand Avenue, in Flatbush, Brooklyn. A bunch of kids whom I had never met before jumped me, pummeling me to the ground, while making a profound theological query: "Why'd you kill God?" I had no answer for them. At that moment I didn't know what they were talking about. Only later, while tending to bruises and scrapes (some) and checking for broken bones (none), did I realize that they were talking about Jesus. Thus ends my first experience with witnessing.

My bruises and scrapes healed a long time ago. Still, fifty-three years later, I am still hurting. But the pain of being picked on as a child is nothing compared to how I feel now when friends and colleagues in the missions and Messianic Jewish world, most of them Jews, beat up on the Jewish people. It isn't any prettier when we lump the Jews or any group of Jews into a distrusted, despised class, than it was for those Irish kids to beat me up one cool and clear autumn in New York.

I confess that, in part, I am missiologically directed and driven by my sensitivity to theological Jew-bashing. I know we all agree that this should have absolutely no place in our outreach to our people. But, beyond contradiction, most of us are well practiced in bashing Jews and Judaism. These old and deep prejudices are mostly hidden from us. In this paper I want to show that this is true, and outline a better way for us to think about our people and serve them in Yeshua's name.[1]

I have expanded my assigned topic, "What is the gospel?" to "What Is The Gospel We Should Be Commending To All Israel[2] In These Times Of Transition?" It is in four parts: Matters of Context, Matters of Content, Matters of Controversy, and Cumulative Conclusions. My argument is inductive, making its case moving from particulars to a general conclusion; cumulative, because each component contributes to the credibility of the whole; and synergistic, because the contribution of each component can only be rightly perceived through appreciating how the components work together, with the whole being greater than the sum of its parts. Only by keeping the parts and the whole dynamic tension will readers rightly understand, evaluate, and most important, respond to what I say here.

Today I want to pull the covers off a sleepy movement, arousing all of us to a unified, demanding, and sacrificial evangelistic mandate, appropriate to our times, to the whole counsel of God, and to our identity as the Remnant of Israel. Mine is a call to inconvenience: it is a call to radical change. Mine is a call to sacrifice: it is call to risk and discomfort. And above all, mine is a call to seek, speak, and live a gospel that is good news for all Israel.

Matters of Context

We communicate an eternal gospel3 in the midst of time. Therefore, we can only do so at specific times, in specific places, and to specific people. "Context" should not be dismissed as a trendy buzzword: it is instead our unavoidable reality. Since only those who properly analyze the soil have a right to expect a good harvest, we would be foolish to omit this step in our rush to sow the seed. Since we must begin by assessing the soil of our context, I begin by examining five contextual issues demanding our attention: Living in Times of Eschatological Transition; New Paradigms, New Tensions; The Bad News Gospel; Individualism, Community and Consummation; and, Implications of Adopting a New Creation Eschatology.

Living in Times of Eschatological Transition

The first of our five contextual factors identifies five signs that these are eschatological times, with the consummation of all things is drawing near. God's agenda has begun to shift from a focus on the ingathering of the fullness of the Gentiles to thc ingathcring of the fullness of Israel.

The Founding of the Modern State of Israel—The Prophet Zechariah tells us that at the time of the end the Jewish people will be living in the Land, with all the nations of the world gathered against them.[4] This could not have happened for 1900 years, and only became a possibility again in 1948, with the establishment of the Jewish State. This is a sign of the times. We should be anticipating and preparing for the consummation of all things.

The Liberation of Jerusalem—The prophets remind us as well that Jerusalem will be a Jewish city in the end-times. This was a non-issue for two millennia, until the Liberation of Jerusalem in 1967. This too is a sign of the times.

The Re-gathering of the Jews to Israel From the Land of the North—Part of the nexus of events in the latter days is the re-gathering of Jewish exiles not only from the nations in general, but also explicitly "from the land of the north," commonly associated with the heartland of the Former Soviet Union. Many of us are old enough to remember when it was front-page news when one Jew from the former Soviet Union immigrated to Israel. But all of this changed forever with the advent of glasnost and perestroika under Mikhail Gorbachev in the 1980s, and the astounding break-up of the former Soviet Union (FSU) in 1991. It was Ronald Reagan who said, "Mr. Gorbachev: tear down this wall," but God swung the hammer.

Since the 1980s, well over a million Jews from the FSU have immigrated to Israel. When we combine this statistic with others such as the massive airlifts and repatriation to Israel of over 85 percent of Ethiopia's Jews, can we be blamed for seeing these events in the context of this prophecy from the Prophet Jeremiah?

> *So then, the days are coming when they will say, "As surely as the LORD lives, who brought the descendants of Israel up out of the land of the north and out of all the countries where he had banished them." Then they will live in their own land. (Jer. 23:7-8)*

The Repentance-Renewal of the Jewish People — Deuteronomy 30 and Ezekiel 36-37 are among the texts connecting this return to the Lord with a renewal in covenantal faithfulness, when God will spiritually renew his people and cause us to "again obey the voice of the LORD, and keep all his commandments ... and his statutes which are written in this book of the law."[5] Today, we are seeing this spiritual renewal becoming a manifest reality, at least in nascent stages. Ever since the Liberation of Jerusalem in 1967, Jews have begun coming to Yeshua-faith in increasing numbers. Many who have come to Israel from "the land of the north" are already Yeshua-believing Jews. Today it is impossible to find an Israeli congregation of Jewish Yeshua-believers that does not include a substantial number of Russian speakers. In Israel today, greater numbers of Jews are coming to believe in Yeshua that at any time since the first century. Mitch Glaser estimates that the numbers of Israeli Yeshua-believers have grown by three or four hundred percent in the past ten years, with sixty or seventy percent of this growth among Russian speakers. Something is happening which Scripture foretold, and the times are changing.

A New Concern for Messianic Jewish Covenant Faithfulness—In recent years, the issue of Torah-based covenant faithfulness has moved to the forefront of Messianic Jewish discussion. On July 31, 2002, the Union of Messianic Jewish Congregations ratified a definitional document including these words: "Messianic Judaism is a movement of Jewish congregations and congregation-like groupings committed to Yeshua the Messiah that embrace the covenantal responsibility of Jewish life and identity rooted in Torah, expressed in tradition, renewed and applied in the context of the New Covenant."[6] The reference to "covenantal responsibility of Jewish life and identity rooted in Torah, [and] expressed in tradition" is nothing short of revolutionary. Such a sentence would never even have come to mind when I came to Yeshua-faith in the early 1960s. The statement contravenes the older consensus that Torah observance was to be regarded as strictly a matter of personal preference, and to only be pursued in circumspect moderation.

Can it be that such indicators are heralding the promised shift of God turning His attention from accomplishing the fullness of the Gentiles, to pursuing the fullness of Israel? I think so! More than that, I am convinced it is so. Now is a time when both the church and the Remnant of Israel need to reexamine their priorities and embrace paradigms and priorities suited to the times.

New Paradigms, New Tensions

Times of transition not only bring new missional dynamism; they are also times of destabilization, threat, and jockeying for power.

Any of us who have been change agents in times of transition can attest to the controversies, denunciations, and resistance attending such efforts. For example, have we forgotten how many in the conservative Christian world resisted what Jews for Jesus stood for in its early days? As one ridiculous example, Moishe Rosen had a file of letters from Jack Wyrtzen exhorting him to have the Jews for Jesus guys cut their hair and shave their beards. Of course he had chapter and verse to back him up. And I'm sure that all of us who are leaders of groundbreaking Yeshua-groups have been called on the carpet by concerned or outraged critics not only differing with us, but also denouncing us in some way. It's still going on. Today you can discover "proof" on the Internet that many of us are involved in a one-world, one-religion conspiracy! Yes it's news to me, too.

Because we represent groups birthed in God-ordained times of transition, we have all had to learn to live with opposition and vilification. Now new and different transitions are upon us—and with the growth of new paradigms, new tensions have arisen. Now the tensions and vilifications are not from outsiders, but among ourselves.

David Bosch traces the past and future of mission theology under the overall concept of paradigm shifts. Beginning with the writings of Thomas Kuhn, the father of modern paradigm theory, he explains reasons why advocates of new paradigms always meet with denunciations and resistance. We may see our situation magnified and clarified through the lens of his words:

> [A shifting of paradigms] seldom happens without a struggle, however, since scientific communities are by nature conservative and do not like their peace to be disturbed; the old paradigm's protagonists continue for a long time to fight a rearguard action … Proponents of the old paradigm often just cannot understand the arguments of the proponents of the new. Metaphorically speaking, the one is playing chess and the other checkers on the same board.
>
> This explains why defenders of the old order and champions of the new frequently argue at cross-

> purposes. Protagonists of the old paradigm, in particular, tend to immunize themselves against the arguments of the new. They resist its challenges with deep emotional reactions, since those challenges threaten to destroy their very perception and experience of reality, indeed their entire world.[7]

Bosch and Kuhn are reading our mail. This is us, and this is now.

The Bad-News Gospel [8]

Because our sojourn in Christian space, particularly the evangelical camp, affects all our missional thinking and doing, we must recognize how Christendom has not presented the gospel as good news for all Israel since the end of the first century, and what this should mean for us now.

In the famous Christmas story, we read words so familiar we miss their import. They provide a core insight we must embrace if we would be faithful messengers:

And in that region there were shepherds out in the field, keeping watch over their flock by night. And an angel of the Lord appeared to them, and the glory of the Lord shone around them, and they were filled with fear. And the angel said to them, "Be not afraid; for behold, I bring you good news of a great joy which will come to all the people; for to you is born this day in the city of David a Savior, who Christ, the Lord.[9]

Notice the phrase, "good news of a great joy which will come to all the people." It is too easy to misread the reference as "good news of great joy which will come to all the peoples of earth," but that is not the referent here. The context speaks of one people in particular, the Jewish people. Many will recoil from this aspect of our text due to reflexively regarding the Jewish people as fundamentally spiritually lost, eternal losers, and the coming of Christ as not being good news for *the* Jewish people, but at best, good news only for *some* Jews, exceptions to the rule.

Although this is the position most of us adhere to, it raises problems. Let one suffice for now. The year before Yeshua died and rose, faithful Jews needed only seek to live faithful to God, trusting in His faithfulness to Israel and in the provisions he had made through the Temple sacrifices. Under such an arrangement, certainly there must have been tens of thousands, hundreds of thousands, or even millions of Jews whose status with God was assured, in this life and the next.

But with the coming of Christ, all that changed. Now, according to the prevailing paradigm, all of these Jews were fundamentally lost, unless and until they accepted Christ as their personal Savior. Is this the kind of gospel we preach? And if so, how is *this* gospel good news for all Israel rather than for a spiritually enlightened elite minority? It will not do to respond that Yeshua is good news for all Israel, as a medicine might be for seriously ill patients, who must take the medicine if they would recover. To speak thus is to read back into the context something which is not there: the angelic messenger assumes the gospel to be good tidings for Zion for whom the triumphant and vindicating reign of their God is becoming evident in the birth of the Son of David.[10]

Terrance Tiessen reminds us that holding to the evangelical paradigm that salvation is a matter of one-by-one destiny, with no salvation except for those who accept Christ as their personal savior, means the coming of Jesus was bad news for the Jews of his generation, as myriads of formerly saved Jews and perhaps God-fearers slipped into perdition or least into eternal jeopardy, because the basis of salvation had changed and narrowed with Yeshua's incarnation, crucifixion, resurrection, or ascension, take your pick.[11] This is like your car warranty becoming invalid because the warranty holder went out of business, with you needing to buy a new warranty involving new stipulations and costs if you want coverage. Is this good news for you? And is the one-by-one gospel good news for all the people of Israel? Hardly.

Donald Anderson McGavran, founder of the Fuller Seminary School of Intercultural Studies, took as his watchword "πάντα τά ἔθνη—panta ta ethne," all the nations. Today I urge that we take as our own a neglected biblical mandate, παντὶ τῷ λαῷ —panti tow laow, all the people of Israel.

As will become clearer later, we have cropped and narrowed the gospel message due to our focus on individual soul salvation. The eternal lostness of who fail to accept our "medicine" is always the backdrop of our presentation, even if not stated. This means that the message we deliver to a Jewish "contact" is not only of the opportunity for him or her to be "saved," but also of the certain perdition of the vast majority of the descendants of Jacob, likely including fifty generations (two thousand years) of his or her family. How is such a message "good news of a great joy which will come to all the people (of Israel)?"

Years ago, Mark Kinzer made an off-hand comment, the seed of what I am saying: "I just think that somehow the coming of Yeshua the Messiah must have advanced the condition of the Jewish people." Do we believe that with the coming of the Messiah, the condition of the Jewish people as a whole took a great leap backward? It *is* an interesting question, don't you think?

I am suggesting that our paradigms and presentations of the gospel are imbalanced and misshapen. Part of the problem is that our gospel is shrunken and distorted. How and why this is so will become clearer as we proceed. For example, consider the phenomenon of category mistakes.

Category Mistakes

One reason for our confusion about Jews, Judaism and the gospel, is the category mistakes the church, mission, and Messianic Jewish communities make about Jews and Judaism. The term "category mistake," devised by English philosopher Gilbert Ryle, names "cases where we talk of something in terms appropriate only to something of a radically different kind."[12]

Many Christians, many of us, and many of our constituents, act and think as if the seed of Jacob is a nation like any other, and Judaism a religion like any other religion, except for Christianity. This attitude is a legacy from supersessionism, infused like dye throughout the warp and woof of much of our theologizing. According to such assumptions, Jews no longer enjoy the status they once did now that Christ has come "and his own received him not."[13] Of course, we would protest that the Jews remain a unique and chosen people, referencing numerous texts highlighting the unique status of the Jewish people.[14] No doubt all of us here avoid this particular category mistake: we see the Jewish people as still a unique and chosen people.

Yet many of us make the same kind of category mistake whenever we feel and think of Judaism as being a religion no different from other religions, and by extension, Jews who do not believe in Yeshua as no different from other people when it comes to knowledge of God, spiritual experience, status, and salvation. In feeling, thinking, speaking, and writing, many view the Jews as simply non-Christians, categorically bound for hell, without hope and without God in the world, effectively pagans, even if religious ones. Whenever we do so, we slot the Jewish people into a category Paul applied not to Israel, but to Gentile pagans. Still, some regard Judaism as a fruitless religion, no different categorically from Hinduism, animism, or Buddhism. They consider Judaism to be a dead, false religion, devoid of the Spirit, and its practitioners, wasting their time on a religion that can neither save them, commend them to God, nor mediate to them any measure of true knowledge and experience with Him. This negation of Jewish religion is axiomatic for some of us, and woe to the person who questions such a position or takes an opposing stance. He or she is sure to be regarded as deviant, dangerous, and at best, confused.[15]

But something is very wrong here. Judaism is *not* a religion just like all the others, any more than Israel is simply a people like all the others. Just as the Jews remain the chosen people, Judaism remains the context of this people's trans-generational communal devotion to the God and Father of our Lord Yeshua the Messiah, and their covenantal bond with him.[16] Can this be said of any other people and their religion? Of course not! No, the Jewish people are in a different category from any other people, and their religion is not simply just another non-Christian religion.

John Howard Yoder helps us here, correcting our category mistake and that of Christendom, by referring to Judaism as "a non-non-Christian religion."[17] We are not speaking here of a two-covenant theory, or of the alleged impropriety or superfluity of gospel proclamation to this people. When we say that the Jewish people are a non-non-Christian people, we correct the category mistake of simply thinking of Jews as non-Christians and Judaism as a fruitless and fundamentally false religion, equivalent to any other world religion one might name. Paul was closer to the truth, speaking to Herod Agrippa the Jews and Judaism as his own people and religion:

> My manner of life from my youth, spent from the beginning among my own nation and at Jerusalem, is known by all the Jews. They have known for a long time, if they are willing to testify, that according to the strictest party of *our religion* [not *their* religion] I have lived as a Pharisee. And now I stand here on trial for hope in the promise made by God to our fathers, to which our twelve tribes hope to attain, as *they earnestly worship night and day*.[18]

How many Jewish mission newsletters would publish articles categorizing religious Jews as "earnestly worshipping [God] night and day?" How many would refer to the Judaism practiced by other Jews as "our religion." None, I would imagine. And this is because our categories have changed. But if we would rightly commend the gospel to the Jewish people we must repudiate the colossal category mistakes of ham-fistedly thinking of the Jews as just like any other non-Christian people, and Judaism as no different from any other non-Christian religion. Although most Jews are not categorically Christians, Judaism is a non-non-Christian religion, and we might even term Jews "non-non-Christians." To paraphrase the Prophet Balaam, "Ours is a people … and a religion … that dwells apart, that shall not be numbered with the nations nor with pagan religions."[19]

Crypto-Supersessionism

In some ways, the river of Jewish missions and much Messianic Jewish thinking flows between the banks of unawareness on the one side and denial on the other. Ironically, this flows from our Zionism, our conviction that the Jewish people remain God's chosen people, and our vigorous opposition to supersessionism. Because we denounce supersessionism, we imagine ourselves to be axiomatically positive about the Jewish people in contrast to most of the church. But again, there are problems.

Consider the teaching, popular in some of our circles: that the Law of Moses is categorically rendered inoperative, and that, since the death of Messiah, the only Law that applies to Yeshua-believers is the Law of Christ. Since the church too is subject only to the Law of Christ, is it not clear that this teaching postulates the expiration of a major status marker that formerly attached to the Jewish people? Yes, I know there are those who would say that the Abrahamic Covenant with the promise of blessing and the Land remains in effect, but in practical terms, the jettisoning of the Law of Moses and the substitution of what is termed "the Law of Christ" means abolishing Judaism for Jewish Yeshua-believers and assimilating them into a code of conduct and way of life indistinguishable from Gentile Christians—the same Law, the Law of Christ. I must protest, and suggest you join me. It will not do to imagine that maintaining pride in Jewish lineage, or attending periodic Jewish Yeshua-believer meetings will sustain Jewish identity for us and our descendants.[20] It will take more than nostalgia about our Jewish ancestors and the expectation of a Millennium to come to inform and sustain Jewish continuity, covenantal living, and trans-generational identity. If we accept that we are subject to no religious law other than the same Law of Christ to which the average white-bread Gentile in Tulsa subscribes, then we are fitting Jewish community and continuity into a plain pine box. It's time to say *Kaddish.*

This doctrine of the expiration of the Law of Moses for Messianic Jews is but one example of crypto-supersessionism, an unconscious cluster of presuppositions which assume the expiration, setting aside, or suspension of that status and those status markers formerly attached to the Jewish people. Unlike supersessionism itself, crypto-supersessionism is a virus epidemic among those who repudiate supersessionism. This plague casts its cold shadow across almost all of the Jewish missions and Messianic Jewish world, leaving behind a trail of misdeeds and misstatements. Examples surround us like Spanish moss in the bayou.

For example, a contemporary Jewish mission newsletter said this:

> Scripture teaches that God has called a social community into being, a community comprised of both Jews and Gentiles, what one early church writer even called a "third race." … We are not advocating that Jewish believers distance themselves from their Jewish heritage. May it never be! But our primary spiritual and social home must be among those whom we allow to influence us the most and that should be the body of believers.[21]

While I applaud the author's caveat concerning not distancing ourselves from our Jewish heritage, his wider context and choice of language enfeebles its force. The Jewish covenantal calling is a communal calling, requiring of us an ever-renewed engagement with the wider Jewish community, rather than the standoffish caution proposed here. The author further vitiates our covenantal calling by terming it our "heritage." Whenever the holy obligations of the Jewish people are treated like cultural souvenirs instead of mandates from on high, we encounter crypto-supersessionism.

More alarming still is the author's telltale reference to Christians as "a third race." This expression from the second century *Epistle to Diognetus*, is used to mean that in Messiah, Jews are no longer Jews, and Gentiles no longer Gentiles, that the two constitute a third race. I imagine we all find this rather repugnant when so stated. The concept feels Neo-Platonic, treating Jew and Gentiles in the Body of Messiah as discarnate and denationalized souls, negating the persistence of Jewish communal identity. Only the virus of crypto-supersessionism could cause a Jewish Yeshua-believer to issue a caution against bonding with the Jewish community, advocating a superseding bonding with the church, in view of the third race nature of the people of God.

Dan Juster's views, while not identical, greatly overlap mine in regard to crypto-supersessionism. His preferred term, "hidden replacement theology," is interchangeable with mine, although his area of concern is the persistence of these views in the church, while my concern is with Jewish missions and Messianic Jews. Juster refers with approval to the views of Michael Wyschogrod on this matter:

> Wychogrod's assertion that "The Church will not have fully repented of its replacement theology until it teaches its baptized Jews that they are responsible to live a Jewish life based on Torah." [Wyschogrod] realizes the logic that anything less is still replacement theology.

Our light for evaluation [of Wyschogrod's position] is based on Romans 11:29, where Paul argues that the gifts and call of God to Israel are irrevocable and Romans 11:5 where he calls Jewish disciples of Yeshua the saved remnant of Israel. Therefore, if we want to see the growth of identifiable Jewish disciples of Yeshua, and do not desire to see Israel diminished, it would seem that Wyschogrod's argument is airtight.[22]

Individualism, Community, and the Consummation

Post-Enlightenment individualism corrupts our relationship with our people and our understanding of their status. Such individualism, endemic in our time, blinds us to the communal context of our gospel proclamation. Bosch strikes a necessary balance here, and we need to hear his critique of how individualism corrupts our perceptions and activities:

The gospel is not individualistic. Modern individualism is, to a large extent, a perversion of the Christian faith's understanding of the centrality and responsibility of the individual. In the wake of the Enlightenment, and because of its teachings, individuals have become isolated from the community that gave them birth.[23]

How many of us are isolated from the community that gave us birth? And how many of us preach a gospel that isolates Jews from the Jewish community? While at first we recoil from the suggestion, further thought should leave many of us shuddering with recognition.

We need to recover again or discover for the first time a deep sense of communal identity and responsibility, and of the communal nature of God's eschatological purposes for Israel and the nations. This sense of the Jewish communal context is summarized nicely for us in Ezekiel 37:21-28, where five facets of God's eschatological purpose for the Jewish people are named. In these times of transition, we can only faithfully serve God's purpose among the Jewish people by treating each of these facets as a non-negotiable priority. Notice that they are all communal—good news for all Israel, not as individuals, but as a whole, *communal* good news.

Ezekiel lists the facets of this good news in this order:

- ✓ The re-gathering of the Jewish to our homeland, Israel (thus, Aliyah)
- ✓ The restoration of the unity of the people of Israel
- ✓ Repentance-renewal24 for the people as a whole
- ✓ Messiah reigning in the center of this gathered people
- ✓ Torah living as the communal life of this people

God is to be praised that each of these priorities is being widely reflected in the Messianic Jewish movement, although, in most cases in an inconsistent and rudimentary manner. Yet for others, this is no description of their current mentality, practice and message because they are infected with crypto-supersessionism and individualism. In broadest outline, this is the kind of gospel we should be proclaiming to the Jewish people, seeing Yeshua in his reigning role, bringing communal blessings to the whole people of Israel. And God is calling us, infused with his Spirit, to vigorously, joyously and communally incarnate and serve these synergistic priorities. Anything less and anything other than this is at best someone else's gospel. Our people will rightly continue to find an individualistic message of soul salvation which fails to highlight God's continued commitment and consummating purposes for the community of Israel to be stale, irrelevant, and foreign—far less and far other than God's invitation to participate in the anticipated vindication and blessing of the seed of Jacob. We must repent and return to this perspective.

Adopting a New Creation Eschatology

Craig Blaising identifies another habit of thought to recognize and forsake: the explicit or tacit acceptance of a spiritual vision eschatology. Spiritual vision eschatology is that view of the final state "which sees eternal life as timeless, changeless, spiritual existence consisting primarily in the human soul's full knowledge of God … a direct view, a beatific vision."[25] Such a vision sees the redeemed with spiritual bodies composed of some sort of spiritual substance, and views earthly life as a symbol (and preparation) for these eternal realities. Because "a future for Israel literally has no place in a spiritual-vision eschatology,"[26] when we hold to these assumptions, we are desensitized to the prophetic expectation that drove the apostles. Even tacitly, our sympathies for a glorious and eternal future for Israel are weakened.

Some want to have it both ways, seeing the physical promises for Israel fulfilled in a Millennium, with the eternal state being some version of spiritual-vision eschatology. Without dismissing millennial beliefs, I concur with Blaising's critique, that "a limited duration [millennial] kingdom alone does not do full justice to the Biblical vision for Israel and the Gentiles."[27]

New creation eschatology restores the communal dimension individualism destroys, providing a holistic vision of time and eternity fully compatible with the thrust of this paper:

> New creation eschatology emphasizes the liberation of the cosmos from sin, the bodily resurrection and glorification of the righteous, and the liberation of the cosmos to share in the liberty of the children of God. It does not see the eschaton as simply a continuation of the past, but does emphasize its continuity with the past as seen in the resurrection of the body. New creation does not see the eschaton as a timeless, changeless or essentially visionary-like epistemic state. It is not eternal in the classic timeless sense but everlasting. New creation has a place for the earth, the cosmos, for the fullness of created life, but especially for resurrected human life living under the lordship of the resurrected Jesus Christ in fellowship with the Triune God. It would see human life in created wholeness—not as

> undifferentiated individuals but as differentiated individuals. But neither would it see them as just differentiated individuals, but rather differentiated in ethnic and communal dimensions as well, since these form an essential aspect of our identities. And what will we find here except Israel and the Gentiles who are together blessed by God, living under the lordship of Jesus Christ to the glory of God.[28]

Blasing's views point us to the outreach revolution that summons us. Such views not only uproot post-Enlightenment individualism, they also unseat a tunnel-vision focus on heaven and hell issues, while disempowering the seduction of crypto-supersessionist assumptions such as third-race ecclesiology. Instead, we see a panorama of the covenantal and communal future of the Jewish people, and the promise of resurrection to communal life in a new heavens and a new earth where righteousness dwells. God is glorified not simply by the salvation of nationals, individuals extracted from the nations and incorporated into a homogenous people of God, but by his saving work among nations and people groups, all destined to retain their creational distinctiveness into the eschaton: resurrected, glorified humans in community, not a non-differentiated crowd of souls gazing forever in adoring wonder before the Throne.

John Stackhouse reminds us that "Salvation is about heading for the New Jerusalem, not heaven: a garden city on earth, not the very abode of God and certainly not a bunch of pink clouds in the sky. … And salvation is not only about what is to come but also about what is ours to enjoy and foster here and now."[29] His last phrase, "ours to enjoy and foster here and now" lies at the heart of the outreach revolution that I believe God is calling us to in our remnant role. We are being called to prepare the way of the Lord by being a sign, demonstration and catalyst of God's consummating purpose for Israel.

Second Peter the dynamic tension between waiting and preparing:

Since all these things are to be dissolved in this way, what sort of persons ought you to be in leading lives of holiness and godliness, waiting for and hastening the coming of the day of God, because of which the heavens will be set ablaze and dissolved, and the elements will melt with fire? But, in accordance with his promise, we wait for new heavens and a new earth, where righteousness is at home.[30]

Matters of Content

When I first learned of my assigned topic, I was uneasy. Charles Dickens explains why.

In the second chapter of *Hard Times,* Dickens draws an indelible portrait of Victorian education at its worst, describing how the strict school master Thomas Gradgrind torments sweet little Sissy Jukes over her inability to satisfactorily define a horse. Sissy's father works with horses, and she certainly knows and loves them. But the abrasive Gradgrind gets her flustered and tongue-tied.

Predictably annoyed, Gradgrind turns instead to a pupil more to his liking, a lad named Bitzer, who does not disappoint him.

"Bitzer," said Thomas Gradgrind. "Your definition of a horse."

"Quadruped. Graminivorous. Forty teeth, namely twenty-four grinders, four eyeteeth, and twelve incisive. Sheds coat in the spring; in marshy countries, sheds hoofs, too. Hoofs hard, but requiring to be shod with iron. Age known by marks in mouth." Thus (and much more) Bitzer.

"Now girl number twenty," said Mr. Gradgrind. "You know what a horse is."[31]

Didn't Sissy Jukes know better than either Gradgrind or Bitzer what a horse is? Did Bitzer's definition really capture the wonder that is a horse? Is it not clear that Bitzer's definition, however accurate, remains wholly inadequate? Obviously, we all want to avoid duplicating Bitzer's blunder in "defining" the gospel.

Conditioned by evangelicalism and post-Enlightenment conceits, we may at first think that defining the gospel is a straightforward matter, and simple, really: begin by quoting 1 Corinthians 15:3-4, and throw in some discussions of the etymology and uses of *evangelion.* I advise against this approach! The gospel should not and cannot really be defined in the same manner as other terms. We must not convert the wonder that is the gospel into some slot in our systematics. We can define philosophical terms, because they are constructs of the mind devised to facilitate thought, but the gospel is something else entirely—it is fundamentally a report we have received and which we pass on, an authoritative, empowered, but always fragmentary report concerning God's saving intervention in Jesus Christ.

Which brings us to 9-11.

We all saw news reports about the 9-11 tragedy. Some of us were eyewitnesses, or nearly so, while others of us were a continent or even an ocean away, glued to the television. But, whatever the case, whenever we speak of 9-11 we are exchanging impressions, perceptions and something always greater than what we know, think, and say.

The gospel is not a concept, nor even a term to be defined. Rather, the gospel is fundamentally a report (Isaiah 53), good tidings of great joy for all the people of Israel (Luke 2), and yes, a message to be delivered (1 Cor 15), which is always a reduction of the reality being reported. Although the gospel is not whatever one says it is, nor everything in general, it is and always will be more than we can grasp and define. After all, when we speak of the gospel, angels bow.

In *Be My Witnesses,* Darrell Guder repeatedly visits this issue:

> Only through its pilgrimage through time can the church discover the vast dimensions of the meaning and application of the gospel. The early Christian community, although evangelized and instructed by the apostles themselves, did not fully grasp what the gospel meant. In fact, the church has not yet grasped the full meaning of the gospel.[32]

Reflecting further, he calls for a theological modesty seldom found in our ranks:

> It would be wise for us to approach with modesty the task of gospel definition. … When we assume that our confidence is to be placed in the accuracy of our dogmatic formulations, the reliability of our particular confessional definitions of the gospel, or a particular version of the inspiredness of Scripture, we have transformed the gospel into a subtle kind of Gnosticism.[33]

Theological immodesty and certitude-addiction leads to truncated, mangled truth. Worse still, convinced partisans often will denounce and attack others, who may, like Sissy Jukes, actually sense or know aspects of the gospel invisible to them.

Matters of Controversy

Before turning to a summary and concluding report, or description, of the gospel, we should clear from our path matters of controversy blocking our way.

"Find Heaven, Avoid Hell"

In 2000, I attended the meeting of the Evangelical Theological Society at the Opryland Hotel in Nashville, Tennessee. Riding from the airport to the hotel, a missionary to the Jews whom I hardy knew, without any warning whatsoever, badgered me with one question: "Do you believe that a Jew who does not believe in Jesus goes to hell?" Aside from being put off by his abrasive approach, I was mystified as to why, of all questions he might have selected, he chose *this* one to test of my orthodoxy? Why this preoccupation with the population of perdition?

Of the eighteen evangelistic sermons in the Book of Acts, none uses the find-heaven-avoid-hell approach as a motivation either for missional engagement by the apostolic messengers, or for repentance by their hearers. Neil Rees, International Coordinator for World Horizons International, forcefully reminds us that "the basic apostolic kerygma fails to mention hell as a motive for accepting the gospel message," adding that "the apostles were perfectly capable of evangelizing without threatening their hearers with hell … [and] this is never developed in evangelistic preaching."[34] He states further that using the prospect of others going to hell as a goad for missionary action or financial support "succeeds only in producing feelings of self-condemnation rather than considered and solid commitment."[35] Should not these facts make us suspicious of a fixation on heaven and hell issues?

"You Are Going to Destroy the Engine Driving Outreach to the Jews"

I would not and do not deny the reality of hell, nor minimize its significance in Holy Writ. But I do question why this was such a focus of attention for my tram-mate and for many others, whether explicitly or implicitly, considering its total absence from the apostolic kerygma. It seems current vehemence surrounding this issue stems from how this doctrine has been long-used to spur missional action, support and response, and how it is used to inform polemical sparring. My guess is that some imagine that my call to ease off on this approach is nothing less than an attack on mission to the Jewish people, through disassembling its engine.

The reverse is true. Instead, I want to replace this non-apostolic engine with an older one—better rooted in the Bible and better behaving on the road God is calling us to. This engine has four "pistons" helpfully summarized in the opening verses of "The Lord's Prayer."

The First Piston of Our Missional Engine: Sharing Our Relationship with God

The Lord's Prayer begins "Our Father." Our first motivation for missional action is to call others to the depth of relationship with God we ourselves enjoy. A moment's thought will prove that this is what energized the apostles. Through their encounter with Messiah and their infusion with His Spirit, God had become so luminously real to them that they could not but tell others what they had seen and heard, which had brought them to this joy, this power, this intoxication. Our first missional motivation should then be to share with others the vital relationship with God driving us. But what is *our* experience with God? The early church was awash in wonder. Are we? Or are we practiced professionals, with a Bible verse and answer for anyone who asks us for a reason for the hope that is in us, while, to tell the truth, we're out of touch with the God of hope. I know that when I was in my forties, I had to repent of how my relationship with God had become peripheral to me, even while I was preoccupied with "ministry." Can anyone relate?

The Second Piston of Our Missional Engine: The Doxological Motive

The second phrase of the Lord's Prayer, "Hallowed be Thy Name," names what missional literature terms "the doxological motive," a passion to see God glorified and worshiped. Contemporary scholars are nearly unanimous in emphasizing this to be the most powerful piston of all, able to drive the entire engine, and do it well.

After tracing throughout the Bible the centrality of the glorification of God, Steve Hawthorne applies his findings to the contemporary missional task, contrasting the doxological motive with other motives, including "find-heaven-avoid-hell." "Guilt-based appeals to care for billions of people continue to soften our hearts a little. In practice, however, they weary and harden believers to a minimal token obedience. … Now more than ever believers need to be nurtured into a jealousy for God's glory."[36]

Today, John Piper is the leading advocate of the preeminence of God's glory. His perspective is a much-needed counterbalance to task-oriented and statistically driven approaches:

> Worship is ultimate, not missions, because God is ultimate, not man. … Worship, therefore, is the fuel and goal of missions. It's the goal of missions because in missions we simply aim to bring the nations into the white-hot enjoyment of God's glory. The goal of missions is the gladness of the peoples in the greatness of God.[37]

Some might imagine that Piper wins adherents to his view from Reformed circles alone. However, this is not the case. In a fascinating article, fundamentalist pastor and educator, Sam Horn (B.A., M.A., Ph.D. Bob Jones University!) tells how he encountered, resisted, and was eventually converted to Piper's views. Using the same metaphor of the missional engine, he makes the issue unmistakable:

> I was also forced to consider that God's desire to be worshipped by men of all nations is actually the engine that drives biblical missions rather than the need of lost men to be saved from an eternal hell. In short, my perspective on missions was too man-centered.[38]

He goes on to highlight a related concept that Mark Kinzer and I highlighted in our flyer, "The Emerging Messianic Jewish Paradigm," and not without controversy. We said this: Such outreach proclaims the Name of Jesus, not the neediness of Jews.

Sometimes mission approaches to the Jewish people include the assumption or even declaration of the emptiness and inadequacy of Jewish religious practice and faith. In contrast, the apostolic motivation for outreach to Jewish people was driven by the realization that in Yeshua, the long awaited Messiah had come. The oft-quoted passage, "There is no other name given among mortals by which we must be saved," comes in a context where Peter and John were seeking to lift up the name of Jesus rather than put down the Jewish people: "for we cannot keep from speaking about what we have seen and heard" (Acts 4:12, 20). We would do well to imitate their example and lift up the name of Yeshua without denigrating the holy things already given to the Jewish people (see Rom. 3:1-4; 9:1-5).[39]

Sam Horn helps to silence outcries against our call to leave off a preoccupation with Jewish "neediness" and instead uplift the name of Yeshua.

At the heart of Biblical revelation is God's self-revelation to man. Part of what God chose to reveal in the Scriptures concerns His primary motive for the activities ascribed to Him in the words of the Book. That motivation can be summed up in the phrase, "God does what He does for the sake of His name." God's primary motive in the salvation of lost men is doxological, "for the sake of His name" (Isa. 63:7-14; Acts 15:14; Rom. 1:5). The Scriptures reveal God's primary motive in delivering His children from their troubles is "the sake of His name" (I Sam. 12:22; Ps. 106:8). God's primary motive in showing mercy to sinning people is "the sake of His name" (Isa. 48:9; Ezek. 20:44). God's primary motive in dealing with the wicked is "the sake of His name" (Exod. 9:14-16; Rom. 9:17). Finally, God's primary motive in His dealings with saved men is "the sake of His name" (I John 2:12; Acts 9:16).[40]

Sam Horn, John Piper, and Steve Hawthorne are right in redirecting our attention to the centrality of lifting up the name of God and the name of Yeshua. Can we deny that the supremacy of Yeshua's name rather than the alleged spiritual bankruptcy or neediness of the Jewish people or of a hell-bound Sanhedrin was uppermost in the minds of Peter and John? I challenge all of us to examine deeply why it is that some of us fight so energetically to maintain our habitual preoccupation with the neediness of Jews, a habit that leads to repeatedly proving to ourselves and to others the alleged futility, vacuity, and impotence of the Jewish way of life. This is not the engine that drove the apostles who lived to glorify Yeshua and the One who raised him from the dead. Isn't this focus and motivation good enough for us?

The Third Piston of Our Missional Engine: Hastening the Consummation of All Things

When we speak of ourselves as "the Remnant of Israel," what do we mean? And what relationship does this have to the consummation of all things?[41]

Dan Johnson[42] demonstrates how Scripture presents two different modalities of remnant identity, one being survivors of a time of judgment, the other being the seed from which God's continuing purposes will be realized. Both of these perspectives are to be found in Romans 9 to 11. Johnson finds the earliest reference to the remnant as the seed and earnest of future blessing in the verb form used in Genesis 7:23, "only Noach was *left* (*vayisha'er akh noakh*), along with those who were with him in the ark," the term, *vayish'er* being elated to the term *sh'erit* (remnant). As Noach/Noah, his family, and the animals in the left with them in the Ark (as a remnant) were a sign of God's continuing purpose for the earth, and instruments for its realization, so the eschatological remnant of Israel of Romans 9 to 11 is meant to be a sign, demonstration and catalyst of God's continuing purposes for the Jewish people—a seed of good things to come. This is our calling.

In Romans, chapters nine to eleven, Paul speaks of two "fullnesses," "the fullness of the nations" (11:25) and "the fullness of Israel" (11:12). Paul calls Israel's fullness greater than the fullness of the Gentiles (**πόσῳ** μᾶλλον τὸ πλήρωμα αὐτῶν … "How much greater will their fullness be?" (Rom. 11:12). Therefore if the fullness of the Gentiles is associated with the Great Commission, the fullness of Israel, that "greater riches" God will bring to pass, may be termed "the Greater Commission," as this reality affects our Remnant responsibilities.

Because we are so used to operating out of an older paradigm, these concepts, and terms like "the Greater Commission" may come as a shock. However, these reflect biblical realities. The Great Commission might more properly be termed "the Penultimate Commission," for it is the magnificent prelude to something greater. The Greater Commission is our Remnant calling. God is calling us to prepare the way for the fullness of all Israel.

But are we listening? If we are nearing the pivotal juncture when the gigantic wheel of God's purpose is turning toward the fullness of Israel, we cannot simply go on with business as usual, living by older paradigms. Our responsibility is as great as our privileges.[43] Our role in the consummation of things is crucial and pivotal. I don't know about you, but this heats up my blood!

The Fourth Piston of Our Missional Engine: Obedience

Obedience to God, "thy will be done, on earth as it is in heaven," is our fourth powerful piston. And even if this were the only one, it would be more than enough to drive our engine. We must speak to our people about Yeshua because we have been commanded to do so. Paul's words apply to us: "For if I preach the gospel that gives me no ground for boasting. For necessity is laid upon me. Woe to me if I do not preach the gospel!"[44] Cannot such a piston drive our engine? Of course it can! And beyond that, should we not be passionate to "bring about the obedience of faith for the sake of His name" among all the people of Israel, as was Paul's passion for the nations?[45]

Such a mighty missional engine roars at the curbside like a Maserati, its door open, waiting only for us to get in the driver's seat to go zero-to-sixty in five seconds flat. By comparison, the find-heaven-avoid-hell motivation seems like a donkey, energized by a carrot and a stick! I may be taking away our donkey, but our Father in heaven has given us the keys to the Maserati. Let's take her out on the road! [46]

"The Law of Moses Has Been Rendered Inoperative"

On the basis of the lexical meaning of *katargeo* ("render inoperative"), some argue that the Law of Moses has lost all force and authority, having now been replaced by the law of Messiah, by extension making inoperative any argument for God's preordained return to Torah-based covenant-faithfulness by the seed of Jacob. Is there any answer to this objection? Actually, there are many answers.

First, defining "the Law of Christ/Messiah" as "all the individual commandments from Christ and the Apostles applicable to a New Testament believer"[47] should not be regarded as either the unanimous or majority view of the exegetical community. Todd Wilson introduces his survey of recent opinion on the matter in a manner that should at least give all of us pause before confidently asserting the Law of Messiah is a code of law replacing the Law of Moses. "While the phrase [the Law of Christ] has traditionally been harmonized with Paul's negative portrayal of the law by treating the phrase either as a circumlocution for Christian living or as a reference to some other "law," a growing number of interpreters want to treat the "law of Christ" as a reference to the *law of Moses.*" Wilson also surveys the widening group of exegetical opinion viewing Paul's "law of faith" and the "law of the Spirit of life" as referring likewise to the Law of Moses.[48]

My point here is not to summarize or advocate for any of these arguments in the literature but instead to caution against accepting as self-evident a position which is by no means a settled issue. We still have homework to do. [49]

But I have a stronger argument against those who would confidently discount the persistence of the Law of Moses on the basis of the alleged meaning of *katargeo*.

D.A. Carson names sixteen word fallacies, of which the eighth is "false assumptions about technical meaning," in which cases, "an interpreter falsely assumes that a word always or nearly always has a certain technical meaning—a meaning usually derived either from a subset of the evidence or from the interpreter's personal systematic theology." He notes that one of this fallacy's corollaries occurs whenever such interpreters "go one step further and reduce an entire doctrine to one word which they have understood to be a technical term."[50] Later, he names and discusses a related error, "unwarranted restriction of the semantic field," by which he means "misunderstanding the meaning of a word in a particular context by illegitimately restricting the word's semantic range."[51]

The heart of the matter is that words are best defined not from lexicons but always from contexts—and often, slightly differently from context to context. Besides, lexicographers have theological commitments, interpretative traditions, and communal interests affecting their interpretations of word meanings. This being the case, those who base their doctrines and stances on lexical data may wrongly attribute objectivity and dependability to lexicons neither objective nor dependable. Furthermore, we who consult lexicons have our own theological commitments, interpretive traditions, and communal interests, all of which cause us to eagerly welcome lexical "evidence" when it appears to confirm our preferences. Lexical evidence is helpful, to be sure, but must always be regarded as provisional, its validity contingent upon rigorous historical, cultural, and semantic analysis of each separate textual context.

It seems to me that those who base their "proof" of the nullification of the Law's authority, alleging that *katargeo* means "to render inoperative," commit methodological error. They illegitimately and prematurely foreclose discussion on a matter that can only be rightly resolved by means of exacting examination of each context where the word is used. Such contexts may illumine or may, on the contrary, contrast with one another in how the term in question is being used elsewhere. And Carson notes that despite our best interpretive efforts, disputed interpretive matters may not be resolved at all, and surely not by a lexicon: "The fallacy lies in thinking the correct interpretation of a passage can be discovered anyway; and in many instances, that is not possible"[52] This calls for us to exercise far greater exegetical caution than is our habit.

Theological positions must be founded on rigorous and self-critical inter-communal exegesis, not on the verdicts of lexicons. Even these hard-won exegeses are not always certain. Therefore, the jury should be recalled on many arguments that have, in the past, seemed settled on lexical grounds. These cases deserve to be reopened, and discussion resumed, not only to define terms, but also to rightly understand both how each specific context influences, shades, and determines meaning, and how these contexts may properly be compared with one another.

Nor does this exhaust the problems created by those who confidently assert that *katargeo* spells the death-knell of the Law of Moses. They can be refuted by what I call "Fruchtenbaum's Criterion." It was Arnold Fruchtenbaum from whom, thirty-five years ago or so, I learned the foundational argument against those who dismiss any distinction between Jew or Gentile on the basis of Galatians 3:28, "There is neither Jew nor Greek, there is neither slave nor free, there is neither male nor female; for you are all one in Christ Jesus." Arnold indicated that we must always ask in what *sense* there is neither Jew nor Greek, neither slave nor free, and neither male nor female. Applying Fruchtenbaum's Criterion to the case at hand, we must be careful to ask, "In what sense, under what conditions, and for whom is the Law of Moses rendered inoperative now that Messiah has come?" The blade of Fruchtenbaum's Criterion cuts down those who, on etymological grounds, confidently assert the demise of the Law.

Two more arguments, briefly noted. First, it is not possible to separate the Law from the narrative of the Older Testament, where the narrative justifies and explains the setting and rationale of the laws there imbedded. The law can no more be successfully extracted from the narrative (or vice versa) than the skeleton can be extracted from a human without killing the patient. Second, and closely related, if the Law of Moses is rendered inoperative, does this not have implications for messianic prophecy? Is this too rendered inoperative now that Messiah has come? And if not, on what basis do we make an exception for the persistence of messianic prophecy from within a body of law and inextricable narrative now declared inoperative?

"Aren't You Arguing for 'The Wider Hope'?"

I argue not *for* the wider hope as much as *against* the wider ego.

It has been decades since I have heard anyone in our circles, speaking on a theological or missiological issue, say, "I don't know." Not many manage to mumble these monosyllables. But wouldn't our relationships with each other be vastly improved if we learned to so speak? As it stands, those who say, "I don't know," especially when asked questions about the census of the redeemed, are regarded as confused, deviant or dangerous. I am suggesting that this kind of marginalization and stigmatization of the diffident is uncalled for, likely rooted not only in theological commitments but also in an appalling lack of theological humility—the wider ego.

I have been encouraged to discover that even missiological giants like David Bosch and Paul Hiebert had smaller egos. We would do well to heed these, who, being dead, yet speak:

Our theologies are partial, and they are culturally and socially biased. They may never claim to be absolutes. Yet this does not make them relativistic, as though one suggests that in theology—since we cannot really ever know "absolutely"—anything goes. It is true that we see only in part, but we do see (Hiebert). We are committed to our understanding of revelation, yet we also maintain a critical distance to that understanding. In other words, we are in principle open to other views, an attitude, which does not, however, militate against complete commitment to our own understanding of truth. We preface our remarks with, "I believe," or, "As I see it" (Hiebert). It is misleading to believe that commitment and a self-critical attitude are mutually exclusive.[53]

Applying such theological humility to our missional task, Bosch says further, "The commitment we give to any theological paradigm is therefore wholehearted and provisional, wholehearted because we hold back nothing from our Lord, provisional because our Lord makes us his witnesses, not his know-it-alls."[54]

I wonder if we got the memo.

Some no doubt remain dissatisfied, demanding a verdict on the status of others, even hypothetical others. Again, I must demur, especially in the case of God's chosen people, whom he hardened for his purpose, but who remain beloved for thc sake of the fathers. The full outworking of the drama of the Jews and the Holy One remains to be played out. A cloud of incense obscures our view of the mercy seat—by divine design. I prefer to echo the roar of another giant, Lesslie Newbigin, one of the most seminal missiologists of the past hundred years. We would do well to hear him:

> I confess that I am astounded at the arrogance of theologians who seem to think that we are authorized, in our capacity as Christians, to inform the rest of the world about who is to be vindicated and who is to be condemned at the last judgment. … I find this way of thinking among Christians astonishing in view of the emphatic warnings of Jesus against these kinds of judgments that claim to preempt the final judgment of God. Nothing could be more remote from the whole thrust of Jesus' teaching than the idea that we are in a position to know in advance the final judgment of God. It would be tedious to repeat again the innumerable warnings of Jesus in this matter, his repeated statements that the last day will be a day of surprises, of reversals, of astonishment. In his most developed parable of the last judgment, the parable of the sheep and the goats, both the saved and the lost are astonished. Surely theologians at least should know that the judge on the last day is God and no one else. … If a theologian is really serious he must learn to understand the impossible possibility of salvation.

In St. Paul we find this same tension of confidence and awareness of the abyss that lies underneath. Paul, who is certain that nothing can separate him from the love of God in Christ Jesus, also tells his friends that he has to exercise severe self-discipline "let having preached to others I myself should be disqualified'' (I Cor. 9:27). The Christian life, lived in the magnetic field between the two poles of the amazing grace of God and the appalling sin in which I share, has a corresponding synthesis of a godly confidence and a godly fear.[55]

Perhaps we should exchange our wider egos for wider souls—like that of Newbigin. I would trade. Would you?

Cumulative Conclusions

Some important disclaimers, lest all I have said be misconstrued:

1. When I speak of the gospel as good news for all Israel, I am neither saying nor implying that all Jews will be in the world to come. I am no more entitled to claim expertise on the census of the redeemed than are others to claim foreknowledge of the roll call of perdition. God alone is judge, and many surprises await us all. I am instead calling us back to a fundamental theme of both Testaments ignored or marginalized by the Church and by Jewish mission for centuries, if not for millennia. The Law and the Prophets point to a glorious hope for all Israel. This concern motivated the apostles and informed their preaching, and is entirely absent from our evangelistic practice, expectation and communal life.[56]
2. When I speak of the gospel as good news for all Israel I am not saying or implying that helping Jews come to Yeshua-faith is a superfluous non-issue. It is a matter of sharing with others our intimacy of relationship with God, of glorifying him, of our remnant responsibility in helping to bring in the consummation, of obedience, and allegiance to the Son of David. Neglect of this responsibility is a matter for which we will all give an account of ourselves to God.
3. I have sought to avoid demeaning anyone of our number or of our broad circle of associates. If I have failed in that regard, I ask forgiveness.
4. I am not saying that my approach alone is worthwhile, with all others bogus or passé. But I am certainly alleging that we have been grossly negligent in not pursuing such an approach deeply aligned with the whole counsel of God, with these times of transition, and with the prophesied consummation.
5. Although there is no mention in this paper of God's will for the nations, this must not be taken to mean that I am unconcerned about the nations or that the Great Commission has no place in my missiology. Nor should my silence on these maters be taken to mean that I am negative about the Church and/or its role. I have focused solely on the people of Israel in keeping with the nature of our symposium, concentrating on our role as part of the Remnant of Israel.

Integrational Thoughts

First, I affirm that repentance and faith play a central role in the message we are called to proclaim. But I also believe that mission culture has had an inconsistent and sub-biblical concept of what repentance means and what it entails for Jews. R. Kendall Soulen helps us with this clarifying statement:

According to the biblical witness, God's work as Consummator takes enduring shape in the history that unfolds between the Lord, Israel, and the nations. Accordingly, *human sin is never merely the sin of the creature against the Creator-Consummator. Human sin is also always the sin of Jew and Gentile, of Israel and the nations.*[57]

The sins of Messianic Jews and of all Israel are far more dire and extensive than simply the record of individual human failings. The sins of all Israel, including Messianic Jews, include and indeed are foundationally our failure to live in covenant faithfulness with Israel's God.

Do Jews need the atonement Yeshua provides? Yes, by all means, yes, but for reasons deeper than we have yet realized and proclaimed. Jewish missionaries and Messianic Jews have always called for other Jews to repent and believe. But we fail to ask, "Repent for what?" By default, we would say, "Repent for being a sinner, for your sins," or perhaps, "Repent for not recognizing the Messiah whom God sent for us."

But this will not do, for we finally only know what sin is when we compare our conduct with what God demands of us. We, the seed of Abraham and Sarah, whose ancestors, standing at the foot of Sinai, said "na'aseh v'nishmah—we will do and we will hear/obey—all that the Lord has spoken we will do"—must repent not of being sinners in general, but of being *Jewish* sinners specifically. The sins of all Israel, including Messianic Jews, include continual and pervasive neglect of the covenant to which we are all obligated (Deut. 29:10-15). Although we may confidently say "There is therefore now no condemnation for those who are in Messiah Yeshua," we may *not* say "there is therefore now no responsibility for those who in Messiah Yeshua." "Yeshua paid it all," but not that we might go back to each of us turning to his own way (Isa. 53:6). Surely, if our sin includes covenant violation, should not our repentance include, not simply faith in the sin-bearer, but also a return to that covenant-faithfulness from which we departed? And is it of no significance that it is precisely to the restoration of this kind of obedience (communally) that God's consummating actions are directed?

Second, under the influence of Enlightenment rationalism, evangelicals have for too long been too focused on the gospel being true news. We zero in on apologetics and Messianic prophecy, good in their own right. However, when the subtext of our message is the certain perdition of the vast majority of the Jews who ever lived, including the intimate family members of those whom we evangelize, anyone who is reasonably astute, or who has been influenced by those opposing our message, is likely to turn to us a deaf ear. The "truth" of the gospel is not likely to make inroads when the news is unwelcome, oppressive, and when it implies, or even theologically *requires*, that the evangelized be eternally separated from their people, axiomatically viewed to be lost forever. Nor will it do to try and hide these implications from those we evangelize: Jewish people are not stupid, and, sooner or later, they know when they have been duped. With our prevailing propositions, we have news for the Jew standing before us: God is going to take her away from her family for ever and ever to be in heaven with him, with most if not all of her loved ones tormented eternally in the lake of fire. Not so good. Can we get back to a gospel that is good news for all Israel without betraying the text of Scripture? I believe we can and I believe we must. And I have tried to help point the way.

Third, we have been too focused on the salvation of individuals, and on individual response, both of which are nevertheless crucial, since all of us will give an account of ourselves to God—individually. But in the process, we have forgotten that the Bible portrays the gospel as good news for *Zion.* It is news of the vindicating and merciful reign of God displayed and accomplished in the One whose goings forth have been from of old, from everlasting days, whose incarnation, death, resurrection, ascension, High Priestly ministry and Davidic reign need to be restored in our thinking to their central place as the means toward prophesied national blessings.

Fourth, we have been too focused on the gospel as atonement, as if this were all there is or the main point, failing to see atonement as part of a "package deal" of sorts, which includes the re-gathering, renewal, reunification, return to covenant faithfulness and messianic fulfillment of all Israel. We have also seen atonement as monolithically individual, which is a strange concept considering the biblical evidence. (See as but one example the prophecy in Daniel 9, which couches the atonement in this broader context of national vindication and salvation.)

Who Has Believed Our Report? Toward a Gospel For All Israel

With all of this in view, consider the following description of the gospel we are being called to commend to our people at this time of transition.

1. The gospel of God for the Jewish people is above all else good news for *all* Israel rather than for a fragmentary spiritually enlightened elite.

2. It is not entirely new news, for the arm of the Lord has rescued Israel time and time again. But it is the good news of God, in covenant faithfulness, doing again what he has done before—coming to rescue his people—but outdoing Himself this time, in the foretold ultimate deliverance, through the faithfulness of Yeshua the Messiah in his incarnation, atoning death, resurrection, and ascension as Great High Priest and ruling Son of David.

3. It is the good news of God vindicating his name and his people Israel in the sight of all nations in victorious strength and faithfulness, to be consummated in the re-gathering, reunification, repentance-renewal, and return to Torah-based covenant faithfulness of the community of Jacob, gathered around Yeshua the Son of David, resurrected and renewed in a new heavens and a new earth where righteousness dwells and joy prevails, in the sight of all nations.

4. Therefore, if our communities and we are to be gospel messengers, we must passionately honor these priorities in our own communities, and, as Remnant people, celebrate, catalyze and advance these priorities in the life of wider Israel.

5. And so, in this fashion and toward such ends," all Israel will be saved." Does this mean every single Jew? Not likely. Rather, Paul is answering the question, "What is going to happen to the Jews as a whole?" For details, see the Letter to the Romans, chapter nine to eleven, against the background of the testimony of the Law and the Prophets to eschatological blessings promised to Israel as a whole.

Related Implications

1. And what of Jewish people who refuse the message? That of course is a serious matter, as has always been the cases whenever our people have rejected or been unresponsive to the saving acts of God. But it is interesting that the Apostles, in their preaching to Jews, never pass a verdict that their rejecting hearers are going to hell. Rather they *warn* them to be careful concerning the possible consequences of such hardness of heart. Giving warnings and delivering verdicts is not the same thing. Again, God alone is judge.

2. Under this paradigm, we need to view ourselves not as missionaries but as prophets. Missionaries come from outside a community with a foreign message: prophets come from within the community, calling the people back to communal standards of faithfulness to God. However, our evangelism will fail if it is only a sales pitch. We must ourselves exemplify the faithfulness to which we are calling others, living for those things which Messiah is bringing to pass—the re-gathering, unification, spiritual repentance renewal, and Torah obedience of all Israel.

3. Our evangelism will involve the following:

    a) Developing modalities (communal expressions) where Yeshua-faith and the power of the Spirit are realities making our pursuit of these goals qualitatively different from what people are likely to encounter elsewhere.

    b) Seeing evangelism as recruiting and involving other Jews in the passionate pursuit of these priorities, we will be agents sensitizing them to the difference made by Yeshua and the Holy Spirit, and inviting them to Yeshua-faith.

    c) Cooperating with and commending Jews of all kinds in their pursuit of whichever of these priorities they are committed to. We are not in competition with them. We should seek out opportunities for cooperation. In such contexts too, our Yeshua-faith and the influence of the Spirit will be made known.

d) Operating within such a model, even if Jewish people do not receive our witness of Yeshua, they will know that we are committed to the well being of the Jewish people and that our gospel is proclaimed as good news for all Israel.

Some Questions To Consider

1. Do we spend far less time speaking with Jews about Yeshua than we do speaking with Yeshua-believers about Jewish evangelism? Why is this? (Try to identify at least two unflattering answers.)
2. Does the approach here presented make you more eager to go out and share the gospel as here defined than you normally are under other paradigms? Why might this paradigm be more energizing?
3. Would most Jewish people we encounter be likely to perceive the message of the gospel as we normally present it as being good news for Jews as a whole? Why/why not?
4. Is our communal life good news for the Jewish people, or a doorway to or evidence of Jewish communal disintegration?
5. Without this vision, what are we left with, and how successful have we been/are we likely to be with our usual approaches?
6. A friend[58] suggests that prevailing approaches self-select those Jews alienated from their own Jewish covenant responsibilities. Do you agree, and is this a good thing?
7. If this evangelistic vision is biblically supportable, and something God is calling us to, would you be willing to implement it despite the social and financial consequences? What might some of those consequences be?

Epilogue

A week ago I received a phone call from a friend, illustrating the burden of this paper. She is an outspoken Messianic Jew in Los Angeles, and an effective witness of her faith. She had been invited to visit the *sukkah* of an Orthodox rabbi active in the area who had been trying to win her back to mainstream Judaism, while she had been witnessing to him.

She had been meeting with him and his family for some time, and this time was quite unsuccessful. He saw that she was "a lost cause" from his point of view. At that point she mentioned Hashivenu, and encouraged him to visit our website. She also mentioned me. It turned out he knew of me, but how?

About two years ago, the Moderator of the General Assembly of the Presbyterian Church (USA) visited Los Angeles to speak at a local church on the divestment issue. Advance publicity indicated that his perspective was bad news for the Jews. I wrote a letter to two rabbis in town. One was Orthodox, but has shown himself willing to go outside the box. The other was a Reform rabbi with a strong social justice record, whom I had met previously. In my letter to these two rabbis I proposed that we picket the Presbyterian Church or the local Presbyterian Church (USA) headquarters in protest of their position on divestment, as highlighted by the planned visit of the denominational dignitary.

I never heard back. But the truth came out in the *sukkah.* As I mentioned, my friend's rabbi friend knew of me. And the reason he did was that "all the rabbis in town had discussed my letter, and had decided it was too loaded an issue to picket with a bunch of Messianic Jews."

What shall we say about this? Should we say, "That just goes to show you. The rabbis will never accept us and only want to convert us back and protect their people from us." Should we say that the letter was a wasted effort and a total loss? To say such things would be a grave mistake. It just will not do for the Remnant of Israel to fold up its skirts and scuttle back into it own enclaves, or seek solace in the lap of the church!

I would say that it is wonderful that all the rabbis in Los Angeles know that the people at my congregation, Ahavat Zion, care about Jewish concerns and stand for the issues that matter to them. I am going to be sending more such letters in the future, and meanwhile develop a synagogue that actively incarnates the glorious future God has for all Israel: gathered, united, repentant, renewed, faithful to his statutes and ordinances, around Yeshua, the reigning Son of David.

Is this not good news for all Israel?

ENDNOTES

1. To prevent abuses of my own, I have chosen to leave unnamed the authors or published sources I criticize in this paper. Anyone requiring further identification of these sources may contact me.
2. "All Israel" is a term borrowed especially from Romans 11:26, connected in this paper to "all the people [of Israel]" in Luke 2:10-11. It is a phrase found 149 times in Scripture. In the present discussion, I believe the sense of the term is equivalent to "Israel as a whole," rather than "every single Jew." This is compatible with the Talmudic view: "All Israel has a share in the world to come: the following (out of Israel) do not have a share in the world to come" (M. Sanhedrin 10:1).
3. Rev. 14:6.
4. Zech. 12:1-3, 9; 14:2,3; Mic. 4:11-13.
5. Deut. 30:8-10, also Ezek. 37:24, "They shall follow my ordinances and be careful to obey my statutes."
6. From the statement affirmed by the Delegates to the 23rd Annual UMJC Conference on July 31, 2002.
7. David Bosch, *Transforming Mission: Paradigm Shifts in Theology of Mission.* (Maryknoll, NY: Orbis, 1992), 184-5. In part, Bosch's argument paraphrases Paul Hiebert, "Epistemological Foundations for Science and Theology," *Theological Students Fellowship Bulletin* (March), 9, and Paul Hiebert, "The Missiological Implications of an Epistemological Shift," *Theological Students Fellowship Bulletin* (May-June), 12.
8. Another aspect of the bad-news gospel is Christendom's habit of denigrating Jewish faith and sancta, postulating that these are worthless when compared with the church's patrimony. This too is bad news, not treated here for the sake of space.
9. Luke 2:8-11.
10. See Isa. 52:7.
11. Terrance L. Tiessen, *Who Can Be Saved? Reassessing Salvation in Christ and World Religions.* (Downers Grove, IL: InterVarsity Press, 2004), 199. Tiessen will argue for "accessibilism," which asserts, "God does save some of the unevangelized, but he has not raised up the world's religions as instruments for achieving this" (Tiessen, 47).
12. Definition accessed on line September 20, 2007 at http://www.philosophyprofessor.com/philosophies/category-mistake.php. For a related study on the history of Christian negative categorization of the Jewish people and Judaism, see Averil Cameron, "Jews and Heretics—A Category Error?" in Adam H. Becker and Annette Yoshiko Reed, *The Ways that Never Parted.* Texts and Studies in Ancient Judaism 95. (Tübingen: Mohr Siebeck, 2003), 345-360.
13. John 1:12.
14. See Deut. 7:6, 14:2, 32:8; Ps. 33:12, 147:19-20; Isa. 43:20, 65:22; Amos 3:2; Rom. 3:1-2, for example.
15. One does not have to look hard or long to find explicit, bald and strident statements from within the Jewish missions and/or Messianic Jewish world denouncing Judaism as categorically no different from other non-Christian religions. Thus, one missionary to says this on his website, "Rabbinic Judaism is a false religion. The synagogues of today are deceptions, which lead Jewish people away from the way of

salvation into a system that rejects Torah, substitutes Torah with human tradition, and leads them into destruction. Rabbinic Judaism is as much a false religion as any other false religion" (Reference available upon request).

16. Along with Mark Kinzer, I believe Judaism to be a house still inhabited by Yeshua even though he is yet to be recognized and explicitly honored by the majority of those living there.
17. John Howard Yoder, *The Jewish-Christian Schism Revisited*, ed. Michael G. Cartwright and Peter Ochs (Grand Rapids: Eerdmans, 2003), 147-159.
18. Acts 26:4-7.
19. Num. 23:9.
20. Although they say much on other matters for which I am grateful and with which I heartily concur, Darrell Bock and Craig Blaising are among those who unwittingly grease the skids for the assimilation of Jewish believers in Jesus when they say "progressive dispensationalism ... teaches that Mosaic covenant law has ended dispensationally, it also teaches that it has been replaced by new covenant law" (Craig L. Blaising, Darrell L. Bock, *Progressive Dispensationalism.* [Grand Rapids: Baker, 1999), 1999. If this is so, then the on-the-ground distinction of Messianic Jewish life and community rests on an exceedingly narrow bed. In their paradigm, in practical terms of lifestyle and legacy, how are Messianic Jews fundamentally different from other Yeshua-believers?
21. Reference available upon request.
22. Dan Juster, "Do We Want the Jews to Disappear?" at http://tikkunministries.org/newsletters/dj-jan06.asp (accessed Sept 27, 2007).
23. Bosch, *Transforming*, 410-411.
24. I hyphenate the two terms, because repentance itself is the fruit of the Spirit at work, and the renewal we value and long is evident in repentance and not possible without it. The two realities, repentance and renewal, are inseparably hand-in hand, and as perceived by the human observer, they can occur in either order.
25. Craig Blaising, "The Future of Israel as a Theological Question," *Journal of the Evangelical Theological Society 44,* no. 3(2001): 448.
26. Ibid., 449.
27. Loc. cit.
28. Ibid. For a fuller treatment on the roots and contrast between spiritual vision eschatology and new creation eschatology, see Craig A. Blaising, "Premillennialsm," in *Three Views of the Millennium and Beyond,* ed. Darrell L. Bock (Grand Rapids: Zondervan, 1999), 160-81.
29. John G. Stackhouse, Jr., ed., *What Does It Mean to be Saved? Broadening Evangelical Horizons About Salvation* (Grand Rapids: Baker Academic, 2002), 10.
30. 2 Pet. 3:11-13.
31. Charles Dickens, *Hard Times*, "Chapter Two - Murdering the Innocents," found on-line at http://www.mtholyoke.edu/acad/intrel/hardtime.htm (accessed September 28, 2007).
32. Guder, Darrell L. *Be My Witnesses: The Church's Mission, Message, and Messengers.* (Grand Rapids, MI: Eerdmans, 1985), 39.
33. Guder, 76.
34. Neal Rees, "*Snatch Others from the Fire and Save Them": An Examination of Belief in Hell as a Motivating Factor in Missions."* Unpublished paper, originally

submitted as a term paper to William Carey International University, http://web.archive.org/web/20050228025757/perso.wanadoo.es/

34. neil/Hell.htm, Accessed on line Sept 20, 2007.
35. Rees, n.d. 12. After providing a succinct and helpful historical survey of Protestant motivations for mission, Gailyn Van Rheenen traces the contemporary shift in such motivations in his aptly titled essay, "Changing Motivations for Missions: From 'Fear of Hell' to 'the Glory of God.'" In Michael Pocock, Gailyn van Rheenen, and Douglas McConnell, eds, *The Changing Face of World Missions: Engaging Contemporary Issues and Trends,* (Grand Rapids, MI: Baker Academic, 2005), 161-181.
36. Steven C. Hawthorne, "The Story of His Glory," in *Perspectives on The World Christian Movement: A Reader*, Ralph D. Winter and Steven C. Hawthorne, eds. (Pasadena CA: William Carey Library, 1999), 15, a pdf found on line September 24, 2007 at www.waymakers.org/_files/glory/StoryGlory.pdf.
37. John Piper. *Let he Nations Be Glad! The Supremacy of God in Missions.* [Second Edition]. (Grand Rapids: Baker Academic, 2003), 17.
38. Sam Horn, "The Heart of Biblical Missions" on his website *Sharper Iron.* http://www.sharperiron.org/2006/10/05/the-heart-of-biblical-missions/ Accessed September 2007.
39. Stuart Dauermann and Mark Kinzer, *The Emerging Messianic Jewish Paradigm* (2005).
40. Horn, *loc cit.*
41. Stuart Dauermann, *Seeds, Weeds, and Walking the High Wire: The Role of the Remnant—Embodying Israel's Destiny.* Unpublished paper from the Hashivenu Forum (Hashivenu: Pasadena, CA, 2006).
42. Dan G. Johnson, "The Structure and Meaning of Romans 11." *Catholic Biblical Quarterly*, 46(1), 1984:91-103.
43. "Every one to whom much is given, of him will much be required; and of him to whom men commit much they will demand the more" (Luke 12:48).
44. 2 Cor. 9:16.
45. Rom. 1:5, 16:26.
46. Johannes Verkuyl, writing thirty years ago, reached similar conclusions, naming six motivations for mission, including all four I identified. His list, in order: obedience; love, mercy and pity; doxology; the eschatological motive (where he makes mention of the Lord's Prayer!); haste; and the personal motive—the arousing of ourselves through arousing others. Verkuyl was the pre-eminent missiologist of the mid-twentieth century *(Contemporary Missiology: An Introduction.* [Grand Rapids: Eerdmans, 1978]), 164-168.
47. Arnold G. Fruchtenbaum, "Messianic Congregations May Exist Within the Body of Messiah as Long as They Don't Function Contrary to the New Testament," In *How Jewish is Christianity? 2 Views on the Messianic Movement.* Stanley N, Gundry and Lois Goldberg, eds. (Grand Rapids: Zondervan. 2003), 121.
48. Todd A. Wilson. "The Law of Christ and the Law of Moses Reflections on a Recent Trend in Interpretation." *Current Issues in Biblical Research.* (London, Thousand Oaks CA and New Delhi: SAGE Publications. Volume 5.1:125-144. Found on line at http://cbi.sagepub.com/cgi/reprint/5/1/123 (Accessed September 23, 2007).

49. Some of our finest minds have done much of the groundwork for us, although space does not permit a review of their argumentation here. Among them, see John Fischer, "Messianic Congregations Should Exist and Be Very Jewish: A Response to Arnold Fruchtenbaum" in *How Jewish is Christianity? 2 Views on the Messianic Movement.* Stanley N, Gundry and Lois Goldberg, eds. (Grand Rapids: Zondervan. 2003), 129-139; "Torah" in David L. Stern, *Messianic Jewish Manifesto.* Third Edition. (Clarksville, MD: Messianic Jewish Publications, 1997), 125-158; Dan Juster, *Jewish Roots: A Foundation of Biblical Theology for Messianic Judaism.* (Rockville, MD: Davar Publishing, 1986), and Mark S, Kinzer, *Postmissionary Messianic Judaism: Redefining Christian Engagement with the Jewish People* (Grand Rapids: Brazos, 2006). For succinct, illuminating treatments of all the relevant texts, see David L. Stern *Jewish New Testament Commentary: A Companion Volume to the Jewish New Testament.* (Clarksville, MD: Messianic Jewish Resources International, 1996). For a detailed presentation of the Law of Messiah as an alternative code to an inoperative Law of Moses, see as well, Arnold G. Fruchtenbaum, *Israelology: The Missing Link in Systematic Theology.* Revision 2001. (Tustin, CA: Ariel Ministries) 2001.
50. Donald A. Carson, *Exegetical Fallacies* (Second edition). (Grand Rapids: Baker, 1996), 45, 47.
51. Carson, 57.
52. Carson, 60.
53. Bosch, 186-7, quoting Hiebert, *Epistemological Foundations*, 9.
54. Bosch, 47.
55. Lesslie Newbigin. *The Gospel in a Pluralist Society.* (Grand Rapids: Eerdmans, 1989) 177-8.
56. In the first chapter of *Dispensationalism, Israel and the Church,* Darrell Bock speaks of "The Reign of the Lord Christ." His stated goal is "to argue that any reconstruction of New Testament eschatology [indeed of Messianic eschatology] must take into account the perspective of both Acts 2 and Acts 3" (37). In discussing the kingdom concept in Luke's gospel, he stresses the immanence of the Kingdom, and the fact that kingdom period begins with Jesus' ministry and message. "While the kingdom has not arrived in its fullness, it has come in its initial stages. In that inauguration the deliverance of God has come, and the future full rule of God has been guaranteed" (40). Bock sees in Luke-Acts a tension between kingdom present and kingdom to come [Acts 1:6]. When seen in context, the time of the consummation of the Kingdom *vis-a-vis* Israel is tied in with Yeshua's return [v.11]. Bock sees Acts 2 and 3 as being answers to the disciples question in 1:6, demonstrating the already of Jesus' kingdom reign [Act 2], and the not yet when the political promises to Israel will be consummated [Acts 3]. What we should not miss is the seamless connection between the gospel and the consummation: the one who tabernacled among us will return to consummate God's good news for all Israel. This deserves to be central to our gospel during these times of transition. See Darrell L. Bock, "The Reign of the Lord Christ," in Craig A. Blasing and Darrel L. Bock, eds., *Disepnsationalism, Israel and the Church.* (Grand Rapids: Zondervan, 1996), 37-67.
57. R. Kendall Soulen, *The God of Israel and Christian Theology.* (Minneapolis: Fortress Press, 1996), 153, emphasis added.
58. Jon Cline.

THE CONDITION OF SALVATION FOR JEWS AND GENTILES IN THIS AGE

Arnold G. Fruchtenbaum, Th.D., Ph.D.
Founder of Ariel Ministries

The purpose of this paper is to answer the question, "Exactly what must one do to be saved?" According to the Scriptures, what is it that a person must do to be saved?

The key point as emphasized by the *Brit Chadashah* is that faith is the one and only condition for salvation. In more than 200 cases where a condition is given for salvation, faith or belief is stated to be the only condition.

One example is John 1:12: but as many received him, to them gave he the right to become children of God, even to them that believe on his name. This verse states that the ones who become the children of God are those who received him. What does it mean to receive the Messiah? The second part of the verse explains that to receive the Messiah means to believe on His name, to believe he really is the Jewish Messiah. Simply by believing what one must believe, one receives salvation. That is the way one becomes a child of God, and believing is the only condition mentioned here.

Another example is Acts 16:30-31: and brought them out and said, Sirs, what must I do to be saved? And they said, Believe on the Lord Jesus, and you shall be saved, you and your house. In verse 30 the question is asked: what must I do to be saved? The Apostle answers in verse 31, the only condition is to believe on the Lord Jesus. If they believe on the Lord Yeshua, then they will receive salvation.

Now what exactly must one believe on the Lord Yeshua? Paul spells out the full content of faith in I Corinthians 15:1-4. In verse one he reminds them he had spelled out the gospel to them, and in verse two he reminds them it is by believing the gospel that they are saved. Then in verses three and four he goes on to spell out the full content of the gospel that involves three basic points: first, Messiah died for our sins; secondly, he was buried (the evidence of his death); and, thirdly, he rose again from the dead. So that is the content of the gospel one must believe for salvation, and it applies equally both for Jews and Gentiles.

The Messiah As Substitute

What this shows is that faith must be placed in the Messiah as our substitute for the penalty of our sins and our Savior from the penalty of sin. Salvation is not merely believing that Yeshua existed. Some of the most pagan atheists believe that a man named Yeshua of Nazareth existed. Merely believing that Yeshua existed, and merely believing that he died on the cross, merely believing that he rose again from the dead does not save anyone. Rather a believer's faith must be placed in the Messiah as a substitute for and as a savior from the penalty of sin.

In other words, one needs to trust the Messiah for one's salvation. One must believe that he has accomplished the salvation work on one's behalf. To be saved, one must believe not just that he died, but he died for one's own sins. If one believes that Yeshua the Messiah died for his sins, that presupposes that one has confessed that he is a sinner. If Yeshua died for one's sins, obviously it means that he is a sinner. So one must believe that Yeshua died for their sins as their substitute, was buried and rose again, and therefore, has provided salvation. Thus, one trusts Yeshua for his salvation.

This is the condition of salvation: Faith must be placed in the Messiah as one's substitute for it and as one's Savior from the penalty of sin.

The Greek Words Used

There are three main Greek words, which are used in emphasizing what the condition of salvation is:

1. Pistis

The first main Greek word is *pistis*, which is used 243 times in the New Testament. It always has the meaning of "faith," with only four exceptions: Acts 17:31, where it has the meaning of *assurance*; II Thessalonians 2:13, where it is translated as *belief*; Titus 2:10, where it has the meaning of *fidelity*; and Hebrews 10:39, where it is translated *belief*, although some translations have *faith*. Except for these four occasions, the word *pistis* always has the meaning of "faith."

2. *Pisteuo*

The second key Greek word is *pisteuo*, which is used a total of 246 times in the Greek New Testament. It always has the meaning "to believe," except for nine times: once it is translated as *believers* (Acts 5:14); and eight times it is translated as either *commit, committed* or *entrusted* (Luke 16:11; John 2:24; Rom. 3:2; I Cor. 9:17; Gal. 2:7; I Thess. 2:4; Titus 1:3; I Tim. 1:11).

3. *Peitho*

The third main Greek word is *peitho*, which means, "to cause belief in a thing." This word is used 50 times in the Greek New Testament, and it is translated in nine different ways. It is translated as *persuade* 22 times; as *trust* ten times; as *confidence* nine times; as *obey* seven times; as *believed* three times; as *assure* one time; as *yield* once; as *made free* once; and as *access* once. But in spite of these nine different translations, the root meaning of the word remains the same: "to cause belief in a thing."

By combining these three Greek words, one can clearly determine what the condition of salvation is in reference to faith. First, it means, "to believe." Secondly, it means, "to be persuaded of." Thirdly, it means, "to place confidence in." And fourthly, it means, "to trust in the sense of relying upon." These are the four facets of faith when one places his faith in Jesus the Messiah.

The Content Of Faith: Past And Present

There are three facets of salvation that always remain the same.

First, the *basis* of salvation was always Messiah's death in the sense that from the divine viewpoint, God was always saving people based upon what Messiah either will do or did do. Second, the *means* was always faith; one had to actually believe in order to receive eternal life. Third, the object of faith was always God, as was the case with Abraham who believed God and it was reckoned to him for righteousness (Gen. 15:6).

But what changes based upon progressive revelation, what God had revealed up to that point of time, is the *content* of faith: What exactly did one have to believe to be saved. That was based upon God's progressive revelation, how much God had revealed up to that point of time.

So what was the content of faith under the Law? This is spelled out in Isaiah 43:10-12. One had to believe two things for salvation: First, he had to believe that the God of Israel was the only God (and if one believes that it would rule out both polytheism and idolatry); and, second, he had to believe that this God of Israel is the only Savior (and if one believes that it would rule out works as a means of salvation). Thus it was not essential to convert to Mosaic Judaism per se and take the obligations of the Law, though that would give the person the privileges of enjoying the blessings of the Jewish covenants. Thus, the men of Nineveh and others did not need to go so far but they had to believe these two basic points, Israel is responsible to be God's witnesses (i.e. Jehovah's witnesses) of these truths.

However, with Messiah's coming, and with Messiah's death the content of faith that one must believe now is clearly spelled out in I Corinthians 15:1-4 passage.

The Jewish Question

Does this apply to Jews today? Especially Orthodox Jews? Can they not obtain salvation by means of the practice of their own Judaism? After all, Jews did not need to believe in Yeshua prior to his coming and were still able by grace through faith to receive salvation, is that now still possible for Jews today? On this issue the New Testament gives a decisive answer, and the answer is no.

A very key verse is Acts 4:12:

> *And in none other is there salvation: for neither is there any other name under heaven, that is given among men, wherein we must be saved.*

Peter clearly declares to the Sanhedrin that there is no other name given under Heaven by which one could be saved than Yeshua, and therefore, they must put their faith in that person for their salvation. It should be noted that he is speaking to Jews and not Gentiles, and furthermore, he is speaking to Orthodox Jews and not secular Jews. Thus even the most Orthodox Jew who claims to believe in the God of Israel, if he does not also believe in the Messiahship of Yeshua and Messiah's death for his sin, he is just as lost as any pagan Gentile would be. Thus in Acts 2-9, the gospel is consistently declared to those who are Jews or those who are proselytes to Judaism who would certainly affirm their belief in the God of the Hebrew Bible, yet apart from Yeshua they had no salvation.

Is it true that while the Bible affirms that those who believe in Yeshua are clearly saved, but leaves silent the question of those who do not believe? Especially of Jews who do not believe? Here again, the opposite fact is the truth. In John chapter three he does affirm several times that only those who believe have eternal life. Is he silent about those who do not believe? Not at all. Therefore the one who believes not has already been judged because he did not believe on the name of the only begotten Son of God (verse 18). Therefore, the one that fails to believe simply has "the wrath of God abiding on him" (verse 36).

The same truth is taught in many other passages. John the Baptist declared that for those who believe in the one he identifies as the Messiah, the Spirit will baptize them; but those who do not believe will be baptized into unquenchable fire.

In John 5, clearly identifying himself both as the Son of God and the Son of Man, Yeshua points out it is those who believe on this Son of God and Son of Man that will undergo the resurrection of life and those who have not done so will undergo the resurrection of judgment (verses 25-29). Furthermore, their failure to recognize him as the Messiah was their failure to believe what Moses actually wrote, because had they truly believed Moses, they would also have recognized who He is and what He teaches is truth (verses 46-47). It should be noted that he is addressing a Jewish audience and not a Gentile audience in this context.

In John 6:40 it is those who believe on the Son that have eternal life and they are the ones that will be resurrected into the immortal and glorified state. This problem simply does not apply to those who do not believe on him.

In John 10, still addressing a Jewish audience, he declares, "I am the door of the sheep". Those who enter through him are the ones who are saved and those who come in "may have life, may have it abundantly." But those who do not enter by that door are the ones who do not have this life (verses 7-18).

Luke 10:16 declares that those who reject Yeshua also reject God the Father who sent Yeshua, again that is still strictly a Jewish context.

In John 10:22-39, the Jews who believe in him are the ones who are his sheep and therefore, only they have eternal life and therefore they shall never perish. The promise is simply not applied to that part of the Jewish audience that did not believe on him.

In John 11:26, Yeshua declared that those who believe on him, even though they die physically, they have the promise of the resurrection.

The above examples of course could be multiplied many times over but I chose to limit our discussion within the gospels (even then it is not exhaustive) to keep it within the Jewish context. For example, Paul writes in Galatians 2:21, “For if righteousness is through the law, then Christ died for nothing.” The fact remains, whether one is a Jew or a Gentile, without faith in the person of the Messiah who died for our sins, there is no salvation; there is no eternal life.

Conclusion

If it is possible to be saved in any other way, especially if one provides a way of salvation for Orthodox Jews who do not accept the Messiahship of Yeshua, then we, Messianic Jews, have no special message to give. In a different context Paul writes that if we do not believe in the resurrection, then we are chosen to believe for nothing. The same applies specifically to us as Messianic Jews: Those of us who have chosen to believe in the Messiahship of Yeshua, chosen to be rejected by members of our family, by the Jewish society, especially by Orthodox Jews, then we have believed for nothing. The whole reason for establishing Jewish ministries is that there is only one way of salvation for both Jews and Gentiles. This is a message that simply cannot be compromised.

THE VIEW FROM HERE

Rabbi John Fischer, Ph.D., Th.D.
Rabbi of Congregation Ohr Chadash, Clearwater, Fla
Executive Director of Menorah Ministries,
President of the International Messianic Jewish Alliance,
President of the Union of Messianic Believers

The entire issue of soteriology is a highly nuanced complex of theological subject matter—or at least it should be. To some it resembles more a minefield than a reasoned enterprise. It begs for answers to questions that may not have adequate answers this side of eternity. When "combatants" enter this fray, it might be helpful to understand from which direction they choose to approach.

Before stepping into this theological minefield, therefore, I want to identify the perspectives that inform my observations of these vital and volatile issues. I am firmly convinced of, and committed to, the following: 1] "The Bible alone, and the Bible in its entirety, is the Word of God written and is therefore inerrant in the autographs." 2] "God is a Trinity, Father, Son, and Holy Spirit, each an uncreated person, one in essence, equal in power and glory."[1]

Among other things, over the years of extensive examination I have also concluded that: 1] The Torah was authored by Moses and is not the compilation of multiple editors. 2] There is but one human author of Isaiah, of Zechariah, and of each of the rest of the prophets. 3] Daniel was written in the Persian era and not in the Maccabean period. 4] The Exodus occurred in the fifteenth century BCE and not in the thirteenth. 5] All four Gospels were written in the first century. 6] The Rabbi Paul wrote all of the letters directly attributed to him. 7] The entire Newer Testament canon was written by Jews before the fall of Jerusalem in 70 CE. These are some of the perspectives that inform my thinking and which I then bring to the matter at hand.

Furthermore, I do not intend to provide answers to each of the interrelated questions involved in this discussion. My purpose is limited to sketching some observations and outlining some perspectives I find relevant to these issues. I do not claim that these observations and perspectives are entirely original, nor are they final.

In fact, many of them are derived from the thoughts and work of others from whom I have benefited and whom I will endeavor to cite faithfully.

One further matter concerns me. All too often the question—or questions—under discussion is intended to discredit rather than to inform. It is raised not to seek answers to honest questions but rather to provide the pretext to make accusations or cast aspersions about the person questioned, or to evaluate the quality and merits of his or her theology. However, I intend to proceed as if in answer to an honest inquiry.

Initially some general observations are in order. A primary consideration in dealing with these issues is that God is fair in all he does; in fact, he is absolutely fair and just, and more fair than we could ever hope to be. Abraham based his bargaining with God on this foundation. "Shall not the judge of all the earth do what is right?" he said (Gen. 18:25). God deals with all people with absolute equity and complete appropriateness.

Further, all people have some "light," some vital information about God, whether that comes from conscience and/or creation. Some knowledge of God, or gods, naturally seems to pervade all cultures. The near universal, normal response of humans—unless expressly educated otherwise—acknowledges the Divine in some fashion. Additionally, a sense of moral "oughtness," some standard of right and wrong, appears across cultures. And, this is usually connected to some set of perceived Divine expectations or guidelines. The ancient Rabbi and the Psalmist address these two perspectives in several biblical texts. "What may be known about God is plain to them. For since the creation of the world God's invisible qualities—his eternal power and divine nature—have been clearly seen, being understood from what has been made" (Rom. 1:19-20 NIV). This apparently serves as Rav Shaul's commentary on David's comments about the role of creation or nature in informing humans about the existence of God: "The heavens declare the glory of God; the skies proclaim the work of his hands" (Ps. 90:1 NIV). The Rabbi then adds concerning the impact and role of conscience: "Indeed, when Gentiles, who do not have the law, do by nature things required by the law, they are a law for themselves, even though they do not have the law, since they show that the requirements of the law are written on their hearts, their consciences also bearing witness, and their thoughts now accusing, now even defending them" (Rom. 2:14-15 NIV). To responsive and open people creation and conscience testify to God's existence and to the moral necessity of behavioral standards.

Moreover, Scripture teaches that God judges people based on the "light" or information they have received. "All who sin not having the law will also be judged apart from the law, and all who sin having the law will be judged by the law" (Rom. 2:12; cf. Luke 23:34). Or as Peter expressed it: "I now most certainly understand that God shows no partiality. But, in every nation God welcomes the one who fears him and does what it is right" (Acts 10:34-35). God is the judge of all people. He judges them on the basis of what they do know and what they have done with that knowledge. Yeshua addressed it this way: "An hour is soon coming in which all who are in their graves will hear His [the Son of Man's] voice, and will arise; those who did good deeds to a resurrection of life, and those who committed evil deeds to a resurrection of judgment" (John 5:28-29). On the whole, it appears that many people have merely set aside the truth they are aware of as it relates to God, or so Romans 1:25 intimates. "They exchanged the truth of God for a lie, and worshipped and served created things rather the Creator" (NIV).

However, this raises the question about the minority—regardless of how small or how large it may be. What about those who respond positively and correctly to the information they do have, and have not yet heard about Yeshua—or have not encountered a clear and accurate presentation of his message? Again the biblical texts provide some guiding principles. God makes a way to get these positively responding individuals the information necessary to take the next step. In fact, it appears that he often "goes out of his way" to do so. In Acts 10 Cornelius had responded properly to the information and understanding he had about God. God then gave both him and Peter special visions in order to bring them together, and so Peter presented to Cornelius and his family the message they needed to hear in order to complete their journey to God. Of all the people in Jericho Rahab seems to have been the only one who understood and appreciated that God was clearly with Israel (Josh. 2:11-13). So God made sure the spies arrived at *her* house. She heard the rest of the story from them and consequently was rescued from the destruction that fell on the rest of the city. Ruth lived in Moab, a place where Israelites would (and should) not normally be found (Num. 25, Deut. 23). Yet Naomi and her family went there and impacted Ruth's life. Ruth had apparently been prepared for this encounter and undoubtedly had responded to

God previously to the best of her ability. Already sensitized to God, she was ready to respond to Naomi (and to God) with that ringing commitment: "Your people will be my people, and your God my God!" (Ruth 1:16). Apparently God brings people together and brings the needed information—whatever or how much that might be, he knows far better than we—to those who are already in the process of responding to him. As the author of Hebrews maintains: "He is the rewarder of those who seek him" (Heb. 11:6). After all, the Torah does promise: "If you seek the Lord your God, you will find him if you search with all your heart" (Deut. 4:29). In Jeremiah (29:13) God confirms this promise when he announces: "You will seek me and find me when you search for me with your whole heart." There are also contemporary examples of previously unreached, primitive peoples welcoming "missionaries" with greetings similar to "We've been waiting for you to come and tell us the news about God."[2] God seems quite willing to use unusual means, and to go to great lengths, to reach people who are responsive to him based on what they already do know. He is, after all, "not wishing that any should perish, but desires that all should come to repentance" (2 Pet. 3:9).

But, are these people safe (with respect to their eternal destiny) until they have heard "the rest of the story?" They clearly are not certain, settled, and secure about this issue until they have heard and responded. Several examples illustrate this important perspective. Mahatma Gandhi, for all his devotion and accomplishments, stated in his autobiography: "It is a constant torture to me that I am still so far from Him whom I know to be my very life and being."[3] Mother Teresa, a globally respected symbol of saintly devotion, could nevertheless write: "When I try to raise my thoughts to heaven, there is such convicting emptiness that those very thoughts return like sharp knives and hurt my soul. There is such terrible darkness within me, as if everything was dead."[4] A weeping Yohanan ben Zakkai could say on his deathbed: "Moreover, two roads lie before me, the road to Gan Eden [Paradise] and the road to Gehinnom [Hell], and I don't know on which road I am to be taken—shall I not weep?" (Berachot 28b). No sense of certainty or assurance of a settled and secure relationship with the Almighty surfaces in these statements. In other words, a sensitive, responsive person usually senses his or her failings. Those without the Gospel—regardless of their piety and responsiveness—remain in great uncertainty and many in grave danger. However, the final word may not yet have been given with respect to their circumstances and destiny.

This raises an important question, particularly with respect to ben Zakkai. Is it just possible that he—and others—were still living circumstantially or functionally in an Older Testament "theological" context even though living chronologically in a post-resurrection historical situation? To be more specific, it would seem that many first century people actually lived during the time after Yeshua's resurrection, yet they could be accurately described—given the concrete reality of their lives and the very recent "arrival" of the Gospel on the historical scene—as living in OT times with respect to the accessibility of, and their access to, Yeshua's life-giving message. They simply had as yet no opportunity for contact with the Gospel; it had not spread to them during their lifetime. And Jews in these circumstances could still tap into the earlier covenant promises and what is described as "the gospel to Abraham" (Gal. 3:8) or "the gospel" in the wilderness (Heb. 4:2) as they had previously. The liturgical and rabbinic materials often express this same grace-based understanding. During Shacharit (the daily morning prayers) we pray: "Sovereign of all worlds! Not because of our righteous acts do we lay our supplications before you, but because of your abundant mercies." At Mincha (the daily afternoon service) we add: "Our Father, our King, be gracious unto us and answer us, for we have no good works of our own; deal with us in graciousness and loving kindness, and save us." The Sages remind their students: "David said, 'Some trust in their fair and upright deeds, and some in the works of their fathers, but I trust in you.' Although I have no good works, yet because I call upon you, you answer me."[5] The Rabbis comment further: "Deal with your servant according to your grace (Ps. 119:124). Perhaps you take pleasure in our good works? Merit and good works we have not; act towards us in grace" (Tehillim Rabba on 119:123). Every Shabbat morning synagogues around the world pray: "Enlighten our eyes in your Scripture, and let our hearts cleave to your commandments, and unify our hearts to love and revere your name that we might never be put to shame. Because we have trusted in your holy, great and revered name, we shall rejoice and be glad in your saving power."[6] While this connection to God may have provided a relationship with the Almighty, it was clearly transcended by "the surpassing greatness of knowing Yeshua the Messiah" (Phil. 3:8), as Rav Shaul had experienced it, and by "the life abundant" (John 10:10) Yeshua offers.

Is it just possible then that some people alive today—and many who lived in earlier generations—nevertheless still live circumstantially in an OT context? If so, then God may well deal with them in the same way as he dealt with those who actually lived in the similar pre-resurrection OT situation.

Two significant observations seem quite pertinent at this point as they bear directly on this question. The first is dictated by Daniel Juster and comes from within Messianic Jewish circles:

> The New Testament shares a general pessimism concerning the opportunity (not impossibility) of salvation apart from the preaching of the Good News. Why?
>
> 1. Its verdict in Romans one is that most have not responded to the revelation of God in nature. Humans go on in their self-centered existence.
>
> 2. Many have not responded rightly in Judaism. The truth is there. But many have not responded to God's righteousness but have sought instead to set up a different way of righteousness. Romans is clear on this. Having a zeal for God, they nevertheless sought to establish righteousness in a way that caused a failure to submit to God's righteousness. There is still more light here and possibility of response, but never so much as to blunt the urgency of the Good News.
>
> So the Bible does not preclude responding to God and being connected to Yeshua in some non-specific way by seeking Him, but it leads us to believe the chances are slim that many will. We comfort ourselves on our grandparents and hope they survived. We hope that those in the camps really turned to God, and there are wonderful stories of supernatural revelation. However, outside of explicit faith in Yeshua we simply do not know. We do have some hope. But the general condition of all is desperate need for the Good News. Besides that, the progress of the Kingdom through the

> Good News is the key to moving history toward the return of Yeshua and the fullness of the Kingdom.[7]

The other observation comes from Harry Ironside, pastor of Moody Bible Church in Chicago in the 1930s and 1940s and a leading evangelical scholar of the early 20th century:

> I like to tell the story of a dear Jewish friend of mine, Mark Lieb, who, when he was a little boy of twelve in Odessa, Russia, came into a room where his aged grandmother sat with her Hebrew Bible on her lap and he saw tears on her face. "Mark," she said, "I want to read something to you," and she read from the Bible these words from Isaiah 53 [quoted in Acts 8:32-33]. Then she turned to him and said, "Mark, these words refer to our Messiah, the Messiah of Israel. Some day He is coming and He will suffer for our sins. Mark, I have been looking for Him for over forty years, but He hasn't yet come. But you are just a little boy. He may come in your day. Keep these words in your heart and wait for Him, for He will surely come and fulfil God's Word." That dear Jewish lady went out into eternity without hearing of Jesus. But who can doubt that her faith in the Word of God was just as real and acceptable to God as if she had heard of Christ and accepted Him as Saviour! She was saved through believing in the name of the One who, to her, was yet to come.[8]

Both the Bible and experience seem to indicate that there is genuine hope for a legitimate, though limited, relationship with God possible for those who genuinely respond to him based on the knowledge they have of him. And, God will see to it that they then receive whatever further information and understanding is necessary to cement that relationship. For this, we can trust God explicitly.

There are some further considerations I would like to address, some of which are based on my previous reflections.[9] These may serve as a preliminary response to the issues at hand. The final answers we happily leave to God!

Foundationally, all of God's actions are perfect and without even the faintest hint of unfairness. The Torah makes this an unambiguous claim. "His works are just. A faithful God who does no wrong, upright and just is he" (Deut. 32:4). Therefore, we can be absolutely confident about God's character and his assessment as he deals with people. While denying that all religions are equally valid, or that all people do have an adequate relationship with God, we heartily acknowledge that God will treat every person with complete love and perfect justice. The Psalmist described God's treatment of people as "righteousness and peace kissing each other" (Ps. 85:10). Or, as Elihu reminded Job: "Far be it from God to do evil, for the Almighty to do any wrong" (Job 34:10). Simply put, it is unthinkable to maintain that God will treat any person of any time, place or circumstance at all unfairly. The Judge of all the earth will do what is right!

Unequivocally, Yeshua is the definitive and fullest revelation of God. In other words, God has revealed himself to some extent in creation and conscience, perhaps even to some small degree in some other religions, and certainly at least partially in historical Judaism. However, God has fully and most definitively revealed himself in Yeshua alone, as Hebrews 1:1-3 makes quite clear: "In the past God spoke to our ancestors through the prophets, at many times and in various ways. But now in the end of days he has spoken to us by the Messiah, the Son, whom he appointed the heir of all things and through whom he made the universe. The Son is the full radiance of God's glory and the flawless manifestation of his reality. He sustains all things by his powerful word. After he made atonement for sins, he sat down in the place of authority beside the Majesty in heaven." And with this authority Yeshua will judge all other claims of revelation as well as the ultimate status of all individuals, as he pointed out: "The Son gives life to all he pleases. The Father has entrusted all judgment to the Son" (John 5:21-22; cf. Matt. 13:41-42).

No other means of full atonement exists apart from what God provided through Yeshua's death and resurrection. Unquestionably, Yeshua's all-sufficient atoning work remains undeniably necessary and clearly central to the issue of man's relationship with God. The discussion swirls around whether Yeshua's sacrifice can be efficacious and applied for people who have not sufficiently known and specifically accepted his provision of atonement. This would include such people as those who lived before his resurrection, infants who die, mentally challenged individuals intellectually incapable of understanding the gospel, and people who have had no real, clear opportunity to hear an accurate presentation of Yeshua and his life-giving message but have responded positively to God based on the information they have.

Clearly, while God is infinite and beyond full comprehension, humans remain finite and fallible. And, all too often, people speak far too quickly and dogmatically about matters beyond their purview. Job expressed it well. “Surely I spoke of things I did not understand, things too wonderful for me to know” (Job 42:3 NIV). Therefore, we all need to cultivate a significant measure of hermeneutical humility and theological tentativeness. This is not to argue for skepticism or agnosticism, nor to plead for the cessation of vigorous interaction. Instead, it is the reminder and recognition of what God declared: “As the heavens are higher than the earth, so are my ways higher than your ways, and my thoughts beyond yours” (Isa. 55:9). Rather than speak too definitively and quickly, we need to step back and respond humbly as Rav Shaul did. He marveled: “How unsearchable are his judgments and how inscrutable are his ways! For who has understood the mind of the Lord?” (Rom. 11:33-34). While we tend to be driven to arrive at clear-cut answers to life’s (and theology’s) complex questions, some questions have to go unanswered in this life.

The Rabbis remind us of this tension-relieving approach to difficult matters when they remark: “When the Messiah comes, he will tell us.” We correctly insist that the Bible remains God’s revelation. However, this does not mean that it answers every question that nags us. Furthermore, not all things in the biblical texts are equally clear, nor, by any means, are they equally clear to all readers. Certainly we can arrive at a sufficient—even if not perfect—understanding of what is vital for life with and under God. On the other hand, we should remind ourselves that while the Scriptures are infallible, the interpreter—and hence his or her understanding—is not. Moreover, a high view of divine inspiration does not automatically guarantee a high level of accurate interpretation. Thus, theological modesty remains a quality for all to cultivate.

Consequently, we retain the challenge and responsibility to disciple every people and nation. Yeshua’s charge to us all remains; “Everywhere you go, and as you are going, disciple all peoples” (Matt. 28:19-20; et al.). So we must guard against any loss of nerve or motivation to proclaim and explain the life-giving, life-changing message of the Jewish Messiah who remains the very source of life itself.

Based on these considerations, we need to steer a path between claiming too much and saying too little. The former can easily lead to a needlessly harsh—and over-dogmatically self-confident—position that drives people away from, rather than attracts them to, the person and power of the Gospel. The latter may lead to subtly minimizing the uniqueness and centrality of Yeshua. To remedy this we hold two biblical principles together. God desires that no one should perish, but rather that every person be rescued and transformed by coming to know him (1 Tim. 2:4; 2 Pet. 3:9). And two, Yeshua alone is the only way to experience such rescue, transformation and relationship with God (John 14:6; Acts 4:12). Exactly how these two principles fully integrate and interweave with one another only God knows.

According to many interpreters, it does seem likely that some people have been "saved" exclusively by Yeshua even though they may not have explicitly called upon Yeshua, i.e. the afore-mentioned infants, the mentally challenged, and OT types. Others will similarly add to this group those who respond faithfully to that knowledge they do have of God. To paraphrase C. S. Lewis from *Mere Christianity* regarding this position, "We do know that no person can be saved except through Yeshua; we may not know that only those who explicitly know him can be saved by him."

In an interview Terrance Tiessen, a missionary and the author of *Who Can Be Saved? Reassessing Salvation in Christ and World Religions* (InterVarsity Press), further unwraps this perspective:[10]

> About ten years ago, I became convinced, much to my own surprise, that God may save people whom he does not reach with the gospel. For some years I expressed my thought in terms of the widely used typology of exclusivism, inclusivism and pluralism. … *Accessibilism* [a term from an article by William Lane Craig] struck me as capturing very nicely what I have come to believe. Salvation is accessible wherever God chooses to apply the work of Christ by his Spirit, and he can do this even where new covenant revelation is not known.
>
> The good news concerning Jesus is God's ordinary means for bringing sinners into relationship with himself and maturing them in communities of faith that provide a small foretaste of life in the kingdom of

God. Evangelism is not just about getting individuals saved from eternal condemnation, it is about bringing into being new covenant communities of people in and through whom God is working to turn back the ravages of sin—personal and social—and to establish his reign on earth. … I believe that we should rejoice in the thought that some of God's elect are among those whom the church, in its weakness or disobedience, has not reached with the gospel … Few things are more exciting to a missionary than the surprise of finding that God has been at work before we arrive with the gospel and the people's hearts are already turned toward God and eager to receive his fuller revelation. Why would it disturb us that God may have saved some of these people, particularly ones who had lived and died in the years before we got there?

It fascinates me though, that people who show this much admirable sympathy for infants seem much less concerned about the large number of adults who live and die without any knowledge of Jesus. I see these as groups within the general class of the "unevangelized." They are sinners who need salvation but who do not know the gospel. I argue that our doctrine of salvation should account for all of the groups of the unevangelized and that it should do so in a consistent way. I hear a clear biblical statement that every human being is a sinner who needs God's salvation and that the only means by which God ever saves anyone is by grace through faith. There are no exceptions to this principle and so we have to unpack how it works in the varied situations of human existence.

I am not saying that the various religions of the world are agencies that God has raised up as means of his saving work in the lives of any of their adherents. I am not saying that there is a second chance for people after death if they have rejected God's revelation up to the end of their lives, although I do postulate that some

> who have been previously saved by faith (including infants and other unevangelized) will first place their faith in the person of Christ when they meet him at death. I am not saying that because God can and does save some apart from the church's witness to Jesus, we need not make costly sacrifices to bring to everyone in the world the gospel, which God uses with saving power and which marvelously transforms the lives of individuals and whole communities.

Tiessen has clearly articulated here some very important and consistently biblical considerations.

Before concluding I want to quote a friend and colleague with whom I have worked and interacted for over 30 years. Dr. Michael Schiffman has very pointedly and perceptively addressed the issues under discussion:

> This is my view … to this point.
>
> First, I believe that NO ONE gets into the Kingdom of Heaven without Yeshua. He is the Only WAY through which people can be saved. Having said this, I must also affirm that I do NOT believe that every Jew who does not believe DIRECTLY in Yeshua (i.e., naming the name) automatically goes to hell. This may be heretical for some of you, but I honestly do not believe that, based on Scripture as well as Yeshua's own words and actions regarding our people, as well as all the other Scriptures regarding Israel. I base this upon the fact that the Jewish people have a covenant with G-d that is still in effect, that is not based upon them, but upon G-d Himself, and do not find a setting aside of the Jewish people in Scripture. I do not believe in selling my people down the river to make my theological formulae work. I will yield to Scripture always, but not to theological constructions, which are human and often blind sighted at times.
>
> Our people have a covenant with G-d. This covenant itself is NOT a covenant of salvation; however it DOES set our people apart from the nations in several

respects, among them being that we are a people with a relationship OF SOME KIND with G-d, and should not be viewed as the other peoples of the earth. This is the imagery in Matthew 25:32-42 of the final judgment, as well as the imagery of the life of Joseph and his BRETHREN. In both cases, our people are not seen as outside the love and protection of G-d.

In my understanding, this DOES NOT mean that Jewish people have another way of salvation other than through Yeshua. I believe in John 14:6 that Yeshua is the Way, the Truth and the Life and that NO ONE comes to the Father but by HIM. But if you look at the grammatical construction and language of that verse, it could be also understood, and with the same weight be translated "BY ME" or "BY WAY OF ME." The former is the favorite understanding of the Church, because it fits their theology, and is on some level self-serving. It follows the philosophy that there is no salvation outside the Church, therefore all must come in. The down side to this view is that this understanding robs people of the hope that IS in Scripture. It reduces salvation to a contractual agreement and leaves almost no room for G-d to be merciful and gracious. This is why we hear people commonly say of a deceased unsaved relative or friend, "Of course we don't know what happened in the last moments of life … " as if Yeshua was going to reveal Himself as the last few brain cells die. This is not only unbiblical, it is a pathetic attempt to give some hope to someone for a loved one who obviously did not do what the John 14:6 contract required.

If you understand John 14:6 to mean "BY WAY OF ME," the imagery of Yeshua is understood not as the DOOR of salvation, but the DOORKEEPER of salvation. While Yeshua did say I AM THE DOOR in John, He is also pictured as a doorkeeper in Revelation. The value of understanding the verse in this way restores in our understanding Yeshua's right to make a judgment call. WE only see the outside, but G-d looks upon the heart.

While I do not speak here of all Jews, I know of Jewish people of faith who truly believe in, and LOVE, the G-d of Israel. They are not pagans, who worship a false G-d, but people who have a knowledge of G-d, be it a limited knowledge. Paul said they have received from G-d a BLINDNESS IN PART. Many of us in the past have understood this in a self-centered way to mean that the larger part of Israel was blind (totally), but WE, the remnant, are those who are not blind, hence there being a blindness in part. I do not believe Paul was speaking in this manner. I think he was saying the Jewish people have a knowledge of G-d, and a love for G-d, but it is a partial knowledge because they DO NOT see Yeshua.

We know that Yeshua is G-d and the agent of creation. HE is the G-d who was at Sinai and gave the Torah to Israel. He is the one who was with our people through the wilderness, in the Land, and the One to whom our people prayed and directed their worship. When the Jewish people pray to G-d, they ARE praying to Yeshua, without realizing it. This is why Mark Nanos in his *The Mystery of Romans* says the weaker BROTHERS are Jewish people who have not yet come to the knowledge of Yeshua.

During the first century many, but not most, of the world Jewish population came into contact with Yeshua, and of those who did, it would be possible to say that many rejected HIM. Since that time, as our people encountered an increasingly non-Jewish Yeshua and totally gentile movement of His followers, it cannot be said they rejected the real Yeshua. In fact, their NO to Yeshua could be understood to be a YES to His Father. IT was a demonstration of faithfulness, not unfaithfulness, although it missed the mark severely. Yet I believe that G-d who knows all hearts not only judges right from wrong, but He understands

> when we do the wrong things for the right reasons, and the right things for the wrong reasons.
>
> It is quite possible that on the Day of Judgment, many of our people who never encountered the real Yeshua, who really loved G-d and trusted in HIM, could be speaking with a man at the door, and have the feeling they know Him and have spoken to HIM before. He knows they loved Him and some went to their deaths with even the partial knowledge they had of Him, and He says, "We have spoken before. 'I am your brother Joseph. Come near to me. I will take care of you.'"
>
> As to those who say, "Then why does anyone need to accept Yeshua? And why should we bother sharing our faith with other Jewish people?" my understanding is, NOT TO PROVE SOMEONE'S theological point! The reason anyone should accept Yeshua is more than salvation as concept. IT is RELATIONSHIP. That is the reason for the Torah. That is the reason Yeshua came. Atonement in concept is closeness to G-d. The whole point of the Jewish religion is that we might be close to G-d, and every mitzvah is designed to bring us closer to HIM. Yeshua brings us incredibly close to G-d, by the fact of our relationship to G-d and the forgiveness of our sins. All Yeshua's parables of the Kingdom point to this. All His critiques of the Pharisees point to this.
>
> No one comes to G-d apart from Yeshua, but we need to give HIM room to make the call. We need to testify of Him and call others to Him because of the closeness He gives us to G-d. Salvation is not just a label or state of being. It is a relationship.[11]

I heartily resonate and concur with Dr. Schiffman's observations.

I want to conclude with several observations. People rooted in the Western world often seem driven to have clear-cut, precise answers to specifically-defined questions, and they desire to cleanly fit sharply-bounded concepts into exacting categories. We want to analyze, organize and systematize. Unfortunately, some issues defy this process, and reality truly is messy. The biblical texts, rooted as they are in a Semitic worldview, tend to treat reality differently. Paradox and tension thrive freely in this world; nuance and complexity flourish happily. Everything need not be reconciled nor understood. Some questions never arise, and others are intentionally and comfortably left unanswered.

I have not answered all the questions and addressed all the issues raised in this discussion; I did not intend to. I have observed and described what I felt I could accurately observe and reasonably describe; other matters simply defy human explanation. The destiny of any particular individual, or group of individuals, is simply beyond our knowledge; it is clearly God's business and not ours. Basically, that's "the view from here." More than this I cannot and will not say. After all, when Messiah comes, he will tell us!

ENDNOTES

1. "Doctrinal Basis" statement of the Evangelical Theological Society.
2. For example, cf. Eternity in Their Hearts by Don Richardson. I have also personally heard similar reports from missionaries from TEAM.
3. Quoted in William R. Bright, Jesus and the Intellectuals, Campus Crusade for Christ, San Bernardino, 1966, 10.
4. Quoted in the St. Petersburg Times, August 25, 2007.
5. Midrash, Psa. 141, ed. M. Buber, 530-531.
6. For a further elaboration on grace and a relationship with God in Judaism, see the following articles by John Fischer:

35. "Torah: Can You Work Your Way to God?" Messianic Outreach, Autumn 1986.
36. "Foundations of Messianic Theology," Mishkan, no. 1, 1995.
37. "Yeshua and Halacha: Which Direction?" Kesher, Summer, 1997.
38. "Jesus through Jewish Eyes: A Rabbi Looks at Jesus," a paper presented at the annual convention of the Evangelical Theological Society, November 2003; available through www.menorahministries.com.

7. Daniel Juster, email posting on the UMJC Leaders Forum, Sept. 1, 2000.
8. H. A. Ironside, Lectures on the Book of Acts, 195-196.
9. For this section I am heavily dependent on Daniel B. Clendenin, "The Only Way," Christianity Today, January 12, 1998, 34-40.
10. Dan Reid, "Salvation, the Unevangelized and the Religions," an interview with Terrance Tiessen in Academic Alert, Winter 2001, InterVarsity Press, 3, 5. The entire interview has direct bearing on our discussion.
11. Michael Schiffman, "Another view on heaven, hell and our sense of justice," email posting on the UMJC Leaders Forum, April 4, 2000.

THE JEWISH PEOPLE AND SALVATION

Michael Rydelnik, Ph.D.
Professor of Jewish Studies and Bible
Moody Bible Institute

In 1996, I received a phone call from my cousin in Israel, telling me that my father had just died. A Holocaust survivor and an Orthodox Jew, he had cut all ties with me when I became a follower of Yeshua. He moved to Israel and refused any contact with me. When he passed away, his only surviving sibling, my aunt, instructed the entire family not to let me know of my father's passing. Gratefully, one of my Israeli cousins refused this last painful demand and called me.

From 1972 until 1996, I had made repeated efforts to reach my Dad, not to share my faith with him but just to restore our relationship. As a result, I had three separate meetings with him, in 1978, 1981 and the last one in 1992, when after speaking together for 10 minutes, the wife he had married in 1977 realized who I was, causing her to assault me and drive from their house. Years later, when my cousin phoned me to relay the details of my father's passing, she noted that just one day before his death, he had reiterated that I was no longer his son and did not want me informed of his soon coming death.

I suppose that was the very first time I began to question the particularist[1] soteriology I had been taught at Bible college and seminary. I had been taught and believed that apart from conscious faith in Yeshua, all people, including Jewish people, including my father, would bc lost for ctcrnity. But if ever someone could earn his way into heaven on the basis of suffering, certainly my father could. He lost his first wife, four sons, and an adopted daughter to the gas chambers at Auschwitz. He himself had suffered miserably in the Lodz ghetto and then several concentration camps. After the war, he remarried and his new wife died while giving birth to my half-brother. Then he married my mother, who was eighteen years younger than he, with whom he had a daughter, my sister Esther, who died in a drowning accident in Berlin when she was two years old. After this tragedy, my parents moved to America and tried to rebuild their lives.

In 1971, my mother went public with her previously secret faith in Yeshua and my father divorced her for this. Within 1 ½ years, I and then my two sisters came to faith in Yeshua, so that he disowned all three of us and moved to Israel to be near his own sister, the only one of his 7 siblings that had not perished in the Holocaust.

After his death, a small voice in my head began to question how God could exclude my father from eternal life. He had suffered so much, he had kept Torah as much as was humanly possible, and then he gave up his second family out of devotion to that Torah and his people. In the midst of my doubts, I had two firm convictions: That Yeshua was truly the promised Messiah and that the Bible, both the Hebrew Scriptures and the New Covenant, was the inspired Word of God.

So it was, that I turned to the Bible to examine my previously held convictions and where I still turn when I am pained by the tragic loss of my father and the continuing unbelief of the vast majority of my people. Must Jewish people consciously believe in Yeshua to have eternal life or are their exceptions to this seemingly biblical requirement? In the next few pages, I will share what I believe the Scriptures say about the Jewish people and salvation.

Before examining those Scriptures, I offer this caveat: In what follows, I do not speak or write as one who has all the answers. I struggle and continually study. I acknowledge my own limitations and I accept the caution that Yeshua gave that we will be surprised by who will indeed attain to eternal life with Him (Matt. 7:21-30; Luke 13:22-30). I recognize that others have different conclusions and respect what motivates them. What follows is my understanding of what I believe the Bible has to say about the Jewish people and salvation. I will frame this by first expressing the reasons this issue is so important, then by examining the biblical evidence, followed by addressing the objections that have been raised to my understanding of the scriptures. Finally, I will present some needed responses to the biblical issues before us.

The Importance of the Issue

In a pluralistic and relativistic [2] society, any statement affirming that one faith asserts an exclusive claim to truth and maintains there is only one way to experience God's forgiveness will certainly raise hackles. Anyone who has lost a loved one who did not trust in the Messiah Yeshua will certainly struggle with particularism. For those of us who have felt the pain of the murder of the Six Million by vicious and cruel Nazis, it is natural that Jewish believers would struggle with any teaching that limits salvation to those who have a conscious faith in Yeshua. It is hard to assert the particularist claims of Yeshua in the face of the Holocaust. Cultural trends, personal grief, and the Shoah demonstrate why this discussion is so important—the exclusive claims of the Messianic faith are *difficult* in that they are both unpopular in society and painful to our people and us.

Besides the difficulty of the issue, it is important because it is *divisive*. Those who affirm particularism often treat those who support a more inclusive soteriology as heretics. This is decidedly unfair. Heresy in scripture requires a denial of an essential truth that would exclude its adherent from the community of faith and the family of God. Inclusivists do not deny Yeshua's deity and absolutely believe in Him as Redeemer. They are part of God's family.

At the same time, inclusivists also can divide by accusing particularists of being close minded, fundamentalists that deny the loving nature of God and fail to practice *ahavat Yisrael* (the love for our people Israel). Sometimes such opinions are expressed with an attitude of intellectual superiority and theological advancement, deriding particularists for their far too literal, old fashioned, or narrow interpretation of the Bible. This subject is so significant because it could potentially tear the messianic movement apart to such a degree, that we will wither and disappear, much as the ancient Nazarenes did.

A third reason this topic is so important is that it is a *decisive* issue. While those holding either position affirm the need to share Yeshua with our Jewish people and all people, certainly the view one takes will affect the amount of urgency there is to that proclamation. It will affect our view of outreach and our sense of "mission." In fact, the decisive nature of this issue is probably why we have gathered here to discuss it.

Since Jewish people and salvation is such an important and weighty issue, we must turn to the Bible as our supreme authority to seek answers.

The Evidence from Scripture

The Bible does indeed address this topic, in what seems to be clear terms. There are four principles that the Scriptures appear to affirm regarding Jewish people and salvation.

The Lost Condition of the Jewish People

To begin, the Bible appears to assert that *Jewish people, in fact all people, are lost without faith in Yeshua as their Redeemer*. Generally, the Scriptures consider humanity to be dead in "trespasses and sins" (Eph. 2:1) and as such separated from God. Isaiah proclaims to Israel that "your iniquities have made a separation between you and your God, and your sins have hid His face from you" (Isa. 59:2). However, some passages require a closer look.

John 3:18

The apostle John[3] considers any individual, including those from the Jewish people, as having been "judged already, because he has not believed in the name of the only begotten Son of God" (John 3:18). Ronald Nash believes this verse so plainly maintains humanity's feeling of being lost without conscious faith in Yeshua, that when he cites it, he fails to comment on its meaning, only stating that this text speaks for itself. [4] Perhaps he is correct, but then again it might be helpful to make some comments.

First, John 3:18 is in the context of a general statement about God's love for the whole world and his provision of the Son of God to save it (John 3:16). It plainly states there that those who believe will be saved. However, John 3:18 presents the alternative circumstance: the consequence of failing to believe, and concludes that the result is judgment.

Secondly, it is unlikely that John considers this to be true only for those who have been evangelized with a loving and clear presentation of Yeshua, since this distinction is not found anywhere in this text. It appears that John is speaking of those who fail to believe in Yeshua regardless of whether they have ever heard of Him or even heard of Him in an accurate way.

Finally, it is a failure to believe "in the name of the only begotten Son of God" which brings judgment, indicating that it is not merely a lack of faith in God but failure to believe explicitly and consciously in Yeshua. To believe "in the name" of a person was to understand their true identity. When the psalmist stated, "Those who love your name may rejoice in you," (Ps. 5:11) obviously he spoke of those who consciously knew the identity of the God of Israel. To make the phrase "believing in the name of the Son of God" exclude conscious faith in Yeshua would seem to violate John's usage as well (John 1:12; John 20:31).

John 3:36

John maintains that "He who believes in the Son has eternal life, but he who does not obey the Son shall not see life, but the wrath of God abides on him" (John 3:36). A person that believes in the Son is assured a place in the age to come. The opposite is also true. A person that does not believe will fail to see life in the age to come. Although John uses the words "does not obey" he uses it in contrast to the verb "believe." It appears that his purpose is to show that failure to believe is in essence disobeying the commandment of Messiah to believe in Him. Leon Morris expresses it well: "Those who believe do in fact obey the Son, and those who do not believe do not in fact obey Him." [5]

Most significant to this discussion is that the "wrath of God" abides on any person that does not believe and obey the Son. This does not refer to an anger distinguished by an "irrational or emotional outburst" but it is used in reference to the effects of a holy God's just response to all unrighteousness (Rom. 1:18). [6] Failing to believe in the Son results in God's wrath abiding on Jew or Gentile alike, without distinction. Apart from faith in Yeshua, all people stand in their sins and justly deserve God's wrath.

John 8:24

In a context that is clearly Jewish, Yeshua told his audience of Jewish leaders, "You shall die in your sins; for if you do not believe that I am *He*, you shall die in your sins" (John 8:24). According to Yeshua, the only way to avoid dying without being forgiven is to have faith. In the conditional clause, Yeshua made clear that He was the proper object of that faith when He said, "if you do not believe ϵγω ϵιμι'." This is an explicit self-declaration of deity. Some have objected that the phrase ϵγω ϵιμι' is not referring to deity but has an implicit completion, such as, "if you do not believe I am who I claim to be" or "if you do not believe that I am not of this world but from above" you are still in your sins. However, Carson correctly rejects those possibilities by pointing out that these translations are unlikely with the absolute usage (no object included) present in this verse. The alternative possibility, that Yeshua was declaring his own deity, is far more likely. [7]

The phrase ϵγω ϵιμι' is probably not a reference to Exodus 3:14 because the LXX translates the phrase "I AM has sent me" with the Greek words ʿο ʿ'ων ("the Existing One has sent me") rather than using ϵγω ϵιμι'. More likely it is taken from the LXX's consistent usage of ϵγω ϵιμι' as the translation of אֲנִי הוּא, a phrase used for God's self-disclosure in Isaiah (Cf. Isa. 41:4; 43:10, 13, 25; 46:4; 48:12). For example in Isaiah 43:10, the LORD says, "In order that you may know and believe Me, and understand that I am He (אֲנִי הוּא)." [8]

To sum up, speaking to a Jewish audience, Yeshua declared that they needed to recognize that He in fact was deity or they would still be in their sins. If there is any doubt that Yeshua was making a claim to deity, the context clarifies that He was. Later in the chapter, John records that Yeshua said that "Before Abraham was, I AM (ϵγω ϵιμι')" (John 8:58). His hearers fully understood the import of these words because "they picked up stones to throw at Him" (John 8:59). This all this relates to the question at hand in that Yeshua told a group of highly committed Jewish people that they were lost and remained in their sins so long as they did not consciously believe that Yeshua was God in the flesh.

Romans 2:17-23

In Romans 1:18-3:20, Paul made the case that all people, Jewish or Gentile, are lost in sin and in need of redemption. In order, he demonstrated that pagans were lost (1:18-32), as are moralists (2:1-16), and then, that Jewish people are lost in sin as well (2:17-3:8). In the section about Jewish sin, Paul's point is that Jewish people who celebrate God's gift of the Torah and teach others to obey it, still failed to keep it themselves. Thus he asked, "You who preach that one should not steal, do you steal? You who say that one should not commit adultery, do you commit adultery? You who abhor idols, do you rob temples? You who boast in the Law, through your breaking the Law, do you dishonor God?"

It may be objected that all Jews do not literally steal, rob temples, or commit adultery. Of course some examples of this kind of behavior may have taken place, but not universally among all Jewish people. [9] However, if the stricter interpretation of the Law is true, as set forth by Yeshua in the Sermon on the Mount (Matt. 5:17-48), evaluating obedience based on the intentions of the heart, certainly not one Jewish person is innocent.

Since Paul's rhetorical questions must be answered affirmatively, then Jewish people are just as lost and accountable to God for sin as are the Gentiles. Douglas Moo captures the import of these words when he writes, "In arguing in this manner, Paul is implicitly contesting the traditional Jewish understanding of the covenant. Whereas Jews tended to rely on their election and works of the law, Paul insists that it is faith—only and always—that is the basis for a righteous standing with God." [10]

Romans 3:9-20

Having made his case that Gentiles, moralists, and Jews are all guilty before God, Paul concludes by stating "that both Jews and Greeks are all under sin' (Rom. 3:9). He follows this with a catena of verses from the Hebrew Bible that show that all people, Jews and Gentiles alike are lost and separated from God. Paul then states categorically that the Law speaks judgment to those who have failed to keep it completely, "that every mouth may be closed, and all the world may become accountable to God" (Rom. 3:19). The universal condemnation of humanity for sin summarizes the point of this section. All people, including Jewish people, appear to be lost and separated from God because of sin. But there is hope that forgiveness is available through faith in Yeshua, which is the second component the Scriptural perspective on Jewish people and salvation.

The Need for Conscious Faith in Yeshua

The New Covenant consistently seems to affirm that Jewish people, or Gentiles, must have conscious faith in Yeshua to experience God's forgiveness and receive the promise of life in the world to come. There are so many passages that can be adduced that it is necessary at this point to limit this discussion to but a few from a number of sections of the New Covenant.

In the Gospel of John

John 3:16 is the most basic verse that asserts the need for explicit and conscious faith in Yeshua, by stating that in love, God gave His Son so that "whoever believes in Him should not perish." Beyond that, it is faith in His name that will result in not being judged for sin (John 3:18). According to John, "He who believes in the Son has eternal life" but without that faith the wrath of God justly abides on him. All these verses from John 3 are in the context of Yeshua's discussion with Nicodemus, a good man, a Pharisee, and a Jewish leader. If Nicodemus needed conscious faith in Yeshua to be born again and forgiven, it would appear that all other Jewish people do as well.

In John 6:28, the multitude asked Yeshua, "What shall we do, that we may work the works of God?" In essence, they wanted to know what God required of them. Yeshua's response is quite simple—to fulfill God's requirements they were to "believe in Him whom He has sent" (John 6:29). This is not just faith in general but faith that has a specific object, namely, Yeshua, the One sent from God.[11]

In Acts

One example in Acts is Paul's sermon to the Jewish community in Pisidian Antioch (Acts 13:13-41). After a long discussion of the history of Israel, Paul argues that the entire plan of God focused on the promised Messiah and that Yeshua of Nazareth fulfilled the promise in his death and resurrection. Paul concludes his message to his Jewish audience with an appeal to believe in Yeshua because it is "through Him (Yeshua) that forgiveness of sins is proclaimed to you and through Him everyone who believes is justified (Acts 13:38-39). Additionally, Paul argues that through faith, a believer in Yeshua receives complete justification, a benefit not available through the Law of Moses.[12]

In Romans

The point of Romans 9:30-10:21 is that, although the Older Covenant only required faith in the God of Israel, now, with the coming of Yeshua the Messiah, He has became the required object of faith for salvation. Although some might object that this would cause many in Israel to lose their salvation since they did believe in God but not in Yeshua, that is not the case. Paul has argued forcefully that even before Messiah came, most in Israel pursued a righteousness that came by works of the Law rather than by faith (9:30-32). Although taught the message of faith in the Hebrew Bible, most of Israel chose to pursue salvation by works of the Law ("But Israel, pursuing a law of righteousness, did not arrive at that law. Why? Because they did not pursue it by faith, but as though it were by works" 9:30-31). As a result, when Messiah came, they rejected Him ("stumbled over the stumbling stone") not because of their faith in God but because of their devotion to works of the Law.

After describing his own heart's desire for Israel to be saved and their need to be saved despite their zeal for God that is "without knowledge" (10:1-2), Paul addresses Israel's problem. He maintains that before the coming of Yeshua, the Jewish people sought to establish their own righteousness (10:3) rather than receiving the righteousness that comes by faith. Bringing the Messiah into the equation, Paul maintains that the goal of the Law was always to point to Messiah, in the words of John Piper, he was "the climactic expression of what the law was teaching all along, namely the message of faith."[13] Quoting Deuteronomy 30:11-14, Paul shows that the faith taught by the Law was always near, "in your mouth and in your heart" (10:6-8).

Having established this principle, Paul shows that Messiah is the fulfillment of this teaching, with salvation being as close as the confession of one's mouth and heart. Therefore, Yeshua has become the proper object of faith for salvation. All people, but in this context, particularly Jewish people must confess Yeshua as God and believe in their hearts that God did indeed raise Him from the dead in order to be saved.[14]

Paul then applies this crucial principle: Since Yeshua is the true object of faith for salvation, therefore He must be called upon for anyone to be saved. And in order to call, one must believe. And in order to believe, one must hear the message. And to hear the message, there must be a proclaimer of that message that is sent with the good news that Messiah has died for sin and has been raised to prove He is indeed God (Rom. 10:13-15). This passage could not be clearer. Jewish people must believe in Yeshua so there needs to be intentional outreach to bring that message to them. There does not appear to be any alternative way for a person to come to a knowledge of that which is necessary to be saved apart from faithful proclamation of the gospel. This age remains a time of "missionary" work among our people whether that word is used or not. Should a "post-missionary" period actually ever arrive, it will make Messianic Judaism die rather than flourish.

Since hearing the good news of Yeshua is essential to believing it, Paul takes up the objection that could be raised, specifically that Jewish people do not believe because they have not heard of Yeshua. Hence Paul asks, "Surely they have never heard, have they? … Surely Israel did not know, did they?" (Rom. 10:17, 19). Paul replies to his own two questions in order. First, he cites Psalm 19:4 to argue that there is sufficient general revelation ("their voice has gone out to all the earth" Rom. 10:18).[15] Secondly, Paul maintains that Israel also knows that God has opened the door of faith to Gentiles so that just as Moses (Deut. 32:21) and Isaiah (65:1) had predicted, Jewish people would be made jealous for the gospel.[16] In other words, Paul argues that although followers of Yeshua are obligated to proclaim the message of Messiah to Israel (Rom. 10:13-15), Jewish people still have sufficient knowledge of revelation so they cannot be excused by ignorance (Rom. 10:16-21).

This section of Romans has affirmed that Jewish people need to have explicit and conscious faith in Yeshua for salvation. Therefore, Yeshua's followers are obligated to share the good news of Yeshua with them. But even if Jewish people do not believe, have not heard or even do not know of Yeshua, Paul deems these excuses as insufficient.

In numerous passages the New Covenant maintains that Jewish people and all people, are lost without Yeshua and need conscious and explicit faith in Him to enter into a forgiven relationship with God. But the New Covenant also adds that Yeshua is the only One who can redeem.

The Absolute Uniqueness of Yeshua

Some might acknowledge the lost condition of Jewish people and even the need for conscious faith in Yeshua. However, they would object that faith in Yeshua is but one way to enter a forgiven relationship with God, maybe even the best way, but certainly not the only way. The Bible does not seem to offer this as an option, especially in two passages.

John 14:6

Thomas asked Yeshua, "Lord, we do not know where You are going; how do we know the way?" to which Yeshua responded, "I am the Way, the Truth, and the Life; no one comes to the Father but through me" (John 14:5-6). The verse, if taken plainly excludes any other possibilities. The use of the article before each of the three nouns dismisses the possibility that Yeshua is but one way, one truth, and one kind of life. The only other alternative is to suggest that Yeshua may be the only way, truth and life but that it is possible to experience His uniqueness apart from conscious knowledge of Him. Not only do the many verses cited in the previous section argue against this possibility, but also it would be contrary to the necessity of faith in Yeshua as presented in the rest of the Gospel of John.[17] It appears that there are no alternatives-Yeshua is the only way to the Father.

Acts 4:12

Peter, at a hearing before the Sanhedrin, declared to this body of Jewish leaders that "There is salvation in no one else; for there is no other name under heaven that has been given among men, by which we must be saved" (Acts 4:12). Geivett and Phillips make four observations that lead them to conclude that these words must be interpreted in a particularist way. First, the use of the phrase "under heaven" indicates how extensively all other names are excluded as possible ways of salvation. Second, the use of the word ανθρώποισ (humanity) implies that the necessity of salvation through faith in Yeshua is all-inclusive, for all human beings. Third, the word δει□ (must) indicates the absolute necessity of faith in Yeshua. Finally, the presence of ὄνομά (name) expresses the fullness of all who Yeshua is in His person and work. Moreover, based on its usage in the New Covenant it includes explicit knowledge of Him (cf. Acts 4:17-30; 5:28-32; 40-41; 8:12, 35; 9:15, 27; 10:43; 19:13-15; 26:9; Rom 15:20; 3 John 7).[18] It seems that if salvation could come apart from conscious and explicit faith in Yeshua, Luke, Peter, and Paul (Acts 16:31) appear oblivious to this possibility in the book of Acts.

Clark Pinnock objects to this interpretation by stating:

> Peter's declaration does not render a judgment, positive or negative, on another question … the status of other religions and the role they play in God's providence or plan of redemption. Now I grant that Peter judges the religion of Judaism, in confrontation with the preaching of Jesus as Messiah in Acts 3-4, to be an inadequate vehicle of God's endtime salvation (the same would hold true, a fortiori, of any other religion in this situation). But Peter does not say what would hold for Judaism or any other religion in the situation where Christ has not yet been named, where the contest has not been joined … Thus we should not see him as denying that there have been and are lesser instances of saving power at work in the world where Jesus' name is unknown. Peter is magnifying a mighty

> act of God bringing in the kingdom, not discussing comparative religions. We should not generalize his remarks so far beyond the context of Acts 3-4.[19]

The problem with Pinnock's objection is that he wants to limit Peter's words to a select group of Jewish people who are found in Acts 3-4. Luke's book will have none of this. He consistently demonstrates that the apostles preached that all need to believe explicitly in Yeshua, both Jews and Gentiles. Accordingly, Peter says to God-fearing Cornelius, that it is "through His name every one who believes in Him has received forgiveness of sins" (Acts 10:43). Conscious faith in the name of Yeshua appears to be the only way.

Moreover, if Pinnock were correct, then Paul would certainly have realized it and would have restrained his determination "to preach the gospel, not where Messiah was already named" (Rom. 15:20) so as not to bring judgment upon those who had never heard. Although Pinnock does affirm the missionary enterprise,[20] his view is logically contrary to it. Proclaiming Yeshua to those who never heard of Him would also bring the possibility of judgment and not only life in His name.

Besides the lost condition of all people apart from Yeshua, the need for all to exercise conscious faith in Yeshua, and the unique claim of Yeshua for salvation, there is one more crucial principle contained in the Scripture regarding the Jewish people and salvation.

The Accountability for Unbelief

All people in general, and *Jewish people in particular, will be held accountable for failing to believe in Yeshua as the Messiah.* This idea is found in several passages, both in the Hebrew Bible and the New Covenant.

Deuteronomy 18:19

Deuteronomy 18:15-19 contains Moses' prediction that the LORD will send Israel an eschatological prophet like Moses. Numbers 12:6-8 clarifies that Moses' unique characteristic as a prophet was that he spoke to God face to face. Therefore, the prophet like Moses would be required to communicate with God in like manner and could not be just any prophet of Israel. Finally, in Deuteronomy 34:10-12, an epilogue added to the Torah many years after Moses (likely during the time of Ezra, at the close of the canon), the epilogue states that "Since then no prophet has risen in Israel like Moses, whom the LORD knew face to face." Thus, at the close of the canonical period, Israel is reminded that no prophet had ever fulfilled the prediction of a prophet like Moses and therefore to keep looking for the Messiah, the eschatological prophet.[21]

The point of all this is that there is a serious warning for Israel attached to this messianic prophecy. Deuteronomy 18:19 concludes by saying, "whoever will not listen to My words which he shall speak in my name, I Myself will require it of him." The meaning is that should the people of Israel not attend to the messianic prophet like Moses, God will hold them to account. If Yeshua did indeed fulfill this prediction, then any Jewish person that fails to hear and obey His words is responsible for this to God.

Psalm 2:12

According to both classical Jewish and Christian interpretation, the Son described in Psalm 2 has been understood as referring to the Messiah. If this is indeed an accurate interpretation (and I believe it is)[22] then the end of the Psalm is significant. It offers blessing to all who take refuge in the Son but warns of the disaster of failing to do so. The psalmist writes, "Do homage to (literally 'kiss') the Son lest He become angry, and you perish in the way, for His wrath may soon be kindled" (Ps. 2:12). Once again, failure to follow the Messianic King will result in facing Him in judgment.

John 5:45-47

At the end of a Sabbath controversy, Yeshua challenged his Jewish audience about their virtual bibliolatry ("You search the Scriptures because you think that in them you have eternal life" John 5:39). As a result of their wrong focus, they failed to understand the Scriptures and to recognize that Yeshua was the Messiah. However, Yeshua warned that only by coming to Him was it possible to have spiritual and eternal life (John 5:40). This failure to recognize Yeshua would bring accountability. Yeshua warned, "Do you think that I will accuse you before the Father, the one who accuses you is Moses, in whom you have set your hope. For if you believed Moses, you would believe Me, for he wrote of Me. But if you do not believe his writings, how will you believe My words?" (John 5:45-47). According to Yeshua, true faith in Moses and the Torah would produce faith in Messiah Yeshua.

It may be appealing to believe that Jewish people have rejected Yeshua out of faithfulness to Torah and thereby have, through loyalty to the Torah, expressed an implicit faith in Him. Yeshua directly rejects this kind of thought. True fidelity to Torah compels faith in Yeshua as Messiah and Lord. Failure to recognize Yeshua from reading the Torah will bring accountability not just to the Father and the Son, but also to Moses, the author of the Torah.

In this evaluation of the Biblical evidence, four principles have become apparent. First that Jewish people are lost without faith in Yeshua. Second, that Jewish people must have conscious faith in Yeshua to be saved. Third, Jewish people have no other means of salvation except by faith in Yeshua alone. Finally, that if Jewish people fail to believe in Yeshua, God the Father will hold them accountable. Because of the severity of these issues, some have offered alternatives and objections. To these we now turn.

The Objections to Particularism

It is absolutely understandable that some have objected to the understanding of Scripture expressed above. Like Paul, whose great compassion for his own people led him to wish himself accursed if it would produce the redemption of Israel (Rom. 9:1-3), so many in the Messianic movement, because of a similar compassion, are longing for a wider hope for the Jewish people rather than the narrow way described in Scripture. Those who object are motivated by love and concern and should be respected for their great desire for Jewish people to experience the world to come in the presence of God. Nevertheless, they should also be evaluated biblically, as best as finite minds are able.

The Possibility of Unrecognized Mediation

Some have expressed the hope that the benefits of Messiah Yeshua's atoning death and resurrection would be applied to devout Jewish people, even if they do not recognize Yeshua as the Messiah. While accepting that Yeshua is the only way to God and that His is the only name by which salvation is possible, this view believes that perhaps God will apply the benefits of Yeshua's atonement to devout Jewish people who do not consciously believe in Him.

All that was written above about conscious faith in Messiah seems sufficient to address this hope. Nevertheless, several passages of

Scripture seem to speak directly to it. One example is Acts 2, in which Luke described the thousands of Jewish people present at the feast of Shavuot as "devout" (Acts 2:5). Yet, despite devotion and spiritual sincerity, Peter still called on them to repent for the forgiveness of their sins (Acts 2:38). If there is any doubt as to the object of their faith, it is evident in that Peter also calls upon them to "be baptized in the name of Yeshua." Peter is not asking for a general repentance for sins committed, but rather repentance for not believing in Yeshua and a conscious turn to Him in faith.

Another case is Romans 10:1-2, in which Paul states that his heart's desire and prayer for the people of Israel is that they might be saved. Paul recognizes that his people are lost without Yeshua but still acknowledges that "they have a zeal for God, but not in accordance with knowledge." It appears that devotion is an insufficient basis for obtaining any unrecognized mediation.

Some appeal to the case of the Roman centurion Cornelius of whom Peter said, "I most certainly understand now that God is not one to show partiality, but in every nation the man who fears Him and does what is right is welcome to Him" (Acts 10:34-35). These verses are claimed to show that God will save people who fear Him and do what is right. If that were the case, then why was Peter directed by the Lord to preach Yeshua to Cornelius? The answer is that despite his devotion, Cornelius was not yet saved. In Acts 11:13-14, the angel is said to have directed Cornelius to send for Peter that he might "speak words to you by which you will be saved." The point of Acts 10:34-35 is not that fearing God and doing good apart from faith in Yeshua is salvific. Rather, that regardless of nationality, those who seek God are welcomed by Him and so God will, in His sovereignty, extend greater light to such people.

As for the value of piety apart from faith in Yeshua, according to John 5:23, ultimately it is inadequate for salvation. There, Yeshua says, "He who does not honor the Son, does not honor the Father who sent Him." Regardless of personal devotion to the Father, without faith in the Son, it falls short.

The Problem of Transitions

This objection is that Jewish people with sincere faith during the Older Covenant before the coming of the Messiah were saved without conscious faith in Yeshua. Nevertheless, Hebrews 10:4 states that the blood of bulls and goats do not take away sin. Hence, the atonement of Messiah had to be applied to the faithful of Israel without their conscious faith in Yeshua. As a result, it is presumed that the blood of Messiah can be applied to Jewish people today who respond in faith to the promises of God but lack conscious faith in Yeshua. Pinnock uses this argument when he writes, "People like Abraham knew God even though they did not know Jesus" and argues for the "salvation of Old Testament saints who lived before Jesus and therefore could not have called upon his name for salvation.[23]

This proposal misunderstands how people have always been saved. There has only been one way of salvation and it remains so in every generation. Namely: **people are saved by grace through faith in the revealed will of God**. Under the Old Covenant, believers in Israel were saved by grace through faith in the God of Israel and the faithful practice of the sacrificial system. This was the revealed will of God for them and they were not required to have a conscious faith in Yeshua as the Messiah. However, since the coming of the New Covenant, God has revealed the truth of Yeshua's Messiahship, deity, sacrificial death and resurrection. All people are called upon to believe this message because it is the revealed will of God today. According to the author of Hebrews, "In these last days, [God] has spoken to us in His Son" (1:2). With the inauguration of the New Covenant, it is no longer possible to rely on Old Covenant circumstances to be saved.

The Fairness of God

Ultimately, this objection rests upon the justice of God. Certainly, God would not hold people accountable for failing to believe in someone of whom they had never had. This is uniquely true of the Jewish people and Yeshua, since for the most part, the only message Jewish people have received of Yeshua is the distorted one proclaimed by the historic Church. The true Yeshua was blotted out by the anti-Torah, supercessionist, anti-Jewish Jesus forced upon the Jewish people for centuries. According to this view, God would be unjust if he failed to overlook Jewish unbelief because the good news of Yeshua was so distorted by the Church.

Needless to say, the Church bears a great deal of guilt for obscuring the message of the true Yeshua to the Jewish people. However, if God will hold pagans accountable for unbelief solely on the basis of general revelation (Rom. 1:18-20), how much more can He expect of the Jewish people who have access to the special revelation of Scripture that predicts the Messiah.[24] This objection could very well be answered with the words of Abraham to the rich man, “They have Moses and the Prophets, let them hear them … If they do not listen to Moses and the Prophets, neither will they be persuaded if someone rises from the dead” (Luke 16:29, 31).

The Exception for Infants

Pinnock chides particularists for inconsistency in that many “hope for the salvation of children who die in infancy, even though babies cannot call on the name of Jesus and the Bible never actually states such a hope clearly.”[25] On the basis of this “exception” to the plan of God, others suggest that there may also be other exceptions for people who do not believe for lack of full information about Yeshua.

In response, it is unfair to compare the lack of faith of those who are incapable of belief (infants) with those who choose not to believe (adults). Additionally, all particularists do not hold the same position with regard to infants that die before reaching an age of accountability.[26] Geisler proposes one possibility on the basis of Romans 5:18-19, which says that “through the obedience of the one man the *many* (i.e. *all*) will be made righteous.” He suggests that Paul does not mean that all were made righteous in the sense of forensic justification, which is only by faith. Rather, it can mean that the imputed guilt brought by Adam’s sin was canceled for all humanity by the work of Messiah. Thus, people are not separated from God until such time as they actually commit acts of personal sin themselves bringing condemnation. He then concludes, “Consequently, since infants have not committed actual sins, they could all be saved even though not yet able to believe.”[27]

Whatever the explanation is for infants that die before they are able to believe, Yeshua did say of children that “the kingdom of God belongs to such as these” (Mark 10:14). This seems to indicate that children are part of the world to come. But there is no similar promise for adult Jews or Gentiles that fail to believe for lack of a clear proclamation about Yeshua.

The Number of the Lost

One final objection to the particularist position is that if it were true, far more people would be lost than saved. This seems contrary to the love of God who does not wish that any should perish (2 Pet. 3:9).

With respect to the love of God, the Bible says that multitudes from every nation will be saved (Rev. 7:9). The Lord does love the world and chooses to embrace myriads of people and nations. Yet, with great sorrow, Yeshua did warn of the danger of following "the way that is broad that leads to destruction and many are those who enter by it." Rather, He taught, that people are to "enter by the narrow gate … for the gate is small, and the way is narrow that leads to life and few are those who find it" (Matt 7:13-14). Although this is painful to accept, it seems that Yeshua is saying that the path to life is indeed narrow.

Additionally, in Romans 11:1-5, Paul identifies Jewish believers as the remnant of Israel. The word "remnant" (λει□μμα) means, "what is left over"[28] and generally, when referring to people, refers to a small group of survivors. The point is that Jewish believers form a small part of the whole of Israel. Paul illustrates the idea of a remnant in this age with the Elijah story in which 7,000 did not bow their knees to Baal. His point is that even in the Older Covenant, the vast majority of Israel did not know the Lord. Rather, God has always worked through a remnant. Therefore, it is not surprising that only a remnant of Israel will be saved today.[29]

For those who know Yeshua, being the remnant and walking on the narrow path ought never to be the source of triumphalism or gloating. Rather it should break hearts and serve as motivation to share the message of Messiah in the most effective way to the most people possible.

Despite the difficulties involved in affirming a particularist view of salvation with regard to all people, and especially Jewish people, it appears to be what the Scriptures teach. If that is so, how should it affect those who have put their trust in Yeshua? The next section will address how a particularist doctrine should be embraced.

The Response to Particularism

Too often particularists are characterized as arrogant or unloving towards the people whom God loves, consigning them to perdition rather than life. Unfortunately, that is how particularists may act sometimes. It seems better for particularists to adopt a different tone and attitude.

Humility

To begin, those who have experienced God's grace should be overcome with humility. Receiving salvation was certainly not a result of any merit on the part of the believer. Becoming a part of the remnant of Israel is a result of "God's gracious choice" (Rom. 11:5). An attitude of humility should prevail.

Once, I appeared on the Phil Donahue Show and as soon as he realized I was a Messianic Jew, he immediately asked me if Jewish people who do not believe in Yeshua all go to hell. My response was to tell him that I am not the Judge and no one will ever stand before me to determine his or her eternal destiny. God is the Judge of all humanity and that I trust Him to judge justly. Yet, I told him, I recognized my own sinfulness and did not feel confident to stand before a holy God on the basis of my own goodness. Therefore, I put my faith in Yeshua for forgiveness. Others may feel more confident in their own goodness and they will have to determine for themselves if they are good enough to face God's judgment on the basis of their own merit. He asked me why I was fudging and I, in turn, asked him why he was trying to make me God. Then he dropped the question.

Some of the believers present with me on the panel did not like my answer. Afterwards, they told me I should have just given a simple yes answer. Others commended me for a slick apologetic. In my opinion, neither of those comments truly understood my response. I sincerely believe that God alone is the Judge of all the earth and it would be presumptuous on my part and arrogant to opine on the destiny of others. I can openly state that I believe that the Scriptures teach a particularist position but still would not be brazen enough to feel that I can determine the fate of anyone. God is the judge and He is wiser than all. I am grateful that I need not serve as an associate justice on the Supreme Court of Heaven. Life might be a better if I let God do His job and I stayed out of His way.

Motivation

If judging the world is God's job, He has made my job clear as well. In the words of Paul, "knowing the fear of the Lord, we persuade men" (2 Cor. 5:11). God has committed to me and to all followers of Yeshua "a ministry of reconciliation." Therefore, we serve as God's ambassadors to a world that He loves, begging them to be reconciled to God (2 Cor. 5:18-20). If we take seriously that the broad way is filled with our people, we will be motivated to fulfill our commission to bring good news to them and announce salvation, and to say to Zion, "Your God reigns" (Isa. 52:7).

Trust

Lastly, if particularism is true, then I need to learn to trust that God is just and knows what He is doing. It is a hard truth and I am not sure I am fully able to comprehend it. That is not to say that I do not understand what the Scriptures say, just that I do not fully grasp God's purpose and plan. But I do trust Him and it is sufficient. I trust that God is supremely gracious and is always extending Himself in love to a world that wants very little to do with Him.

I will end where I began-with two stories about learning of my father's death. After he died, a gentile friend of mine, a pastor's wife from Memphis, revealed to me that she had been so burdened for my Dad that she had spent the previous 12 years corresponding with him in Israel, paying to have her letters translated into Yiddish. She had regularly sent him Yiddish books and tracts and several Yiddish New Testaments. She had never told me because she feared I would not approve. But I was amazed—my father corresponding with a gentile woman about Yeshua! I thought my father had never heard about Yeshua only to discover he had heard far more than I ever had dreamed. God had not left him without a witness.

And now for the second story. When my cousin called to notify me of my father's death, as we were about to hang up, she remembered one last thing she wanted to tell me. She said on the day before he died, a woman from the U.S. entered my father's hospital room to visit her own father in the next bed. She happened to see my father's name on a piece of tape on the wall. So she turned to him and asked if he was related to Professor Michael Rydelnik from Chicago? He responded by saying, "He used to be my son, but he is dead to me." I do not know who this woman is. She has never made any effort to contact me. But according to my cousin, she angered my aunt by coming to my father's deathbed and sharing with him about Yeshua. She told him that he was the Messiah who was his atonement for sin. As far as I know, my father rejected her message, and died the following day of kidney failure. Yet I can see the mercy and grace of God. To the very end, the Lord sent his ambassadors to my father, in the form of a southern pastor's wife and an unknown American Jewish believer. That is why I need to trust God about the Jewish people and salvation. He cares about His chosen people even more than I do and He is doing much more than I ever dreamed to reach them.

ENDNOTES

1. Particularism affirms that "salvation depends on explicit personal faith in Jesus Christ" R. Douglas Geivett and W. Gary Phillips, "A Particularist View: An Evidentialist Approach" in Four Views of Salvation in a Pluralistic World edited by Dennis L. Okholm and Timothy Phillips. (Grand Rapids: Zondervan, 1996), 214. Although sometimes called exclusivism, particularism is more appropriate because of the unwarranted negative suggestions of undue dogmatism.
2. For the sake of clarity, although I reject relativism, the idea that objective truth does not exist, I affirm pluralism in our society. Pluralism does not assert that all faiths are true but that people must be freely permitted to explore and assert what they understand to be true. A colleague of mine has said, "Relativism says that there is no right or wrong. Pluralism says that you have the right to be wrong."
3. Although it is possible that Yeshua directly spoke these words, it is more likely that the quotation by Him ended in John 3:15 with verses 16-21 presenting the theological reflections of John (D.A. Carson, The Gospel According to John, [Downers Grove: IVP, 1993] 203; Leon Morris, The Gospel According to John, [Grand Rapids: Eerdmans, 1971] 228. Assuredly, they reflect the teachings John had received from Yeshua during his earthly ministry.
4. Ronald H. Nash, Is Jesus the Only Savior? (Grand Rapids: Zondervan, 1994), 148.
5. Morris, 248.
6. G Stahlin, "Orge" in Theological Dictionary of the New Testament edited by G. Kittel and G. Friedrich, abridged by Geoffrey Bromily. (Grand Rapids: Eerdmans, 1985) 722-27.
7. Carson, 342-43.
8. Ibid.
9. C. K. Barrett, A Commentary on the Epistle to the Romans, (Peabody, MA: Hendrickson, 1957), 56-57.
10. Douglas Moo, The Epistle to the Romans in the New International Commentary on the New Testament edited by Ned Stonehouse, F. F. Bruce, and Gordon Fee. (Grand Rapids: Eerdmans, 1996), 158.
11. The Gospel of John includes a number of other verses that appear to state plainly the need for conscious faith in Yeshua, some of which are 6:40; 8:24; 10:9, 26-28; 11:25-26.
12. Paul's "distinctive themes of 'forgiveness of sins,' 'justification,' and 'faith'... resound in this first address ascribed to him in Acts just as they do throughout all his extant letters" Richard Longenecker, "Acts" in The Expositor's Bible Commentary Vol. 9, edited by Frank E. Gabelein, (Grand Rapids: Zondervan, 1981), 427.
13. John Piper, Let the Nations Be Glad (Grand Rapids: Baker, 1993), 152.
14. The confession of the mouth is not an insertion of works to salvation but rather an aspect of the expression of true faith.
15. This is similar to what Paul has previously argued about the availability of general revelation to lost Gentiles (Rom. 1:18-20). While not sufficient to save (that is why preachers are necessary) it is sufficient to condemn.

16. This is similar to what Paul will argue in Rom. 11:11-14, that Jewish rejection of Messiah and Gentile faith in Him will provoke Jewish people to jealousy.
17. Particularly John 3:16, 18, 36 (see the discussion on these verses above).
18. Geivett and Phillips, 230-31.
19. Clark H. Pinnock, "Acts 4:12–No Other Name under Heaven" in Through No Fault of Their Own edited by William V. Crockett and James G. Sigountos (Grand Rapids: Baker, 1991), 110-11. Pinnock also raises another objection that will be addressed later in this paper.
20. Ibid., 114.
21. For a more detailed defense of the messianic interpretation of Deuteronomy 18:15-19, see Michael Rydelnik, "Inner-Biblical Interpretation of Messianic Prophecy" MISHKAN (Fall, 1998), 50-57.
22. For a defense of a canonical process approach to reading the Psalms as messianic, see Bruce K. Waltke, "A Canonical Process Approach to the Psalm" in Tradition and Testament, edited by John Feinberg and Paul Feinberg, (Chicago: Moody Press, 1981) 3-18. David C. Mitchell has defended an eschatological/messianic reading of the Psalms in The Message of the Psalter: An Eschatological Programme in the Book of Psalms (Sheffield: Sheffield Academic, 1997).
23. Pinnock, 112-13.
24. See the discussion above about John 39-40, 45-47.
25. Pinnock, 113.
26. See Norman Geisler, Systematic Theology Vol. III (Minneapolis: Bethany House, 2004), 430-54 for an overview of salvation and infant mortality.
27. Ibid., 449.
28. V. Herntrich IV, "Leimma" in TDNT abridged, 523.
29. This does not end the discussion for Paul. He looks forward to the eschatological day of the Lord, when the nation of Israel as a whole will turn to Messiah Yeshua in faith and He, the Deliverer will come. Then, the remnant will become the whole (Rom. 11:25-26). At that time, God's words to Jeremiah will come to pass, "'For they shall all know me, from the least of them to the greatest of them,' declares the LORD, 'for I will forgive them of their iniquity, and their sin I will remember no more."

FINAL DESTINIES: QUALIFICATIONS FOR RECEIVING AN ESCHATOLOGICAL INHERITANCE

Mark S. Kinzer, Ph.D.
Rabbi of Congregation Zera Avraham
Senior Scholar and President Emeritus of Messianic Jewish Theological Institute, Chair of the Hashivenu Board

In *What Does It Mean To Be Saved?* Regent College professor John Stackhouse points to a misunderstanding of salvation that he sees as endemic in the evangelical world:

> In his gracious but penetrating response to the essays in this volume, Oxford professor John Webster wonders whether it is particularly North American evangelicals who need to be reminded that the Bible presents salvation as offering more than getting souls to heaven. My experience of teaching soteriology for several years at Regent College—an international graduate school of Christian studies whose students come from thirty-five countries on every continent except Antarctica—leads me to think that evangelicals far and wide also need their horizons expanded. Over and over, students have betrayed an understanding of salvation that amounted to a sort of spiritual individualism that is little better than Gnosticism.
>
> In fact, we could make an important start simply by teaching that salvation is *not* about "Christians going to heaven." Salvation is about God redeeming the whole earth … Salvation is about heading for the New Jerusalem, not heaven: a garden city on earth, not the very abode of God and certainly not a bunch of pink clouds in the sky … And salvation is not only about what is to come but also about what is ours to enjoy and foster here and now.[1]

According to Stackhouse and his colleagues, evangelicals too often view salvation in negative terms (what we are saved *from*), and as forensic, individualistic, private and pietistic, and spiritualized. In contrast, the authors argue that salvation should be viewed primarily as positive, transformative, communal, relational, cosmic, and embodied.[2]

Even if salvation is far more than "souls going to heaven," we cannot divorce soteriology from eschatology, nor should we minimize the significance of identifying the criteria by which individuals qualify for the final installment of the eschatological gift. Let us formulate our question in a manner that avoids soteriological ambiguity or confusion: What qualifications must individual human beings possess to inherit life in the world to come? Underlying this general question is a more specific one: Do we have grounds for hope that some who do not explicitly acknowledge Yeshua before death will be among those who inherit life in the world to come?[3] Within the Messianic Jewish movement the driving concern is even more specific: Do we have grounds for hope that some Jewish people who do not explicitly acknowledge Yeshua in this life will be among the redeemed in the world to come?

I call this the question of final destinies. In my view, the good news proclaimed and lived by the apostles is primarily concerned with final destiny (in the singular): the eschatological consummation of covenant history and the created order in Messiah Yeshua by God's Spirit. However, that singular destiny is manifold and diverse, and encompasses the destinies of unique individuals. It is these eschatological destinies that will occupy my attention in this paper.

A thorough and compelling response to this question of final destinies would include at least four elements: (1) a study of the explicit biblical teaching on the topic, which would focus on the Apostolic Writings (since reward and judgment in the world to come is not a major theme in Tanakh); (2) a consideration of broader theological issues that have a bearing on the question;[4] (3) an examination of the practical implications of the available responses;[5] (4) a summary of the various responses to the question that have been offered through the centuries, and the reception they have received in the community of faith.[6]

Given length restrictions, I will pursue here only the first of these inquiries: a study of what the Apostolic Writings have to say about final destinies. Even on this point I will need to limit myself to the first two sub-questions: What qualifications must individual human beings possess to inherit life in the world to come? Do we have grounds for hope that some who do not explicitly acknowledge Yeshua before death will be among those who inherit life in the world to come? Our answers to these sub-questions will have implications for the third sub-question (i.e., the case of Jewish people who lack explicit Yeshua-faith), but we will not examine this as a topic in its own right.[7]

Within the Apostolic Writings I find three distinct ways of approaching this topic. They correspond roughly to three spheres of apostolic influence and activity: (1) the apostolic tradition of Peter and James (as reflected especially in the Synoptic Gospels and the General Letters); (2) the apostolic tradition of Paul (as displayed in the letters which bear his name); and (3) the apostolic tradition of John (as embodied in the Gospel and Letters of John).[8] I will begin with the tradition of Peter and James, and then take up the traditions of Paul and of John.[9]

The Tradition of Peter and James

The tradition that derives from Peter and James has much to say on the topic of final destinies—the reward and punishment of individuals in the world to come. It is usually overshadowed by the traditions of Paul and John, and read only in the light of their distinctive terminologies and emphases. This is unfortunate, and constitutes an oversight that we as Messianic Jews (to whom this tradition is especially addressed) are especially well suited to overcome. When studied on its own terms and taken seriously in its own right, the tradition of Peter and James challenges many popular assumptions and raises important questions.

One of the primary themes in this tradition's approach to final destinies is the warning against presumption: the misplaced confidence that *we* will be rewarded at the end, while *others* (who do not possess our qualifications) will be punished. The threatening words of John the Immerser, with which the story of Yeshua's mission begins, are typical:

> John said to the crowds that came out to be immersed by him, "You brood of vipers! Who warned you to flee from the wrath to come? Bear fruits worthy of repentance. Do not begin to say to yourselves, 'We have Abraham as our ancestor'; for I tell you, God is able from these stones to raise up children to

> Abraham. Even now the ax is lying at the root of the trees; every tree therefore that does not bear good fruit is cut down and thrown into the fire." (Luke 3:7-9; see Matt. 3:7-10)[10]

Descent from Abraham—a Jewish genealogy—will not provide automatic entry into the final banquet. Similarly, Gentile descent will not ensure automatic exclusion:

> I tell you, many will come from east and west and will eat with Abraham and Isaac and Jacob in the kingdom of heaven, while the heirs of the kingdom will be thrown into the outer darkness, where there will be weeping and gnashing of teeth. (Matt. 8:11-12)

In Matthew's version of this saying, it is evident that those who "come from east and west" are Gentiles, since the words are uttered in response to the faithfulness of a Gentile centurion (Matt. 8:5-10). Accordingly, the "heirs of the kingdom" are Jews. Like the warning of John the Immerser, this teaching serves as an admonition against presumption based on Jewish identity.[11] Of course, it does not imply that *all* the "heirs of the kingdom" will be excluded, but instead contrasts the final destinies of many Gentiles with that of many Jews in order to challenge the comfortable assurance and exclusivism of the people of the covenant.

Yeshua's admonition against presumption extends beyond the claims of Jewish identity. He issues the same warning to his own disciples, and makes clear that their confession of faith in him as Lord, their public association with him, and even their mighty deeds done in his name will be insufficient to ensure their final destiny:

> Not everyone who says to me, 'Lord, Lord,' will enter the kingdom of heaven, but only the one who does the will of my Father in heaven. On that day many will say to me, 'Lord, Lord, did we not prophesy in your name, and cast out demons in your name, and do many deeds of power in your name?' Then I will declare to them, 'I never knew you; go away from me, you evildoers.' (Matt. 7:21-23)

This is an extremely significant text. It is not addressed to casual hearers of Yeshua, but to those who speak and act publicly in his name—and do so effectively! It is addressed to leaders of the Yeshua-movement—to us! Like the "heirs of the kingdom" in general, we must guard against the presumption that our participation in and apparently fruitful leadership of the community of the (renewed) covenant ensures our final destiny.[12]

Just as hopeful passages regarding the final destiny of Gentiles stand side by side with stern rebukes of Jewish presumption, so the tradition of Peter and James includes hopeful passages regarding non-Yeshua-followers that contrast with the above warning to his disciples. Of special significance is the parable of the sheep and goats (Matt. 25:31-46). As Davies and Allison note, the Gospel of Matthew highlights the importance of this "word-picture of the Last Judgment" by placing it at the conclusion of Yeshua's fifth and final discourse.[13] It is thus the climax of Yeshua's public mission. The beginning of the "word-picture" describes the scene: "When the Son of Man comes in his glory, and all the angels with him, then he will sit on the throne of his glory. All the nations will be gathered before him, and he will separate people one from another as a shepherd separates the sheep from the goats, and he will put the sheep at his right hand and the goats at the left" (Matt. 25:31-33). Whoever "all the nations" may be, they certainly include multitudes that were not part of the Yeshua-believing community during their lifetime. This is confirmed by the fact that they do not recognize Yeshua as the one they helped (25:37) or failed to help (25:44). Yet, many among them inherit the life of the world to come.

The "word-picture" of the sheep and the goats deals with people who have not consciously known Yeshua during their lifetimes. In another saying Yeshua even opens up the possibility of a happy ending for those who have opposed him:

> Therefore I tell you, people will be forgiven for every sin and blasphemy, but blasphemy against the Spirit will not be forgiven. Whoever speaks a word against the Son of Man will be forgiven, but whoever speaks against the Holy Spirit will not be forgiven, either in this age or in the age to come.[14] (Matt. 12:31-32; see Luke 12:10)

Some Pharisees had asserted that Yeshua expelled demons by means of demonic power (i.e., magic). Yeshua sees this as an act of "speaking against the Holy Spirit," that is, attributing deeds that are manifestly good (and thus the work of God) to an evil source. It is to call good evil. According to Yeshua, this constitutes a basic rejection of God. In contrast, merely to speak against Yeshua is a less serious offense. It can be forgiven—that is, some of those who do it may inherit the life of the world to come.[15]

If being a Jew or a public follower of Yeshua is insufficient for inheriting the life of the world to come, and if being a Gentile or one outside the Yeshua-believing community does not exclude one from that life, what are the qualifications for a happy final destiny? The teaching of the tradition of Peter and James shows remarkable consistency in answering this question. Yeshua's words in Matthew 7:21 are emblematic of this answer: "Not everyone who says to me, 'Lord, Lord,' will enter the kingdom of heaven, but only the one who does the will of my Father in heaven." What counts are actions (i.e., words and deeds) that conform to the divine will. Sometimes this tradition places particular emphasis on the action component:

> For the Son of Man is to come with his angels in the glory of his Father, and then he will repay everyone *for what has been done.* (Matt. 16:27)

> I tell you, on the day of judgment you will have to give an account for every careless word you utter; for by your words you will be justified, and by your words you will be condemned. (Matt. 12:36-37)

> If you invoke as Father the one who judges all people impartially *according to their deeds*, live in reverent fear during the time of your exile. (1 Pet. 1:17)

> And I saw the dead, great and small, standing before the throne, and books were opened. Also another book was opened, the book of life. And the dead were judged *according to their works*, as recorded in the books. And the sea gave up the dead that were in it, Death and Hades gave up the dead that were in them, and all were judged *according to what they had done.* (Rev. 20:12-13)

Sometimes the tradition emphasizes that the deeds required are those that conform to the will of God as expressed in the commandments (*mitzvot*) of the Torah, i.e., righteous deeds:

> Then someone came to him and said, "Teacher, what good deed must I do to have eternal life?" And he said to him, "Why do you ask me about what is good? There is only one who is good. *If you wish to enter into life, keep the mitzvot*." (Matt. 19:16-17)
>
> For I tell you, unless your *righteousness* exceeds that of the scribes and Pharisees, you will never enter the kingdom of heaven. (Matt. 5:20)

The most important commandments that lead to life are those that summon us to love God and neighbor:

> Just then a lawyer stood up to test Yeshua. "Rabbi," he said, "What must I do to inherit eternal life?" He said to him: "What is written in the Torah? What do you read there?" He answered, "You shall love the Lord your God with all your heart, and with all your soul, and with all your strength, and with all your mind; and your neighbor as yourself." And he said to him, "You have given the right answer; *do this, and you will live*." (Luke 10:25-28)
>
> Blessed is anyone who endures temptation. Such a one has stood the test and will receive *the crown of life that the Lord has promised to those who love him*. (James 1:12)
>
> Has not God chosen the poor in the world to be rich in faith and to be heirs of *the kingdom that he has promised to those who love him*? (James 2:5)
>
> You do well if you really fulfill *the Torah of the Kingdom* according to the scripture, "*You shall love your neighbor as yourself*" … So speak and so act as those who are to be judged by *the Torah of liberty*. (James 2:8, 12)

The love that fulfills the Torah is not a sentiment, but an action done in the context of a relationship—a relationship with God, and a relationship with other human beings.

We may specify further the character of the love of neighbor commanded by Yeshua that serves as a key criterion for the inheritance of life. In so doing, we come to the heart of the teaching of Peter and James regarding final destinies. From what has been said thus far, one might think that the tradition of Peter and James presents an unattainable ideal of perfectionism that fails to take account of human sinfulness and our constant need for divine mercy. In reality, these texts demonstrate a vivid awareness of our dependence on God's mercy, expressed concretely in the forgiveness of sins. But the way we avail ourselves of this mercy is by showing mercy ourselves:

> Blessed are the merciful, for they will receive mercy. (Matt. 5:7)
>
> And forgive us our debts, as we also have forgiven our debtors … For if you forgive others their trespasses, your heavenly Father will also forgive you; but if you do not forgive others, neither will your Father forgive your trespasses. (Matt. 6:12-15)
>
> Do not judge, so that you may not be judged. For with the judgment you make you will be judged, and the measure you give will be the measure you get. (Matt. 7:1-2)
>
> For judgment will be without mercy to anyone who has shown no mercy; mercy triumphs over judgment. (James 2:13)[16]

Yeshua also conveys this central teaching through the parable of the unforgiving servant (Matt. 18:23-35). A king forgives an enormous debt owed him by one of his ministers, but that same minister fails to forgive a tiny debt owed him by one of his slaves. The parable concludes in this way:

> Then his lord summoned him and said to him, 'You wicked slave! I forgave you all that debt because you pleaded with me. Should you not have had mercy on your fellow slave, as I had mercy on you?' And in anger his lord handed him over to be tortured until he

> would pay his entire debt. So my heavenly Father will also do to every one of you, if you do not forgive your brother or sister from your heart. (Matt. 18:32-35)

All of the above texts provide classic examples of the traditional rabbinic principle of "measure for measure" (*middah keneged middah*). According to this principle, God will treat us in the same way we have treated others. Yeshua takes up this principle, but he applies it to only one feature of our conduct: if we want God to be generous and merciful toward us, we must be generous and merciful to others. This reflects Yeshua's sense that all human beings are in desperate need for mercy. Strict justice will not produce a good result for anyone. This does not lead him to emphasize faith rather than deeds, but instead to emphasize one aspect of how we act toward others—our generosity and readiness to forgive.[17]

According to the tradition of Peter and James, Yeshua also teaches that the final judgment, which determines final destinies, takes account of the unique circumstances, challenges, and opportunities of each individual. The judge assesses not only what the individual has done, but also the relationship between what they have done and what they were given. This aspect of the final judgment is especially prominent in the parable of the talents (Matt. 25:14-30), placed immediately before the parable of the sheep and goats. A master entrusts property to three servants: the first servant receives five talents, the second receives two talents, and the third receives one.[18] The first servant goes into business, and produces an additional five talents for his master. The second servant does the same, and likewise doubles the initial investment. The response of the master in both cases is the same: "Well done, good and trustworthy slave; you have been trustworthy in a few things, I will put you in charge of many things; enter into the joy of your master" (25:21, 23). The third servant returns the deposit without addition, and is rebuked for it. If he had produced one additional talent—thus doubling the master's initial investment—he would have received the same commendation as the other two servants. Thus, the master's pleasure is dependent not simply on what each servant produces, but on what they have done with what they were given.

This principle of relative accountability is likewise reflected in another saying of Yeshua dealing with masters and slaves:

> That slave who knew what his master wanted, but did not prepare himself or do what was wanted, will receive a severe beating. But the one who did not know and did what deserved a beating will receive a light beating. (Luke 12:47-48a)

The slave who did not know what was expected of him is still held accountable—presumably because he should have known! His ignorance is culpable. Nevertheless, his punishment is light in comparison to the slave who knew what his master wanted, and did not do it. The principle of justice illustrated by this example is then stated explicitly:

> From everyone to whom much has been given, much will be required; and from the one to whom much has been entrusted, even more will be demanded. (Luke 12:48b)

Yeshua here teaches that the final judgment will take account of what each of us knew and did not know, of the resources each of us had or lacked. The perfect justice of God will be administered in light of God's all-seeing eye.

The tradition of Peter and James calls for faith in Yeshua as God's elect servant, and insists that the afflicted are healed when they trust in him (e.g., Mark 2:5; 5:34, 36; 6:5-6; 10:52; Matt. 8:10, 13; 15:28). [19] Nevertheless, this tradition nowhere presents explicit faith in Yeshua (or lack of such faith) as a criterion of judgment in the last day.[20] What then is Yeshua's role in the determination of final destinies? In order to understand the perspective of the tradition of Peter and James on this question, we must attend to the eschatological expectations displayed in this tradition. John the Immerser had proclaimed an imminent judgment on Israel as part of the birth pangs of the Messianic age (Matt. 3:1-12). Yeshua came to renew Israel's covenant (Luke 22:20) and to restore the twelve tribes (Matt. 19:28), but first he had to take upon himself the judgment that belonged to Israel so that Israel and the nations might receive divine forgiveness (Matt. 20:28; 26:28). As his death involves the bearing of Israel's judgment, so his resurrection anticipates and secures Israel's ultimate eschatological resurrection (Matt. 27:52-53).

Yeshua's redemptive work thus focuses first on Israel's—and the world's—final destiny. The destinies of individuals receive their particular meaning only within the framework of that singular but multifarious national and cosmic destiny. The mission of Yeshua thus has a direct bearing on the life and destiny of every individual. But does the tradition of Peter and James provide any further insight into what this entails?

This tradition tells us three additional things about Yeshua and the final destinies of individuals that are of great importance. First, Yeshua himself will be the judge who determines each destiny (Matt. 7:22-23; 10:33; 16:27; 25:31-33). His teaching and his example, which provide God's definitive interpretation of the essential requirements of the Torah, will serve as the standard of judgment,[21] and his atoning sacrifice will make available God's forgiveness. But individuals will also encounter him face to face to receive his personal verdict on their lives.

Second, those who hear his call to discipleship and leave all to follow him, and remain faithful to the end, will inherit the life of the world to come (Matt. 19:21, 29; Mark 8:35). Following Yeshua is the perfect observance of the Torah (Matt. 19:16-21), and thus qualifies one for that inheritance. Those who live in a manner that acknowledges before the world their relationship to Yeshua will have that relationship acknowledged by Yeshua the judge before the Father (Matt. 10:32). Even those who hear that call at the end of their lives, and respond sincerely, will be with Yeshua in Paradise (Luke 23:39-43). However, if one becomes a disciple and then, in a situation of stress, denies knowing Yeshua (like Peter in Matt. 26:69-75) and fails to repent (unlike Peter), then Yeshua the judge will deny that person before the Father (Matt. 10:33). This accords with the principle of accountability, "From everyone to whom much has been given, much will be required" (Luke 12:48b).

Finally, as noted above, some who were not conscious and explicit followers of Yeshua will be welcomed at the end by Yeshua the judge with the words "Come, you that are blessed by my Father; inherit the kingdom prepared for you from the foundation of the world" (Matt. 25:34). But, according to this crucial "word-picture of the Last Judgment," these heirs of the kingdom actually had a history of responding faithfully to the personal call of Yeshua, and were inheriting the kingdom because of that response. That call had come through Yeshua's family members—the hungry, the thirsty, the stranger, the naked, the sick, the imprisoned (Matt. 25:35-36, 40). Apparently, what Yeshua had said of the apostles also applies to the needy: "Whoever welcomes you welcomes me" (Matt. 10:40).[22] Thus, even those who are never conscious of Yeshua's presence or call (Matt. 25:37-38, 44), which comes to all people, are judged by how they respond to that call.

To summarize: the apostolic tradition of Peter and James challenges the presumption of Jews and Yeshua-believers regarding final destinies, and insists that the final judgment will involve a just and merciful assessment of everyone's deeds. While the judgment will take account of the particular circumstances, gifts, and limitations of each individual, it will also scrutinize the deeds of all according to the Torah as definitively interpreted by Yeshua. That definitive interpretation places special emphasis on the requirement that we show mercy to others, giving and forgiving. Yeshua himself will be the judge, and his assessment of our deeds will also reveal how we related to him during our lives—explicitly or implicitly.

The Tradition of Paul

It is enlightening to read Paul in light of the tradition of Peter and James rather than the reverse. We find that Paul employs his own distinct conceptual framework and addresses a situation unlike that described in the Gospels (e.g., a mission outside the land of Israel, among Gentiles, which focuses on the establishment of stable Yeshua-faith communities). However, his message on the topic of final destinies departs little from that of the tradition of Peter and James.

The tradition of Peter and James sets the question of the final destinies of individuals within the broader context of the final destiny of Israel's eschatologically renewed national life.[23] The tradition of Paul paints on an even vaster canvas. Creation as a whole suffers in bondage to decay, and longs for the cosmic liberation that will come when the "children of God" are glorified (Rom. 8:18-23). Paul recognizes that God's saving purpose affects "all things," and that God's self-offering to *each* will be definitively bestowed when God rules over *all*: "When all things are subjected to him [Yeshua], then the Son himself will be subjected to him who put all things under him, that God may be everything to every one" (1 Cor. 15:28). To expand our vision beyond the horizons of our narrow individual concerns, God reveals to us the ultimate goal of "all things": "For He has made known to us in all wisdom and insight the mystery of his will, according to his purpose which he set forth in Messiah as a plan for the fulness of time, to unite all things in him, things in heaven and things on earth" (Eph. 1:9-10). Our individual destinies are wrapped up in the destiny of "all things."

But Paul does have much to say about those individual destinies. Like the tradition of Peter and James, he warns sternly against any form of presumption in the face of divine judgment. Physical descent from the patriarchs and matriarchs (Rom. 9:8), the covenantal sign of circumcision (Rom. 2:25-29), and possession and knowledge of the Torah (Rom. 2:17-24) are all privileges of enormous value (Rom. 3:1-2; 9:4-5), but they cannot guarantee the inheritance of the life of the world to come. Gentile Yeshua-believers have been grafted into Israel's tree, but they must not boast arrogantly of their spiritual superiority over Jews, or God will cut their branches from the trunk (Rom. 11:17-22). They also must not revert to their past Gentile life of idolatry and sexual immorality, thinking that their immersion in the Messiah and their participation in his covenant meal will ensure their final redemption; such a return to paganism would resemble the conduct of the generation of the exodus, and would elicit the same judgment as received by those wayward Israelites (1 Cor. 10:1-13). Paul makes clear that even he, an apostle of the Messiah, cannot presume a favorable judgment, but must persevere in faithfulness to his calling (1 Cor. 4:4-5; 9:24-27; Phil. 3:11-14).

Paul likewise suggests that we should avoid hasty conclusions about the final destiny of those outside the community of God's manifest covenantal action in Israel and in Yeshua. In Romans 2 Paul cites the example of virtuous Gentiles in order to chasten the presumption of his fellow Jews:

> When Gentiles, who do not possess the Torah, do instinctively what the Torah requires, these, though not having the Torah, are Torah to themselves. They show that what the Torah requires is written on their hearts, to which their own conscience also bears witness; and their conflicting thoughts will accuse or perhaps excuse them on the day when, according to my good news, God, through Yeshua the Messiah, will judge the secret thoughts of all. (Rom. 2:14-16)[24]

> So, if those who are uncircumcised keep the requirements of the Torah, will not their uncircumcision be regarded as circumcision? Then those who are physically uncircumcised but keep the

> Torah will condemn you that have the written text and circumcision but break the Torah. (Rom. 2:26-27)

Both of these texts have the final judgment in view, as do previous verses in the chapter (see Rom. 2:5-13). Paul does not imply that such Gentiles are perfect in their conformity to the law "written on their hearts," but only that their implicit relationship with the God of Israel will culminate at the end in an explicit acknowledgement of them as servants of the Most High.[25]

For Paul, as for Peter and James, the needle that bursts all bubbles of presumption is the sober expectation that God will judge the deeds of every one at the last day:

> But by your hard and impenitent heart you are storing up wrath for yourself on the day of wrath, when God's righteous judgment will be revealed. For he will repay according to each one's deeds: to those who by patiently doing good seek for glory and honor and immortality, he will give eternal life; while for those who are self-seeking and who obey not the truth but wickedness, there will be wrath and fury. There will be anguish and distress for everyone who does evil, the Jew first and also the Greek, but glory and honor and peace for everyone who does good, the Jew first and also the Greek. For God shows no partiality. (Rom. 2:5-11)

Some see these words as hypothetical and rhetorical, and refuse to take them at face value. Such rejection of the plain sense of Paul's words finds support neither in the wider canonical witness of the Apostolic Writings, nor in the remainder of the Pauline corpus, where a final judgment of our deeds is taken for granted:

> Yes, we do have confidence, and we would rather be away from the body and at home with the Lord. So whether we are at home or away, we make it our aim to please him. For all of us must appear before the judgment seat of Messiah, so that each may receive recompense for what he has done in the body, whether good or evil. (2 Cor. 5:8-10; see Rom. 14:10-12)

Paul's joyful expectation and hopeful confidence never degenerate into presumption, for he knows that "all of us" will give an account for what we have done.[26]

Like the tradition of Peter and James, Paul implies that the final judgment will take account of the particular circumstances of each individual. One will be judged according to what one has done with what one was given. Paul sees this principle at work in the differentiated judgment of Jews and Gentiles:

> All who have sinned apart from the Torah will also perish apart from the Torah, and all who have sinned within the framework of the Torah will be judged by the Torah. For it is not the hearers of the Torah who are righteous in God's sight, but the doers of the Torah who will be justified. (Rom. 2:12-13)

Paul then proceeds to speak about Gentiles who "do instinctively what the Torah requires" and who show thereby that "what the Torah requires is written on their hearts" (Rom. 2:14-15). In verses 12-13 "Torah" includes the detailed ordinances addressed specifically to Israel and the commandments that presume an explicit knowledge of the God of Israel; in contrast, "what the Torah requires" in verses 14-15 consists only of basic moral and religious teaching such as that later codified under the Noachide laws. Those who have been instructed and formed in the Mosaic Torah will be judged in the light of that instruction, whereas those whose knowledge of God and God's requirements is more general will be judged in light of that general knowledge.

The tradition of Peter and James stresses that observance of the Torah prepares one for the life of the world to come, and that the two love commandments constitute the core of that observance. The apostle Paul acknowledges the central role played by love of neighbor in the Torah as a universal and enduring guide to life in the Messiah (Gal. 5:14; 6:2 Rom. 13:8-10), and he sees the fulfillment of this commandment as an anticipation of the life of the world to come (1 Cor. 13:8, 13). As an essential expression of this love, the Pauline tradition echoes that of Peter and James in its teaching about forgiveness (Col. 3:12-14; Eph. 4:1-3, 31-32; 5:1-2). Paul focuses on the way such forgiveness responds to, participates in, and replicates the forgiving love of God in Messiah, but—unlike the tradition of Peter and James—he does not teach about the granting of forgiveness as a condition for receiving forgiveness.

The most distinctive feature of the Pauline teaching on final destinies, in comparison to the tradition of Peter and James, is the role of faith (Rom. 1:16; 1 Cor. 1:21; 15:1-2). The good news of Messiah Yeshua's obedient life, sacrificial death, and victorious resurrection brings God's salvation to Israel, the nations, and all creation, and the saving power of this good news is effective among those who respond with faith:

> The word is near you, on your lips and in your heart" [Deut. 30:14] (that is, the word of faith that we proclaim); because if you confess with your lips that Yeshua is Lord and believe in your heart that God raised him from the dead, you will be saved. For one believes with the heart and so is justified, and one confesses with the mouth and so is saved. The scripture says, "No one who believes in him will be put to shame." For there is no distinction between Jew and Greek; the same Lord is Lord of all and is generous to all who call on him. For, "Everyone who calls on the name of the Lord shall be saved. (Rom. 10:8-13)

We must pay close attention to what Paul says and does not say here. Many bring to the text assumptions about what Paul means by "faith" that are unsupported by his actual words.[27]

First of all, in the Pauline letters faith involves belief in certain key truths. In Romans 10, the key truths concern the resurrection of Yeshua and his enthronement as Lord.[28] In Romans 4, Paul pictures God's giving a son to the aged Abraham and Sarah as a kind of resurrection (4:17, 19), and explicitly compares Abraham's faith in God's promise with our belief that God raised "Yeshua our Lord" from the dead (4:24). Why this focus on Yeshua's resurrection and Lordship? According to Paul, Yeshua rises from the dead as "the first fruits of those who have fallen asleep" (1 Cor. 15:20). His resurrection is the beginning of the resurrection of the righteous, and his glorified humanity becomes the agent of the life-giving transformation of all who belong to him (1 Cor. 15:21-22, 45, 48-49). In this context to believe that God raised Yeshua from the dead is to believe that God will also raise us from the dead in him, with him, and through him.

Second, while this faith involves belief in a set of key truths, it is far more than the intellectual affirmation of a set of propositions. Romans 4 presents Abraham as the model of faith, and his belief in God's promise of a son took the form of heroic trust over many years (4:19-21). His faith (*pistis*) was thus expressed as faithfulness (another meaning of *pistis*), and could also be characterized as obedience (Rom. 1:5; 16:26). Elsewhere Paul speaks about "faith working through love" (Gal. 5:6). Thus, "Paul does not regard faith in purely passive terms: rather, it has very definite moral aspects which determine how the believer should live 'by faith' or 'by the Spirit.'"[29]

Third, Paul often associates faith with water-immersion (Gal. 3:25-27; Eph. 4:5). In fact, scholars commonly view the confession of faith referred to in Romans 10 as an integral part of the ritual of immersion in the early Yeshua-community.[30] This is significant because it implies that Pauline "faith" is enacted in a communal context. It is not merely a private, individual, and subjective experience, but an action realized in a corporate setting.

Finally, this association with immersion also implies that "faith" is one of Paul's ways of speaking about union with the Messiah.[31] Just as Paul connects "faith" and "salvation," so Paul connects union with Yeshua in the Spirit and the final destiny of life in the world to come:

> If we have been united with him in a death like his, we will certainly be united with him in a resurrection like his … if we have died with Messiah, we believe that we will also live with him. (Rom. 6:5, 8)

> If the Spirit of him who raised Yeshua from the dead dwells in you, he who raised Messiah from the dead will give life to your mortal bodies also through his Spirit that dwells in you. (Rom. 8:11)

The importance of belief in the resurrection of Yeshua becomes evident in this context. In the ritual act of immersion, and in suffering affliction for Messiah's sake (Rom. 8:17), the follower of Yeshua participates in his death. We do so in hope that this participation will culminate for us in the resurrection life and glory that Yeshua now possesses as "Lord."

Paul's concept of "faith" thus has enormous depth and scope. It cannot be equated with the acknowledgment of Yeshua as Lord condemned in Matthew 7:21-23, which is compatible with disobedience to God and alienation from the Messiah. It also cannot be equated with the purely intellectual assent condemned in James 2:14-26, which exists independent of any appropriate deeds. In fact, its closest correlate in the tradition of Peter and James is faithful discipleship. As noted above, that tradition proclaims that all who follow Yeshua as his disciples, and remain faithful to the end, will inherit the life of the world to come (Matt. 19:21, 29; Mark 8:35). Just as an intimate and loyal relationship with Yeshua the itinerant Master provides assurance of a happy final destiny, so union with the crucified and risen Lord—in "faith"—offers the same assurance.

If "faith"—signifying a bond of union with the Messiah—leads to a happy final destiny, what leads to a tragic ending? Several Pauline texts address this question:

> Do you not know that wrongdoers will not inherit the kingdom of God? Do not be deceived! Fornicators, idolaters, adulterers, male prostitutes, sodomites, thieves, the greedy, drunkards, revilers, robbers—none of these will inherit the kingdom of God. (1 Cor. 6:9-10)

> Now the works of the flesh are obvious: fornication, impurity, licentiousness, idolatry, sorcery, enmities, strife, jealousy, anger, quarrels, dissensions, factions, envy, drunkenness, carousing, and things like these. I am warning you, as I warned you before: those who do such things will not inherit the kingdom of God. (Gal. 5:19-21)

> Put to death, therefore, whatever in you is earthly: fornication, impurity, passion, evil desire, and greed (which is idolatry). On account of these the wrath of God is coming on those who are disobedient. (Col. 3:5-6)

> Be sure of this, that no fornicator or impure person, or one who is greedy (that is, an idolater), has any inheritance in the kingdom of Messiah and of God. Let no one deceive you with empty words, for because of these things the wrath of God comes on those who are disobedient. (Eph. 5:5-6)

Paul stresses the link between Yeshua-faith and the eschatological inheritance of God's kingdom. However, when speaking about those who are excluded from that inheritance, Paul lists types of behavior that are in fundamental violation of the universally applicable norms of the Torah (in Rabbinic terms, the Noachide commandments). He does not include in the list "unbelief" (i.e., lack of explicit Yeshua-faith). As we inferred earlier from our reading of Romans 2, Paul does not divide the world neatly between Yeshua-believers (who are "saved") and those who lack explicit faith in Yeshua (who are "damned"). Judgment for all will be according to deeds rather than beliefs or experiences, though beliefs and experiences shape deeds. Just as the deeds of the "righteous Gentiles" of Romans 2 demonstrate an implicit Torah inscribed on their hearts, so the deeds of some outside the visible walls of the ekklessia may bear witness to their implicit faith in the crucified and risen Messiah.

In conclusion, Paul addresses a different audience than the tradition of Peter and James, and develops a new concept of "faith." Nevertheless, his teaching regarding final destinies bears a close resemblance to that of his fellow apostles.

The Tradition of John

Like the apostolic tradition of Paul, the tradition of John emphasizes "faith" as the proper response to the person and message of Yeshua. John writes his Gospel with a clear and single purpose, and he conveys that purpose unambiguously at the end of the book: "But these [signs] are written so that you may come to believe that Yeshua is the Messiah, the Son of God, and that through believing you may have life in his name" (John 20:31). What does John mean by "believe"? And what does he mean by "have life in his name"?

As in Paul, faith involves the affirmation of certain truths. In John faith focuses less on particular eschatological events enacted in Yeshua (i.e., his death and resurrection), and more on Yeshua's personal identity.[32] Faith affirms that Yeshua is the Messiah (John 11:27; 20:31; 1 John 5:1), the Son of God (John 11:27; 20:31; 1 John 5:5), who comes from and is sent by God (John 16:27; 17:8, 21). But faith sees Yeshua as more than merely a faithful servant, entrusted with a unique redemptive mission: he is the Holy One of God (John 6:69), who dwells in the Father and in whom the Father dwells (John 10:38; 14:10-11). He is the one who shares the Divine Name and nature (John 17:11-12), and faith in Yeshua acknowledges that he rightly proclaims,

"I Am" (John 8:24; 13:19; see 8:58-59, 18:5-6). In contemporary idiom, we could say that for John the central truth affirmed by faith is the deity of Yeshua.

However, John shows no more interest than Paul in purely intellectual assent to propositional truths. One does not "have life" through affirming creedal formulas. Believing that Yeshua is the way, the truth, and the life (John 14:6) necessarily involves answering an invitation to enter and nurture a relationship. It is the proper human response to a personal encounter with the One who embodies the self-revelation of Israel's God. It involves "coming to" Yeshua (6:35), "loving" Yeshua (16:27), and "obeying" Yeshua (14:21; 15:10; 3:36; 8:51; 12:47-48). As in Paul, so in John faith serves an equivalent role to that played by discipleship in the tradition of Peter and James.[33]

What is the "life in his name" received by those who believe in Yeshua? In the apostolic tradition of Peter and James, "life" refers to a gift bestowed in the future, in the world to come (Matt. 7:14; 18:8-9; 19:16-17, 29; 25:46). Therefore, we might reasonably think that John's primary concern is to assure those who believe in Yeshua of their future destinies. However, close attention to John's usage makes clear that this is not the case. In John "eternal life" is received now, in *this* world. It is a present possession, not one merely anticipated in the future.[34]

> Whoever believes in the Son has eternal life. (John 3:36)
>
> Very truly, I tell you, anyone who hears my word and believes him who sent me has eternal life, and does not come under judgment, but has passed from death to life. (John 5:24)
>
> Very truly, I tell you, whoever believes has eternal life. (John 6:47)
>
> Those who eat my flesh and drink my blood have eternal life. (John 6:54)

The present possession of eternal life gives confident hope for the future world (John 6:40, 54; 11:25-26). However, John focuses not on that future hope, but on the life that those who believe receive *now.*

Yeshua gives eternal life to those who believe in him (John 5:21; 10:26; 17:2). Moreover, the life he gives remains his own after he gives it away, for it is not a "thing" external to his person. Yeshua gives life by giving himself.

> For just as the Father has life in himself, so he has granted the Son also to have life in himself. (John 5:26)
>
> I am the bread of life. Whoever comes to me will never be hungry; whoever believes in me will never be thirsty. (John 6:35; see 6:53-58)
>
> I am the resurrection and the life. (John 11:25)
>
> I am the way, and the truth, and the life. (John 14:6)

Eternal life is not merely Yeshua's gift to us—it is his presence among us and within us. This is why we need to "believe in" Yeshua in order to have that life—since "believing" means coming to him, loving him, remaining with him. When we draw near to Yeshua, we are drawing near to life. It is like the light or heat given off by a fire—one cannot have the light and heat without the fire, and one cannot have the fire apart from the light and heat.

This identification of Yeshua with "life" in John is linked to the book's emphasis on Yeshua's deity. God is the only one who has life "in himself." Yet, God has granted that Yeshua likewise have life "in himself," so that all would honor him even as they honor God. To draw near to Yeshua is to draw near to God, and to draw near to God is to have life: "And this is eternal life, that they may know you, the only true God, and Yeshua the Messiah whom you have sent" (John 17:3).

Just as John focuses on eternal life as a present reality, so he envisions judgment as occurring now and not merely in the world to come:

> For God so loved the world that he gave his only Son, so that everyone who believes in him may not perish but may have eternal life. Indeed, God did not send the Son into the world to condemn the world, but in order that the world might be saved through him. Those who believe in him are not condemned; but those who do not believe are condemned already, because they have not believed in the name of the only Son of God. And this is the judgment, that the light has come into the

> world, and people loved darkness rather than light because their deeds were evil. For all who do evil hate the light and do not come to the light, so that their deeds may not be exposed. But those who do what is true come to the light, so that it may be clearly seen that their deeds have been done in God. (John 3:16-21)

Yeshua comes as light that reveals what we have done and who we really are. Those who flee from the light are those who prefer the darkness. Their judgment is not a future verdict, but a present reality—for in fleeing from the one who is the light and the life, they condemn themselves to darkness (the absence of light) and death (the absence of life).[35]

While believing in Yeshua is the way one receives life (since, as noted above, he *is* the life, and believing means "coming to him"), the reason why people "come to the light" is "that it may be clearly seen that their deeds have been done in God." The converse is also true: those who disbelieve run away from the light in order that "their deeds may not be exposed … because their deeds are evil." One's response to Yeshua reveals who one truly is: if we reject the one who is truth, we show that we are false; if we reject the one who is goodness itself, we show that we are evil. Thus, John dismisses neither the significance of deeds (in supposed contrast to "faith") nor the significance of the way one has lived *before* believing in Yeshua.[36] In this text, judgment is still according to deeds, and belief or disbelief is not so much the basis of judgment as it is *the judgment itself, rendered by the one being judged*!

In the apostolic tradition of Peter and James, no explicit connection is made between "faith in Yeshua" and final destinies. In the tradition of Paul, Yeshua-faith is linked to "salvation," but judgment is rendered according to deeds that violate the Noachide commandments (with no reference to the absence of Yeshua-faith). In the tradition of John, as seen above, faith in Yeshua leads to "eternal life," and disbelief in Yeshua brings condemnation—but both outcomes are viewed primarily as present realized conditions rather than future destinies (though they have definite implications for the world to come). Nonetheless, the novel linkage between "disbelief" and judgment deserves comment.

> Those who believe in him are not condemned; but those who do not believe are condemned already,

> because they have not believed in the name of the only Son of God. (John 3:18)
>
> Whoever believes in the Son has eternal life; whoever disobeys the Son will not see life, but must endure God's wrath. (John 3:36)

Who are those who "do not believe in the name of the only Son of God"? Does this refer to every person in the world who is not explicitly a believer in his name? The second passage above would imply that more than this is meant by "do not believe," as it is the one who "disobeys the Son" who endures "God's wrath," and disobedience requires knowledge of a command and a Commander.

This inference draws support from other texts in John. In John 6:36, Yeshua says, "But I said to you that *you have seen me* and yet do not believe." In the verses that follow Yeshua contrasts these disbelievers with those who believe: "every one who *sees the Son* and believes in him has eternal life" (John 6:40). Just as belief in Yeshua is preceded by an encounter with him in which the person "sees the Son," so disbelief is preceded by a similar encounter. Elsewhere John describes this personal encounter with auditory rather than optical imagery:

> I do not judge anyone who *hears my words* and does not keep them, for I came not to judge the world, but to save the world. The one who rejects me and does not receive my words has a judge; on the last day the word that I have spoken will serve as judge. (John 12:47-48)

The disbeliever hears the words of Yeshua, and rejects Yeshua and his words. Once again, this contrasts with the believer in Yeshua: "Truly, truly, I say to you, he who *hears my word* and believes him who sent me, has eternal life" (John 5:24).[37]

Thus, the Gospel of John says little about *non*-believers, but much about *dis*-believers![38] It deals harshly with those who see the light, recognize it as light, and then turn their backs and run away from the light. It speaks of the condition of those who have encountered Yeshua and rejected him—not of those who have never encountered him at all. What does this mean for our day? To hear and see Yeshua is not just to read a book about him, hear a preacher speak about him on TV, watch a movie about his life, or receive a tract and a memorized speech from a missionary on the street. What we actually perceive in such contacts is shaped by our communal commitments and our personal and family history. To see Yeshua, in the Johannine sense, is to see *the light,* and to recognize its brightness. Such an encounter is required for genuine belief *or* disbelief to occur.

What does this mean for Jewish people who do not believe in Yeshua? Whatever was the case with his own generation who clearly "saw him" and "heard him," and said an emphatic "no" to him, we cannot assume that all future generations of Jews who lack explicit belief in him have encountered him and given that same negative response. Only God can distinguish between a disbeliever and a non-believer; however, even if the distinction were evident to human eyes, the extraordinary circumstances of Jewish history would incline one to extreme caution in assessing the destinies of individual Jews.

What does the tradition of John have to contribute to an inquiry into the future destiny of non-believers in Yeshua? Its assumptions appear to be similar to those discerned above in the traditions of Peter and James and of Paul. Just as the realized judgment enacted in this world through an encounter with Yeshua leads to life or condemnation depending on the previous deeds of the person who sees Messiah's light, so the final judgment will be based on deeds:

> Do not be astonished at this; for the hour is coming when all who are in their graves will hear his voice and will come out—those who have done good, to the resurrection of life, and those who have done evil, to the resurrection of condemnation. (John 5:28-29)

The prologue to the Gospel of John also states that all things were made through the Word who becomes incarnate in Yeshua (John 1:13, 9, 14). In him is the life that is the light of all people (John 1:4-5, 9). Many writers in the early Church understood this to mean that the Son of God had acted in a revelatory and salvific manner outside the history of the people of Israel.[39] It is evident that the tradition of John itself assumed that the Son of God had acted similarly in Israel's own history (John 12:41). In this perspective, all human beings encounter Yeshua's light in some measure, and all will be held accountable for how they respond to the light they receive.

In conclusion, we find that the tradition of John has less explicit teaching about final destinies than the traditions of Peter and James or of Paul. It speaks much about "eternal life" and "condemnation," but these are seen primarily as present realized conditions rather than anticipated future recompense. Belief and disbelief in Yeshua are not so much qualifications for future destinies as they are the judgments that individuals render on themselves in the present by turning towards or away from the light that is revealed to them.

While John differs from the traditions of Peter and James and of Paul in the singularity of its focus on faith in Yeshua as the One in whom God dwells uniquely, and in its predominantly realized eschatological horizon, it offers no teaching on future destinies that conflicts with the other apostolic traditions we have examined.

Mark 16:9-16

The final text to consider, Mark 16:9-16, cannot be assigned to any particular stream of apostolic tradition. While attached to the ending of the Gospel of Mark, a scholarly consensus recognizes that it does not belong to the original composition.[40] Its canonical value has been disputed, but we will not here enter that debate.

Mark 16:15-16 offers the only example in the Apostolic Writings of a passage which explicitly connects final condemnation to lack of faith in the good news: "And he said to them, "Go into all the world and proclaim the good news to the whole creation. The one who believes and is immersed will be saved; but the one who does not believe will be condemned."

Does this text teach that all those who do not believe in Yeshua in this life are destined for final destruction? In context, it is evident that the point of the passage is far more limited. The previous verses tell us what is meant by "not believing." Miriam of Migdol sees the risen Yeshua and goes to tell his followers of her encounter. Though they had been with him for three years, had loved and served him, and had heard him speak of his coming death and resurrection, "they would not believe" (Mark 16:11). Two more come to them with the same report, and still "they did not believe" (Mark 16:13). Finally, Yeshua appears to them himself and admonishes them for their "lack of faith" (Mark 16:14). He then commands them to "proclaim the good news to the whole creation" (Mark 16:15). In this context, it is evident that "the one who does not believe" is one who hears the good news, encounters through it a compelling testimony to the risen Lord, and nevertheless stubbornly and persistently refuses to become a disciple (i.e., be immersed and enter the community of those who love, serve, obey, and trust him).

The teaching on belief and disbelief in Mark 16:9-16 resembles what we have found in the tradition of John. Condemnation awaits those who willfully disbelieve, that is, reject the light that has dawned upon them. These words do not refer to those who lack genuine knowledge or experience of Yeshua, but to those who, like the disciples, know him—see the light—and then refuse to accept what he has done for them. Mark 16:16 does not categorize the whole world into the two groups of "believer" and "non-believer," and consign the latter to eternal perdition. It instead describes the two responses offered by people who have genuinely encountered Yeshua.

Conclusion

At the beginning of this paper I stated that a thorough and compelling response to the question of final destinies would include at least four elements, and that I would here be dealing with only the first of those elements. Therefore, any conclusions drawn at this point must be provisional, to be tested and refined by further theological, practical, and historical reflection. Nevertheless, our study of the explicit biblical teaching on the topic provides us with a preliminary hypothesis that deserves serious consideration.

According to this hypothesis, the apostolic teaching (as witnessed especially by the traditions of Peter and James and of Paul) begins by warning us against presumption regarding our own "salvation" and the damnation of others. It is striking how often the apostolic instruction has been understood by evangelicals in exactly the opposite form: as assuring our salvation and the salvation of others like us (in opinions, experiences, or community affiliations), and the damnation of those unlike us. I think that Soren Kierkegaard was on the right track in his meditation on "fear and trembling":

> I have never been so far in my life, and am never likely to get farther than to the point of 'fear and trembling,' where I find it literally quite certain that every other person will easily be blessed—only I will not. To say to the others: you are eternally lost—that I cannot do. For me, the situation remains constantly this: all the others will be blessed, that is certain enough—only with me may there be difficulties.[41]

Kierkegaard is not here making a doctrinal statement about the salvation of "the others." Instead, he seeks to exemplify the attitude that the good news aims to evoke through its warnings concerning final destinies.

The sharp needle that bursts the bubble of presumption is the universal apostolic teaching that all will be judged according to their deeds. We find this teaching in every strand of apostolic tradition that we have examined. What counts at the end, in the final analysis, is not our lineage, ethnicity, religious affiliation, religious experiences, or religious opinions, but how we lived our lives. Did we obey the divine commandments? Did we do God's will? Did we realize God's purpose for our lives?

God's justice in this final judgment is expressed in God's holding each accountable only for what he or she has received. We are responsible to take what we know and what we are given, and to make something of it. Each must respond to the light of revelation that she or he has been apportioned. This should sober us, who have beheld Yeshua's glory, and likewise temper our assessment of the destinies of others.

God's redemptive purpose for Israel, the nations, and all creation is realized through the person and work of Messiah Yeshua and the gift of the Spirit. Since the destinies of individuals receive their character from the wider corporate and cosmic destiny in which they share, no one may attain a blessed end apart from the saving work of Yeshua. Ultimately, the happiness of the world to come will consist of an eternal community of "all things" with the Father through the Son in the Spirit. In anticipation of that day, God offers us the opportunity to enter into that eternal relationship now. This is what the tradition of Peter and James knows as discipleship, and what the traditions of Paul and John mean by "faith in Yeshua." The judgment of our actions will determine whether we have already begun living in this eternal relationship, implicitly or explicitly, and whether we have continued do so, or whether we have sought the way of escape.

For those without explicit faith in Yeshua, the judgment of their works will reveal how they have responded to the light—or, better, the *Light*—they have been given. All creatures are created and sustained by God through the Divine Word in the Spirit, whether they know it or not. All creatures—and all human beings in particular—encounter God through the Word in the Spirit every day, every hour, every moment. Yeshua is met in the person of the needy; he stands beside everyone who has been wronged, and who must decide whether to bear a grudge or let it go; he speaks to each through the Torah "written on the heart." Most significantly, Yeshua reveals himself explicitly through the proclamation of the good news, through the transmission of his teaching, and through the embodiment of his redemptive mission in the life of the community that bears witness to his name. How have we responded to Yeshua, the living Torah, in all our actions? At the end, he will ask this question of everyone.

What C. S. Lewis says about Yeshua's threats concerning Hell applies equally well to the entire apostolic teaching on final destinies:

> The Dominical utterances about Hell, like all Dominical sayings, are addressed to the conscience and the will, not to our intellectual curiosity. When they have roused us into action by convincing us of a terrible possibility, they have done, probably, all they were intended to do.[42]

In similar manner the Dominical and apostolic promises concerning the life of the world to come rouse us to action—not by alerting us to "a terrible possibility" but by setting before us a glorious hope.

May each of us respond to the Light that has illumined our lives, and may he welcome each of us with the words, "Well done, good and trustworthy servant, enter into the joy of your Master."

BIBLIOGRAPHY

Barclay, John M. G. *Obeying the Truth.* Minneapolis: Fortress, 1988.

Beasley-Murray, George R. Word Biblical Commentary, Volume 36, John. Waco: Word Books, 1987.

Boccaccini, Gabriele. *Middle Judaism.* Minneapolis: Fortress, 1991.

Braaten, Carl and Robert Jenson, eds., *Union with Christ, The New Finnish Interpretation of Luther.* Grand Rapids: Eerdmans, 1998.

Brown, Raymond. E. *An Introduction to the Gospel of John.* New York: Doubleday, 2003.

Campbell, Douglas A. *The Quest for Paul's Gospel.* London: T&T Clark, 2005.

Cole, R. Alan. *Tbe Gospel According to St. Mark.* Grand Rapids: Eerdmans, 1961.

Cranfield, C. E. B. *The Epistle to the Romans, Volume II.* Edinburgh: T. & T. Clark, 1979.

Davies, W. D. and Dale C. Allison, *A Critical and Exegetical Commentary on The Gospel According to Saint Matthew, Volume 3*. Edinburgh: T&T Clark, 1997.

Dickson, Athol. *The Gospel according to Moses.* Grand Rapids: Brazos, 2003.

Dunn, James D. G. *Word Biblical Commentary*, *Volume 38a, Romans 1-8.* Dallas: Word Publishing, 1988.

France, R. T. *The Gospel According to Matthew.* Grand Rapids: Eerdmans, 1985.

Keck, Leander E. *Romans.* Nashville: Abingdon, 2005.

Keener, Craig. S. *A Commentary on the Gospel of Matthew.* Grand Rapids: Eerdmans, 1999.

___________. *The Gospel of John, A Commentary, Volume One.* Peabody: Hendrickson, 2003.

Kernaghan, Ronald J. *Mark.* Downers Grove, Il: Intervarsity, 2007.

Kinzer, Mark S. *Postmissionary Messianic Judaism.* Grand Rapids: Brazos, 2005.

Levering, Matthew. *Christ's Fulfillment of Torah and Temple.* Notre Dame: University of Notre Dame Press, 2002.

Lewis, C. S. *God in the Dock.* Grand Rapids: Eerdmans, 1970.

_________. *The Problem of Pain*, Chapter 8 in *The Complete C. S. Lewis Signature Classics.* San Francisco: Harper, 2002.

McKnight, Scot. *A New Vision for Israel.* Grand Rapids: Eerdmans, 1999.

Pannenberg, Wolfhart. *Systematic* Theology, *Volume 3.* Grand Rapids: Eerdmans, 1998.

Stackhouse, John G. Jr. (editor). *What Does It Mean To Be Saved?* Grand Rapids: Baker Academic, 2002.

Tiessen, Terrance L. *Who Can Be Saved?* Downers Grove: Intervarsity, 2004.

VanLandingham, Chris. *Judgment & Justification in Early Judaism and the Apostle Paul.* Peabody: Hendrickson, 2006.

Von Balthasar, Hans Urs. *Dare We Hope "That All Men Be Saved"?* San Francisco: Ignatius, 1988.

ENDNOTES

1. John G. Stackhouse, Jr. (editor), *What Does It Mean To Be Saved?* (Grand Rapids: Baker Academic, 2002), 9-10.
2. Most Messianic Jews would also consider salvation as dealing prominently with nations, and in particular with the nation of Israel.
3. The distinction between implicit and explicit faith goes back to the Middle Ages. For its use by Thomas Aquinas, see Matthew Levering, *Christ's Fulfillment of Torah and Temple* (Notre Dame: University of Notre Dame Press, 2002), 23-24, 92-93.
4. Relevant theological issues include the meaning and significance of God's attributes of mercy and justice and the relationship between them; the divinity of Yeshua and his mediatorial role in creation, revelation, and redemption; the validity of the traditional doctrine of "original sin," and its implications for a free human response to God's gracious initiative; the implications of the paradigmatic cases of infant mortality and those with severe mental limitations; the nature of Israel's enduring covenant and the ecclesiological bond between the Jewish people and the Christian Church.
5. Practical implications include how the embrace of the various responses affect the following: motivation for outreach; the power and attractiveness of our presentation of the good news; our relationships with those who are outside the Yeshua-faith community (especially our fellow Jews); our attitudes towards the Jewish people through history and the Jewish religious tradition; the formation of personal character that bears the image of Yeshua.
6. For an excellent recent volume that covers much of this ground, written by an evangelical theologian with a missionary background, see Terrance L. Tiessen, *Who Can Be Saved?* (Downers Grove: Intervarsity, 2004).
7. Given the passionate concerns about this topic within the Messianic Jewish movement, it is unfortunate that I am unable to address this question explicitly in the present paper. However, in my view the question of non-Messianic Jews and the world to come must be examined in the broader context provided by the studies undertaken here and in my book, *Postmissionary Messianic Judaism* (Grand Rapids: Brazos, 2005).
8. Some texts (i.e., Acts, Hebrews, and Revelation) demonstrate an overlap of traditions. On the present topic, Revelation shares the perspective of the tradition of Peter and James. Acts and Hebrews are also closest to this tradition, though they likewise have elements in common with the tradition of Paul.
9. My focus in this paper on biblical "traditions" has a twofold purpose: (1) to facilitate the discerning of family resemblances among various strands of teaching in the Apostolic Writings, so as to enable an exegetical treatment that takes account of similarities and differences in language, conceptuality, and focus; and (2) to underline the fact that books whose authors are not themselves apostles (e.g., Mark, Luke) rely upon authoritative apostolic testimony. I am certainly not aiming to ascribe authority to underlying "traditions" apart from the canonical text—and context—in which they are embodied and transmitted. I am also not asserting any grand claims regarding the composition of the individual books. My purpose is in large part heuristic.

10. All biblical citations are based on the NRSV, with my own modifications.
11. The parallel in Luke has a different context, which leads to a different meaning. There the warning is issued to those who heard and saw Yeshua personally, among whom he lived and worked: "Then you will begin to say, 'We ate and drank in your presence, and you taught in our streets.'" (Luke 13:26). Those "thrust out" of the presence of the Patriarchs are not "the heirs of the kingdom," as in Matthew, but "you yourselves" (i.e., those who knew Yeshua; Luke 11:28). In this context, those who "come from east and west, and north and south" are not necessarily Gentiles, but those from outside the land of Israel, who could not have known Yeshua personally.
12. This is a common theme in the tradition of Peter and James. See, for example, 2 Pet. 2:21; Heb. 2:1-3; 10:26-31. 12:25-26.
13. W. D. Davies and Dale C. Allison, *A Critical and Exegetical Commentary on The Gospel According to Saint Matthew* (Edinburgh: T&T Clark, 1997) 3:418.
14. Some exegetes imply that this text may refer only to the period of Yeshua's earthly mission, when he operated "incognito" (R. T. France, *The Gospel According to Matthew* [Grand Rapids: Eerdmans, 1985], 210). However, would the community have preserved such a saying if it had no application to their lives? Such a reductionist explanation derives more from a preconceived doctrinal position that seeks to evade the force of the text than from serious theological exegesis.
15. On the basis of this text, Athol Dickson asks the following questions regarding the final destinies of Jewish people who do not believe in Yeshua: "Is it possible for people of this age who were taught since birth to 'speak against the Son of Man' to be forgiven for doing exactly as they have been trained to do? … Will a gracious God consider their situation, look into their hearts to see if they truly love him, and forgive 'their words spoken against the Son of Man?'" (*The Gospel according to Moses* [Grand Rapids: Brazos, 2003] 253). C. S. Lewis concluded from this text: "Honest rejection of Christ, however mistaken, will be forgiven and healed" (*God in the Dock* [Grand Rapids: Eerdmans, 1970] 111).
16. Texts on *tzedakah* show the same principle at work (e.g., Luke 6:38; 16:9-13, 19-31; 19:8-90).
17. See Gabriele Boccaccini, *Middle Judaism* (Minneapolis: Fortress, 1991), 217-20. Boccaccini exaggerates the difference between the Yeshua tradition and Rabbinic thought on this topic, but his exposition of the teaching of the Yeshua tradition on forgiveness is superb.
18. A talent was worth more than fifteen years' wages of a laborer.
19. In keeping with the usage of the synoptic gospels, Acts 4:9 employs the verb "be saved" (*sosotai*) to refer to bodily healing. It also attributes this healing to the "name" of Yeshua and to "the faith of his name" (3:16). This is the context for Peter's claim, "There is salvation in no one else, for there is no other name under heaven given among mortals by which we must be saved" (Acts 4:12). Obviously, "salvation" has wider meaning here than just physical healing. However, it must include such manifestations of saving power. Given this fact, John Taylor's interpretation of the text has merit: "He was saying that Jesus of Nazareth is the source of every act of healing and salvation that has ever happened. He knew perfectly well that vast numbers of people had been healed without any knowledge of Jesus, yet he made the astounding claim that Jesus was the hidden author of all healing. He was the totally unique savior because he was totally universal" (cited by Tiessen, 85).

20. Of the two possible exceptions, Revelation 21:8 and Mark 16:16, the *apistois* who are cast into the lake burning with fire are not "the unbelievers" (KJV, NASB, NIV) but "the faithless" (RSV, NRSV, NEB, ESV), "the unfaithful" (CEV), or "the untrustworthy" (Stern). JB properly paraphrases as "those who break their word," while TEV has "the traitors." This reading is supported by Revelation's universal use of the positive form of the adjective (*pistos*) to mean "faithful" rather than "believing" (1:5; 2:10; 2:13; 3:14; 17:14; 19:11; 21:5; 21:6). The other possible exception to this generalization (Mark 16:16) will be treated later, for reasons to be explained at that point.
21. Wolfhart Pannenberg notes that the Beatitudes allot the inheritance of the kingdom to categories of people whose character reflects the teaching and example of Yeshua, regardless of whether they have ever heard of him: "The message of Jesus is the norm by which God judges even in the case of those who never meet Jesus personally ... all to whom the Beatitudes apply will have a share in the coming salvation whether or not they ever heard of Jesus in this life. For factually they have a share in Jesus and his message, as the day of judgment will make manifest." (*Systematic* Theology, *Volume 3* [Grand Rapids: Eerdmans, 1998], 615).
22. Exegetes disagree over the identity of Yeshua's "family members" in Matthew 25. Some see them as disciples of Yeshua, either apostles or other suffering members of the community (see, for example Craig S. Keener, *A Commentary on the Gospel of Matthew* [Grand Rapids: Eerdmans, 1999], 604-6). Others, such as Davies and Allison, see them as the needy in general. While I incline to the latter view, it is significant, regardless, that (1) the sheep and goats are those outside the covenant community, and (2) they did not know that they were encountering Yeshua when they cared for his "family members."
23. See Scot McKnight, *A New Vision for Israel* (Grand Rapids: Eerdmans, 1999).
24. James D. G. Dunn underlines the significance of the reference to "my good newsl" in this context: "The introduction of the gospel as criterion is not at odds with the preceding argument, as though in speaking of divine judgment Paul suddenly narrowed the much broader criteria with which he had been operating to the narrower one of faith in Christ. On the contrary, his point is precisely that his gospel operates with those broader factors, with faith in Christ seen as of a piece with a less well defined responsiveness to the Creator ... Faith in Christ is of course the goal of his own mission and preaching (cf. 10:14-17), but as a fuller and normative rather than exclusive expression of such responsiveness" (*Word Biblical Commentary*, *Volume 38a, Romans 1-8* [Dallas: Word Publishing, 1988], 103).
25. See Dunn, 101.
26. The importance of this theme in Paul's teaching has recently been emphasized by Chris VanLandingham, *Judgment & Justification in Early Judaism and the Apostle Paul* (Peabody: Hendrickson, 2006), 175-241.
27. For an insightful and up-to-date study of Paul's use of *pistis*, see Douglas A. Campbell, *The Quest for Paul's Gospel* (London: T&T Clark, 2005), 178-207.
28. "It is significant that it is the Resurrection which is mentioned—an indication that for Paul the belief that God raised Jesus from the dead is the decisive and distinctive belief of Christians" (C. E. B. Cranfield, *The Epistle to the Romans, Volume II* [Edinburgh: T. & T. Clark, 1979], 530).
29. John M. G. Barclay, *Obeying the Truth* (Minneapolis: Fortress, 1988), 236.

30. For example, see Cranfield, 527; James D. G. Dunn, *Romans 9-16* (Dallas: Word Books, 1988), 607; Leander E. Keck, *Romans* (Nashville: Abingdon, 2005), 254. Dunn compares the confession of faith in Yeshua as "Lord" with the Shema: "The confession which follows functions therefore as an (or the) equivalent of the Shema (Deut. 6:4): as he who says the Shema identifies himself as belonging to Israel, so he who says *kyrion Iesoun* [Yeshua is Lord] identifies himself as belonging to Jesus. As a 'slogan of identification' it would no doubt be used at baptism, but also much more widely in worship (1 Cor. 12:3), evangelism (2 Cor. 4:5), and parenesis (Col. 2:6)."
31. Some recent Scandinavian studies of Luther have concluded that the Reformer likewise understood "faith" primarily in terms of "union with Christ." See Carl Braaten and Robert Jenson, eds., *Union with Christ, The New Finnish Interpretation of Luther* (Grand Rapids: Eerdmans, 1998).
32. "Doubtless the prime interest of a gospel … is to set forth the *action* of God in Christ for the fulfillment of his purpose of grace … But the unremitting concentration of [John] the Evangelist on the person through whom God acts makes it plain that for him 'function and person are inseparable'" (George R. Beasley-Murray, *Word Biblical Commentary, Volume 36, John* [Waco: Word Books, 1987], lxxxiv).
33. "'Believe' thus refers to the proper response to God's revelation, a faithful embracing of his truth, as in OT 'faithfulness'; it is a conviction of truth on which one stakes one's life and actions, not merely passive assent to a fact" (Craig S. Keener, *The Gospel of John, A Commentary, Volume One* (Peabody: Hendrickson, 2003), 327.
34. "For the Synoptics, 'eternal life' is something that one receives at the final judgment or in a future age (Mark 10:30; Matt. 18:8-9), but for John it is a present possibility" (Raymond E. Brown, *An Introduction to the Gospel of John* [New York: Doubleday, 2003], 239.
35. See Brown, 239.
36. See Tiessen, 145.
37. This perspective provides the necessary context for interpreting other Johannine verses, such as John 8:24: "I told you that you would die in your sins, for you will die in your sins unless you believe that I am he." As Tiessen notes, "it is important to remind ourselves that Jesus made the statement specifically to people to whom he was revealing his identity. It is critical that we not overextend such statements to the unevangelized, who are, by definition, without such revelation" (85).
38. Ibid., 134.
39. Ibid., 48-52.
40. See Ronald J. Kernaghan, *Mark* (Downers Grove, Il: Intervarsity, 2007), 343-44. Even conservative scholars who argue for its early dating and canonical value agree that it does not belong in Mark: "It may be compared with the story of the woman taken in adultery, in John viii, as an example of an early tradition which may very well be genuine and is undoubtedly primitive, but does not belong to the actual Gospel text as it stands" (R. Alan Cole, *Tbe Gospel According to St. Mark* [Grand Rapids: Eerdmans, 1961], 259).
41. Cited in Hans Urs Von Balthasar, *Dare We Hope "That All Men Be Saved"?* (San Francisco: Ignatius, 1988), 88.
42. C. S. Lewis, *The Problem of Pain*, Chapter 8 in *The Complete C. S. Lewis Signature Classics* (San Francisco: Harper, 2002), 416.

KERUV AS GUIDING PRINCIPLE FOR PROCLAMATION OF THE GOOD NEWS

Tsvi Sadan, Ph.D.
Tenured Senior Lecturer for the Department of
Hebrew and Semitic Languages, Bar-Ilan University

Strategies and methods will always be the outcome of specific worldviews. Let me illustrate what this means. Before the destruction of Gush Katif, leading rabbis proclaimed: it shall never happen.[1] This false prophecy was based upon a certain worldview that assumes a God who operates according to predictable patterns. The strategy and the methods resulting from it were: Since they have God on their side, all the would-be evacuees had to do was to hug their opponents, or as their slogan said: "we have love and it shall win." This was a strategy of compliance rather than resistance. The result of that strategy was a resounding failure.

Now, if present strategies of the proclamation of the Good News and the methods resulting from them are to be understood, we must try to understand what shapes the present and prevalent Messianic Jewish worldview. Only after such a process wherein we are rigorously honest with ourselves and willing to be vulnerable—even to the point of discomfort—can present existing strategies be truly identified and examined for their actual value.

The following is my attempt to explain through my own personal experience, ongoing studies and convictions, how present strategies of proclamation were shaped. I will then evaluate them and suggest alternatives; and here I'd like to call attention to the following: though the descriptions below happened in Israel, much of this could easily be applied to the North American scene as well as to Europe and the former Soviet Union, with only minor modifications. In this regard, Israel is part of contemporary Western culture—these observations fit perfectly.

Scenes that Shape the Messianic Jewish Worldviews

When I came to faith in 1980, those who welcomed me and nurtured me in my new faith were two Mennonite missionaries who were allowed to conduct services in an Anglican Church. This scene that welcomed me was anything but Jewish. At the time, I could care less. I was raised in a secular Kibbutz and was soaked with anti-religious sentiments. My lack of interest in Judaism and my new zeal for Jesus made me easy prey.

Enthusiastically, I drank from the wells of Christianity. My sources of inspiration were Christian figures and Christian books. I familiarized myself with the biography of James Hudson Taylor and the meditations of Oswald Chambers. For the first time in my life, I heard names like Wesley, Spurgeon, and Stott. My teachers, preachers and spiritual leaders weren't Jewish, could hardly speak Hebrew, had no appreciation for Jewish thought and had but little knowledge of Jewish history. Unaware, and out of my new devotion to Jesus, during the 1980s I became a Protestant Christian—*de facto* if not *de jure*. Though this happened to me in the 1980s, similar experiences continue to dominate the "conversion scene" today.

Yet there are some differences between then and now. In the past, Israelis came to faith through sporadic missionary activity carried out by either professional Protestant missionaries or by enthusiastic Evangelicals who came to Israel mainly from England and North America. Today, many of the Israelis come to faith either through Israeli friends or through Israeli missionary-oriented activities. Still, many continue to come to faith (repentance should I say) by encountering Christians—missionaries or not. The result is a steady, albeit slow, increase in the numbers of "Messianic Jews" (a term used here in the broadest possible sense, meaning Jews who believe that Yeshua is the Messiah).

In the past, leadership was largely held by Christian missionaries. Today American Jews, American "wannabe" Jews and American Christians predominantly hold leadership. Where Jewish Israelis are in leadership, they have received their education, if they have any, in Christian institutions either in North America or Great Britain. In addition, with the influx of immigrants from the former Soviet Union in the 1990s, Russian-speaking people began to establish new congregations and assume leadership positions in existing congregations. Yet, though names of people and organizations have changed, in essence, present-day leadership is operating in the same way as their missionary predecessors did. Though now Hebrew is the spoken language in most places, modes of operation and models of leadership that grew out of Evangelical worldviews are still dominating the scene.

In the past, there were few indigenous Israelis in the various congregations. Today, their growing numbers have been a catalyst that fuels a Jewish self-awareness, which was unseen before. Israelis who come to faith face an identity crisis in the status quo—existing Hebrew-speaking Evangelical congregations. Most suppress their frustrations. A few are beginning to express their faith in Jewish terms—not as a missionary ploy but out of an existential need and a sense of integrity.

In the past, most Israelis came from secular backgrounds and were the only ones of their family who accepted Yeshua. Today, second-generation Messianic Jews tend to follow their parents' convictions; they prefer contemporary secular Israeli values (Right-wing liberals) to the values of Israeli religious communities. There are many second-generation Israeli believers, particularly children of mixed marriages, who still feel more at home with the Christian community than with Israeli society. Today, as it was before, most new believers are young (20 to 30), from secular backgrounds and with no university education.

In the past, Israelis in general thought that Messianic Jews were simply converts to Christianity. The general attitude toward them was a complete lack of appreciation or incomprehension, to say the least. Now, the general public seems to accept the fact that there are those Jews who believe in Jesus—and that's okay. There are two primary reasons for the change of attitude. Messianic Jews now fulfill their national duties. They are law-abiding loyal citizens who serve in the army—some in elite units. But the change of attitude is largely due to the expansion of post-modern ideologies. Secular Israeli society sees value in accepting, and even elevating, oppressed minority groups. Liberal values of human rights and democracy steer secular Israelis toward accepting Messianic Jews even when they don't like what Messianic Judaism represents. At the same time, religious Jews of all shades are maintaining the traditional negative attitude toward Jesus-believing Jews.

In the past Israeli believers had a sense of unity because they were few in number and did not question the validity of the Christian beliefs bestowed upon them. In the 1980s, Passover conferences organized by young Israeli believers were able to draw hundreds from all over Israel. Today however, the Messianic community is far from being united. For the most part, division runs along Christian denominational lines. There are also divisions for purely personal reasons. However, the most significant division is that which runs across religions. What characterizes Messianic Jews in Israel is that, though they are called Jews, in practice they resemble Western Christianity in every way. This is why, for example, most Messianic Jews don't care about mixed marriages; and even see value in intermarriage—providing the spouse is a "believer" (based upon Gal. 3:28: "there is neither Jew nor Greek.")

Against this trend there are those who think that loyalty to Yeshua must also mean loyalty to Judaism (in one form or another). This creates a profound division, so much so that one must talk about *two* communities of Messianic Jews. This division transcends mere theological differences in that those who express some form of fidelity to Judaism are viewed by many as heretics, plain and simple. From the other side, there are those "religious Messianic Jews" who tend to view "Christian Jews" through the traditional Jewish lens. The result is that there is hardly any dialogue between the two groups. Presently, those Messianic Jews who adopted the beliefs of Western Christianity are the overwhelming majority.

The dominance of this group can easily be seen through the way Israelis are drawn to the different conferences organized by Charismatic congregations and organizations. In contrast, those who seek to establish deep and meaningful affiliation with Judaism can hardly gather a minyan (10 Jewish men) for a prayer.

Outlining the Way "Mission" Is Viewed

The facts described above make it easier to outline the present dominating worldview of most Messianic Jews concerning what the "Mission" is. Again, taking the risk of presenting myself as a "typical" Messianic Jew, I encountered an enthusiastic young man from the American Charismatic movement who presented Jesus to me in simple terms: he is the one who can save me from the apocalyptic vision of Hal Lindsey's *The Late Great Planet Earth*. But whatever the personal circumstances may have been, upon accepting Jesus, I began to learn the Bible from people who themselves were trained in a particular form of Christianity. Therefore, even with their genuine love toward Israel, they could only teach me what they knew, and what they knew wasn't even remotely Jewish.

Yet, and this is where the difficulty begins, I wasn't aware of the fact that I had been ushered into a particular brand of Christianity. I was told that I was getting the pure "truth." The result was that in addition to my genuine repentance experience, my entire worldview began to be shaped in the image of that of my teachers. In particular, I started to see the world as divided into two groups of people: the good guys—the "believers" and the bad guys—the "non-believers." Among the "bad guys" were, of course, the Catholics and any other Protestant denominations that did not cater to my newly acquired Evangelical mindset. In this tightly knit scheme I viewed the "non-believing" Jews in the same way I viewed any other infidel, be they Muslims, Presbyterians or Buddhists.

And into this new world of mine came also the idea of "evangelism"—a word not found in the Jewish vernacular. Evangelism, as I understood it, meant telling others that Yeshua is the Messiah. The action of the telling itself became of paramount importance to me because of the particular meaning given to the familiar verse, "go and make disciples of all nations, baptizing them in the name of the Father and of the Son and of the Holy Spirit."

The first thing I learned from that verse was that of the few new commandments Jesus gave, this was probably the most important. The highest achievement of any "believer" is to convince others that Jesus is the Messiah. The more people you "bring to the Lord," the better you are in the eyes of God. It is not surprising that the new role models I was adopting were the great English missionaries of the 19th century. I use the term "missionaries" here, though in actuality I was trained to think of two kinds of missionaries. The worse kind were those Catholic missionaries who did all sorts of bad things to the people they wished to convert. The good kind of missionaries were those who were willing to dress up like Chinese or live in the jungles to convince the heathens that the good Lord is a true gentleman.

The second thing I learned from that verse was this: a "true believer" is the one who thinks like you. To turn one into a "believer" meant turning one into a good Evangelical (as it was in my case). Less than that result meant that something was not working out properly in the process of conversion. If, God forbid, one has decided to become a Lutheran, it meant that he wasn't really saved.

The third thing I learned from that verse was that to be completely and absolutely saved, a would-be "believer" had to dress up in white and get himself "immersed," not baptized, by a "spiritual leader" who will dip him in water, back first, and say: "I baptize you in the name of the Father and of the Son and of the Holy Spirit." Anything less than that, if one had water sprinkled over him by a priest or was baptized only in the name of Jesus, his baptism was good for nothing and he was yet to become a true believer.

Being convinced of the absolute importance of evangelism, based on what I was taught, I formed a nice, portable, sound bite of this "good news." In a nutshell (and it was always presented in a nutshell because I had to present it while standing on one foot as it were), the "Mission" was to deliver this piece of good news:

> Jesus is the one promised by the Old Testament's prophets to save all people from their sins. The wages of sin is death and all men sin. But, Jesus' blood has the power to atone for the sins of those who believe that he is Messiah and God. Those who believe that and that he died and rose from the dead are granted forgiveness through God's grace. The "believers" are joined into one Body of Messiah, also called Ecclesia. The "believers" are the only ones to escape God's wrath and are going to enjoy eternal life. In this Body, Jews and Gentiles are united in brotherly love made possible through abolishing divisions of religion, gender and ethnicity. Those who are part of the body are the only ones who serve God in spirit and truth. Therefore, only those who are in the *Ecclesia* are empowered by the Holy Spirit to understand and do God's will.

When I shared this good news with people, the general response was bewilderment rather than the expected hostility. Family members, friends, colleagues and innocent bystanders looked at me in a funny way while they desperately tried to figure out what in the world I was talking about. Generally speaking, while everybody knew something about Yeshu, no one ever heard of Yeshua. Secular friends did not know what to do with sacrifice and religious acquaintances couldn't figure out how Moses managed to disappear from my grand picture.

At first I attributed the bewilderment to "spiritual blindness" and "fat hearts" but slowly I began to realize that they genuinely couldn't understand what was so good about my news. Armed with my newly formed evangelical worldview, I did not even think about the possibility of flaws in my presentation. How could there be flaws if I received the truth straight from heaven's representatives on earth?

But, as I now turn to explain, as far as Jews are concerned, my version of the good news lacked the "good" part of the "news." The most obvious element lacking from that version of the good news was Israel's unique relationship with God. Though the vast majority of Messianic Jews agree that the Jewish people are important, they don't really know what to do with them. After all, if there is a New Covenant, Jews, along with everybody else, need to join the New Israel (which looks suspiciously like the same Western Christianity from which this notion has been birthed). In this kind of worldview, Jews are viewed like any other people. They are like the Zulu, French or Tamil. The only difference is that they once had a glorious past. But after Jesus created the Ecclesia (also known as Church) individual Jews are called to join the Church, just like everybody else. The "Willowbank Declaration" that defines the LCJE's approach to "Mission" says it clearly (Lausanne Consultation for Jewish Evangelism, where not a few Jewish missions and organizations are represented):

> We affirm that much of Judaism, in its various forms, throughout contemporary Israel and today's Diaspora, is a development out of, rather than as an authentic embodiment of, the faith, love and hope, that the Hebrew Scriptures teach. We deny that modern Judaism with its explicit negation of the divine person, work, and Messiah-ship of Jesus Christ contains within itself true knowledge of God's salvation (article III.14.).

In this kind of message, Jesus becomes the forfeiter of the very covenant Jews were willing to die for and not break. And in this regard, all Messianic Jews should remember that all Jews who live today owe their lives to their forefathers' obedience to that covenant that gives them their God-given identity.

So if you are Jewish, what is so good about news which announces that the "Old Covenant" went up in smoke more than 2000 years ago? If you are a Jew who cares about these things, the prospect of a wholesale abandonment of the covenant and people is simply horrendous. Little wonder that such news attracts mostly Jews from secular background. These were the people who at first did not care about such things as a covenant. Yet even they, with their wounded understanding, cannot comprehend a gospel that calls for their demise. This is why even those who insist on calling themselves "Jewish Christians" will not consider erasing the word "Jewish" from this bewildered term.

To summarize: the worldview that shaped the concept of "Mission" which I initially adopted resembled in many ways the classic (even orthodox) Christian worldview. Where the good news is concerned, I saw the Jewish religion in a typical Christian fashion—a pharisaic-legalistic-outdated religion that resents true spirituality. My version of the gospel did not have a place for Judaism or for Jews as a religious entity. I thought that the New Covenant was a total and clean break from the Old Covenant with its outdated Law. My good news called for *sola gratia*, *sola fide*, *sola scriptura* and *solus Christus* as is usually understood. This was my worldview out of which came my good news' proclamation strategy and methods.

Contemporary Strategy and Methods of Good News Proclamation

From the above descriptions it should come as no surprise that the most prevalent contemporary strategy for the proclamation of the good news among Messianic Jews relies heavily upon the 19th century Protestant models of "Mission," particularly the English Missions out of which missionaries like Christian Friedrich (Joseph Samuel) Frey, Adolf Saphir and Paul Levertoff came.

As it had before, today Messianic Jewish Mission activity relies upon Christian theology just as it depends upon Christian resources. Until today, a missionary has always been a paid professional who spreads the version of the good news that he learned from his particular Church (Anglican if you are English, Lutheran if you are German etc.). This means that each mission organization is not truly independent but reflects the theology of those who support it theologically and financially. In the case of Jewish mission organizations, the money that sustains these organizations comes primarily from Protestants whose views toward Jewish Mission is more or less the same as it was before.[2] Practically it means that to sustain their activity, Jewish mission organizations form their identity and activity around Christian parameters. So for example, though today many Christians are in favor of "Jewish expression of faith in Yeshua the Messiah," their tacit expectation is that it will be done in a way that conforms to the basic tenets of Christianity.

Turning to "strategies," "methods" and "effectiveness" of our "proclamation," it should be clear by now that these marked words that initiate our discussion are heavily Christian. "Mission," as was said above, is not simply a word that reiterates Yeshua's command. Rather, "Mission" is a term loaded with presupposed ideas about what the Good News to the Jewish people is. So to repeat, the present-day sense of "Mission":

> To evangelize is to spread the good news that Jesus Christ died for our sins and was raised from the dead according to the Scriptures, and that as the reigning Lord he now offers the forgiveness of sins and the liberating gifts of the Spirit to all who repent and believe. … evangelism itself is the proclamation of the historical, biblical Christ as Saviour and Lord, with a view to persuading people to come to him personally and so be reconciled to God. … Jesus still calls all who would follow him to … identify themselves with his new community. The results of evangelism include obedience to Christ, incorporation into his Church and responsible service in the world (Lausanne Covenant).

To implement this grand vision, the basic strategy is for every "true believer" to do whatever possible by peaceful means to convince every living Jew that Jesus is the Messiah. This strategy is supposed to be implemented through roughly three methods: proliferation of written and verbal "proof texts" that Jesus is the Messiah, adaptation of some form of "Jewish life style" and establishing "good witness."

The distribution of "proof texts" is done primarily by means of a "tract" that can be verbal or written. This "tract" is designed in such a way that it can be delivered quickly and indiscriminately to as many people as possible so that they will immediately learn about the possibility that Jesus is the promised Jewish Messiah. This narrow focus of "tract" distribution does not allow for any nuances, nor can it; the tract and its messenger are forced to present a cryptic version of "good news."

The second item of the strategy entails the adaptation of some kind of Jewish life-style. Its purpose is to better convince "non-believing Jews" that Jesus is not against but for (Messianic) Jews. This method includes not only the use of religious artifacts and costumes but also the use of Jewish religious texts. Converted Jews disgracefully used the last one in the disputations of the Middle Ages; and there are modern examples of that approach as well. Those who use it operate under the assumption that it serves the grand purpose of the proclamation if they will do as Paul supposedly did: "To the Jews I became as a Jew, in order to win Jews" (1 Cor. 9:20). There is much to be said about this kind of approach; the least is that it is dishonest and attributes dishonesty to Paul.

The third method that is now gaining much favor is that of "good witness."

Samples of a good witness include anything from joining the Israeli army to running an honest business and having a good marriage. Donating money to "non-believing" Jewish organizations, which is now gaining popularity, is an example of this "good witness" approach. The underlying assumption here is that "good witness," or living according to a particular understanding of the teaching of the New Testament, has the power of persuasion and conviction.

These three methods do not exhaust all modalities, but it does seem that almost all other methods employed today are coming out of them (these will include Bible studies, home groups, public debates, web pages, books, articles, use of public media and so on). In addition, it should be remembered that every method used today is culturally and legally permissible. Mission activists use these to their advantage under an umbrella of Western liberal values such as freedom of religion, freedom of speech and human rights that are embodied in laws protecting the same. Today the proclamation of the Good News to the Jewish people is possible in an unprecedented scale due to the modern, even post-modern, understanding of democracy. Ironically, the worldview that calls for gay rights also allows for mission activity (at least for now). The use of democracy for the advance of Jewish mission presents an enormous ethical problem since by depending on it, mission activists cannot deny, for example, the right of Muslims for peaceful Jihad.

Keruv as an Alternative to "Mission"

What was described up to this point—and it should be clear by now—is that in truth, much of what calls itself Messianic Judaism in fact resembles an exotic Christian sect rather than a Jewish one. One can argue until blue in the face that the Israeli Supreme Court was wrong when in 1989 it reached the decision that Messianic Jews are people who belong to another religion. Yet the judges were no fools. Long ago the Jewish people had reached a decisive decision to reject the kind of good news described above. They refused the Gospel that in the name of Jesus called them to convert to another religion. They refused the Gospel that in the name of Jesus called them to break their unique covenant with God. They refused the Gospel that forced them to identify with the culture of their historical oppressors. They refused the Gospel that called them to compromise monotheism and reject Talmud, Tradition and their cherished customs.

In the new worldview that has been forming inside me for more than 10 years, I now say: the Jewish people had and still have every possible right to continue to reject this version of the Good News. No sane Jew is willing to forfeit the welfare of his people for the sake of his own personal destiny. This kind of an approach is traditionally called betrayal, and rightly so. Paul was willing to be cut off from the Messiah for the sake of his people. The history of Messianic Jews sadly shows the opposite pattern; more often then not, they quickly adopt the worldview of their former oppressors. Of the few glaring exceptions is the forgotten, misunderstood and tragic figure of Stanislaus Hoga. Hoga, a Polish-born Jew, immigrated to England in the 1820s to work with the London Society for Promoting Christianity Among the Jews. Only after helping Alexander McCaul to write the *Old Paths*—a severe attack on the Talmud and Judaism, he realized how damaging the activity of his day's mission societies was. At a heavy personal price, Hoga left his former friends and re-entered the Jewish fold.[3] Of his former colleagues he said: "they love the Jews so much that they live upon nothing but Jews."[4]

Strategies and methods amount to very little if they are based upon questionable worldviews. Israel's mighty army accomplished very little in Lebanon War II because the IDF worldview didn't have within it elements like "decisive victory." The same is true with the Good News. Who could tell how much money and human effort were spent over the last decade alone in the relentless attempt to save the

Jews? Some say that one billion dollars and countless numbers of people, from professional missionaries to simple folks, were attempting to "spread the good news" in multiple ways. Yet with so much effort, the results are still very much arguable.

The reason for such poor results, as I have tried to explain, is that it does not really matter what strategies we devise and what methods we employ so long as the Messianic Jewish "Mission" is to even insinuate the alteration of Judaism as we know it today. As long as this will continue to be our predominant sense of mission, Messianic Jews will insure the continued rejection of the Good News by the vast majority of the Jewish people.

Instead of this traditional "Mission" approach with its "proclamation of alienation," Messianic Jews should consider replacing it with the "proclamation of Keruv." Keruv is a Hebrew word that comes from Karov, "near." Keruv is a mission to call Jews to draw nearer to God, first by familiarity to their own religion and tradition. The Jewish people, as taught by Yeshua, cannot comprehend the Good News apart from Moses (John 5:46). Bringing the Good News outside of such context is what turns Keruv to "Mission." Accordingly, real keruv has in it elements of reassurance and hope for the Jews as people under covenant.

In his little-known book, *A New Vision for Israel*, Scott McKnight restores the worldview, which can enable to bring in keruv rather than alienation. The good news of Jesus, says McKnight, is that he came to restore national Israel:

> The most important context in which modern interpreters should situate Jesus is that of ancient Jewish nationalism and Jesus' conviction that Israel had to repent to avoid national disaster. Jesus' hope was not so much the "Church" as the restoration of the twelve tribes … the fulfillment of the promises of Moses to national Israel, and the hope of God's kingdom." (10)

According to this understanding, the Good News that the kingdom of God is at hand, and indeed has arrived, is necessarily linked to national Israel's restoration. This being the case, today's national Israel that is called to enter the Kingdom can be identified only through Jewish Tradition (Judaism). It goes without saying therefore that any proclamation that seeks to tamper with the Jewish identity inevitably finds itself at odds with the idea of the restoration of national Israel,[5] and because of it, with Israel as an identifiable, unified entity that enters as such into the kingdom.

Keruv therefore means first and foremost that trustworthy Jews do the proclamation. In this way, the methods of "proof texts," "Jewish life style," and "good witness," comes into play, but from an entirely different angle; it becomes a state of being rather than a method, or a tactic (only) to "win people for Christ." Living as Jews as an existential statement is what turns the "proof text," the "tract" from a method to a living thing. After all, didn't the apostle call us to be a living epistle, a living "tract" rather than using scripture verses as a kind of weapon? Understand what I am and am not saying: these methods listed before should not be simply discarded. What I am saying is that ideas such as "good witness," "proof texts" and "Jewish life style" should become for Messianic Jews a complete, integral, honest state of being rather than tactical maneuvers.

So again, to outline the idea of Keruv more clearly, the "strategy" for our proclamation of the good news (as defined by us) is to live first of all as trustworthy Jews. This can be achieved only if Messianic Jews come to the conclusion that upon the existence of the Jewish people rests the redemption of the world. "The world exists because of Israel since it is written: 'Thus says the LORD: If it had not been for my covenant, I have not established day and night and the ordinances of heaven and earth'."[6] The Messianic Jewish Good News concerning this is that Israel without Yeshua is only a shadow of what it ought to be.

Trustworthy Jews do not despise, ridicule or even hate their religion. "Love the Jews but reject their religion" is an intolerable approach. The Gospel that publically proclaims statements such as "the rabbis are our worse enemies," "the Siddur is poison," "Tefilin, I spit on it," is a Gospel of hate. And it is almost beyond belief to hear a little girl saying she should "throw the Siddur into the garbage cause that's what mom told me I should do."

Instead, Messianic Jews must go out of their way to draw others nearer to a Jewish way of life by personal example but also by making past traditions and beliefs more understandable and friendly to the disconnected and the disillusioned. The Good News here is not that Yeshua came to destroy Judaism but that he is the greatest Sage, the ultimate Tana and it is in his power to rejuvenate our religion so that it can become what it ought to be.

Any community of Jews that fails to restore love and appreciation for their past inevitably will be viewed as hostile to any kind of meaningful Jewish future. This is true not only concerning the Messianic Jewish community but to any other Jewish community that tries to establish itself by reinventing Judaism.

The crisis Zionist Israel faces today is an outcome of an ideology that tried to create a "new Jew" who is free from the shackles of tradition. Yoseph Haim Brenner expressed this new vision best: "Israel has no messiah—let us make mighty soldiers to live without messiah." Today, Israelis in unprecedented numbers are drawn nearer to Judaism and to a spirituality that had not been previously available to them. This trend is a testimony to the depth of the crisis, and to its possible solution. Statistics show that outside Israel, "new Jews" of any kind assimilate themselves into oblivion. Trustworthy Jews on the other hand are those who work hard toward strengthening the Jewish people by first of all helping them to draw near to the religion of their forefathers. Out of this mindset should also follow loyalty to the state of Israel. Messianic Jews should join the IDF, to give but one example, not because this is expected of them from the modern democratic state of Israel. They should join the army and contribute to Israel because it helps to secure the future of the Jews.

"Good witness" is something that further substantiates trustworthiness. Toward the very end of his life Paul was still able to say: "Brothers … I had done nothing against our people or the customs of our fathers." If he did, his witness couldn't be called "good witness" or "trustworthy witness", and he wouldn't have had three Jews to talk to. Yet today, Messianic Jews think they can be a good witness by assuming some kind of moral stand which some call Biblical. Yet, in its religious context, a good witness, a trustworthy witness cannot stand apart from the Torah. This should be explained further.

Until modern times, within the framework of Judaism, no "non-observant" Jew was permitted to give a testimony in a Jewish court of law. Maimonides summarized this position succinctly: "the one who does not live according to Scripture, Mishnah or Derech Eretz, he is held as wicked and is disqualified to bare witness" (Mishne Torah, Hilchot Edut, 11:1). This conclusion is a logical extension of the demands of the Torah, such as "You shall not join hands with a wicked man to be a malicious witness" (Exod. 23:1). So if any Israelite who rejects the Torah cannot testify, cannot be trusted with minor things, who will listen to his testimony concerning the most important things?

One should truly marvel at the fact that only a handful of commentators as well as generally thinking believers pay attention to Yeshua as the example of the trustworthy witness. For his Good News to be heard, to be trusted, he had to be obedient to the Torah (anyone claiming otherwise disqualifies him from being the Messiah). It is the same with all the early apostles and disciples. Jews would have not given Peter the time of day had they known he enjoyed eating pork with Cornelius (as many say he did). If the followers of Yeshua were known to disregard Moses, quite simply, the name of Yeshua would have been forgotten.

And there is no difference today. Messianic Jews cannot be surprised if their witness is ignored at best. They cannot stand in opposition to Moses and speak for God. It is simply incredible to think of the possibility that a Jew can be faithful to God and at the same time unfaithful to Moses. Accordingly, good witness is possible only in the context of trustworthy observant Messianic Jews whose ultimate authority for the two Torahs (shebechtav and shebe'al-peh) is Yeshua: "Torah that man learns in this world is *hevel* before the Torah of Messiah" (Kohelet Raba on Eccles. 11:8). Accordingly, there is great news in telling that he calls Israel: "Come to me, all who labor and are heavy laden" (Matt. 11:29).

Within such contexts it is easier to understand what it means for the Messianic Community to be a living "tract." In a manner of speech, the proof text is in the pudding. One can quote all the right verses in the world in an attempt to convince others that Yeshua is the promised one, but it will be to no avail if the proclamation erases the rest of the promises given to Israel; which is exactly what Christians did for the last 1800 years. Again, it can be said that with Jews, strategies and methods do not work because of their "blindness." But this is really the easy way out, a way to avoid self-examination. A living epistle must live out righteousness, which in turn will give credence to their "proofs." Here again, the Good News is that if the promises concerning the Messiah were fulfilled, surely the promises concerning Israel will be fulfilled as well.

And concerning righteousness, though I do believe that it is Yeshua who made me righteous, it is really incredible to think of righteousness apart from Torah. Righteousness is not a theological concept. It is a life lived according to God's expectations that were outlined for us in the Bible. To say that Yeshua made me righteous and disregard the Mitzvah is not convincing, and this is to say the least.

Just as we believe about Yeshua, the Bresslev Hassids believe that Rebe Nachman of Bresslev is "Tsadik, foundation of the world whose righteousness protects us and all Israel." Yet even so it doesn't even dawn on them that he exempts them from remaining meticulously observant. The same is true for Messianic Jews. They need to learn from the early disciples who didn't think that Yeshua exempted them from observance at all. Rather, they believed that he called their righteousness to exceed that of the Pharisees, an ideal they strived to accomplish. Messianic Jews will do well to learn from them how to become a living epistle.

As a way of life, as an existential statement, the strategy of Keruv as outlined here does not depend upon "results" to validate itself. Noah did not produce any results for 120 years despite the fact that he fulfilled all the requirements needed from a trustworthy witness. If the Messianic Jewish strategies and methods for the proclamation of the Good News are built upon productivity and various business results models, then they inevitably must turn to expensive marketing strategies, with all that it entails (brokers, lawyers, fund-raisers, campaign managers, trade-marking, lawsuits, manipulative slogans etc.).

Finally, because Keruv is a statement of love, it does not need to dress and undress itself to accommodate the desires of the communities to whom it speaks. The good news of Yeshua has the power to speak to the heart of the most adamant secular Jew and to the heart of the ultra-orthodox. I know many Messianic Jews who are all too happy "to be a secular Jew for the sake of the secular Jew" (with the exception of a few Gentiles), but I have yet to see a Messianic Jew who is willing to be an ultra-orthodox for the sake of the ultra-orthodox. The truth is that neither is desirable. Instead, the Messianic Community must form its own unique religious lifestyle in a way pleasing to God, and man. Working upon the principle of Keruv, the Messianic community should be able to produce that sweet scent that will attract others to the kingdom of God, and this scent, it should be obvious, should not come out of our eau-de-cologne but out of the nature of our being.

ENDNOTES

1. This was the cry of former chief rabbi Mordechai Eliyahu, and there were others. The cry itself is based on Ezekiel 20:32.
2. Moshe Aumann, *Conflict & Connection*, Gefen Publishing House, 2003. See also interview with the Christian Embassy's president Malcolm Heading in, Tsvi Sadan, 'Where Is the Christian Embassy Heading?' Kivun, 53 (September-October), 2006, 8-9 [Hebrew].
3. See more on him in Beth-Zion Lask Abrahams, 'Stanislaus Hoga—Apostate and Penitent,' Transactions of the Jewish Historical Society, 15, 1946: 121-149.
4. S. Hoga, 'Jewish Emancipation and the Conversion Society,' The Jewish Chronicle, 3.9.1847, 231.
5. I want to refer the reader once again to Aumann's research in *Conflict & Connection*, where he too concludes that the Church may tolerate Jews but not Jewish sovereignty.
6. Torat Hamincha of R. Yaakov son of R. Hananel Skilli, sermon 21. The translation of Jer. 33:25 follows his interpretation.

THE GOOD NEWS PROCLAMATION BY THE MESSIANIC CONGREGATION

Sam Nadler, D.D.
Congregation Leader, Hope Of Israel Congregation
President, Word Of Messiah Ministries

My thesis is that for me *messianic congregations* best accomplish the proclamation of the Good News to my people. By Good News I understand that in Messiah Yeshua, God has faithfully confirmed His Abrahamic promises to Israel redeeming all who have faith in Him. By congregation (e.g., *kehilah*, *edah*, synagogue),[1] I mean a local community of disciples that gather regularly for prayer and teaching, in mutual accountability to Scriptural authority, as opposed to a weekly bible study or a fellowship meeting, that may also meet regularly, and contain both prayer and teaching, but would lack the mutual accountability to Scriptural authority.[2] By "messianic" I refer to the faith in Messiah expressed in a biblically Jewish frame of reference.[3] There are three basic values generating the *kavanah*-driven methodology that actively proclaims the Good News to my people through a messianic synagogue.[4]

MY VALUES FOR PROCLAIMING THE GOOD NEWS THROUGH A MESSIANIC CONGREGATION

The Value of *Tikkun Olam*: the Promised Good News Repairs the World

The Good News is God's way to restore what sin has destroyed, and I will refer to this restorative work using the common phrase *Tikkun Olam*. God wants the world restored to His purpose and not merely recreated in our own image.

The triune God created us in His image to rule creation.[5] Today, ruling may suggest domination. But pre-sin, ruling was a responsibility best seen in Adam's gardener-training phase by cultivating and keeping[6], that is, to serve and protect it. The surprise is that in creating

Adam in His own image, HaShem then proclaimed that it is not good for man to live alone. I believe we best represent God in loving relationships and these loving relationships are most effectively seen in a caring community—a loving group, not a lone hermit.

We see this loving relationship re-emphasized by the command that HaShem gave Adam and Eve to "be fruitful and multiply, and fill the earth, and subdue it."[7] From the beginning, "God blessed *them*," not just him or her.[8] Adam and Eve were blessed in relationship together. They were created with complete dependence on their Creator to fulfill His will.

However their impact upon the world as His representatives was not yet a restoration, redemption or salvation issue; it preceded their sin. Our faithful service is to represent God for who He is through His word regardless of the world's condition. It is only with the catastrophic fall in Genesis 3 that we have Tikkun Olam. The purpose of Tikkun Olam is to restore this sin ruined world, that is, to restore our severed relationship to God and our divided community with each other. When sin necessitated redemption, God promised a Redeemer from "the seed of the woman."[9]

God focused the promise through His covenant to give Abraham a land, a people, and a blessing,[10] so that in his seed all the nations of the earth would be blessed.[11] The Covenant promises moved Abraham to have a blessed impact on his world. In the midst of pagan Canaan, Abraham "called upon the name of the Lord,"[12] thus applying Tikkun Olam. So also, in representing God, Abraham took disciple making seriously with the 318 servants (or literally, "dedicated ones," חֲנִיכָיו) that "were born in his house."[13] This community of disciples shared in his urgent Tikkun Olam service.[14]

In the Prophets, Tikkun Olam takes on a national urgency, like a responsible watchman (הַצֹּפֶה) warning the Jewish community of impending judgment.[15]

The New Covenant teaches that Yeshua is HaShem's faithfulness to Israel. The Good News of Messiah is the realization of the promise to our fathers[16] and HaShem's eternal will for Tikkun Olam. Messiah's death and resurrection fulfilled God's Edenic promise, and as Abraham's ultimate Seed He sent out His talmidim to make disciples of all nations. The fulfillment of the promise[17] called us to make disciples from the beginning until He returns. His representatives who value Tikkun Olam impact Olam Hazeh through Olam Haba's Good News proclamation to our people.[18]

The Value of Kiddush HaShem: His name is sanctified in Messiah's Good News

Kiddush HaShem values the sanctification of God's name. When we desecrated His name through sin, we were separated from God, even though we were created in His image. The fact is that Messiah lived and died for Kiddush HaShem.[19] The messianic congregation especially values Kiddush HaShem since His name is sanctified through the Good News that is to the Jew first. This priority is critical, for the Good News is validated if God's righteousness is revealed. Paul's theme in Romans is that the Good News of Yeshua reveals God's righteousness.[20] Paul defines the Good News as having three essential elements that demonstrate God's righteousness in Yeshua.

First, the Good News is God's "saving power" in Yeshua. HaShem demanded a consistent righteousness from His people.[21] What He provided in Yeshua's life, death and resurrection is the work of righteousness, required to restore us to a right standing with our Creator.[22] The Good News of Yeshua is the message of God's righteous work that powerfully saves, reconciles and restores the lost nations of the world as well as the lost sheep of the house of Israel.

Second, the Good News is "to all that believe" it.[23] Since the Good News is what God has accomplished and provided in Messiah Yeshua, therefore that same message requires appropriation by faith.[24] Salvation by faith in Yeshua demonstrates God's righteousness for it confirms that God is faithful to His promise for His name's sake. Just as Abraham believed the same promise and it was accounted to him for righteousness, so also those who are His children by faith are likewise reckoned righteous before God. So what God has powerfully done that was witnessed to by the Law and the Prophets is "the righteousness of God through faith in Yeshua the Messiah for all those who believe."[25]

Third, the Good News is "to the Jew first and also to the Gentile." What about that Good News being the righteousness of God demands that it be to the Jew first, or chiefly?[26] The covenant with Abraham and his seed is the only hope of the nations. No other covenant of redemption was made with another people. The Good News is always "to the Jew first" because it is always the fulfillment of the Abrahamic covenant. God could not righteously save anyone apart from what He promised Israel, as corroborated in Romans 9-11[27] and "confirmed" in Romans 15:8.[28] The same covenant that promised blessing for the nations in Abraham's seed also promised Abraham a people and a land. It is one covenant. If God were to fulfill one promise but nullify another He would break the covenant, therefore being unrighteous with Abraham and his descendants.

It is this 3-fold Good News that reveals God's righteousness in Messiah. If we remove any element then you have a different message that defames God's righteous character. Yeshua is the public demonstration of HaShem's righteousness for my people first. In fact by its existence, a messianic congregation demonstrates that the Good News is to the Jew first, since Yeshua is God's faithfulness to our people. If the Apostle to the Gentiles expected the Gentile believers to be unashamed to proclaim the Good News to the Jew first, how can a messianic congregation do any less?

The Value of Am Yisrael Chai: God is faithful to Israel in the Good News.

In Messiah, God faithfulness to Israel is best evidenced in the messianic congregation, through an identifiable community of Israel. *Am Yisrael Chai*—the people of Israel live!—is the outworking of our concern for *kol yisrael* to be saved. Why? The redemption of Israel means having identifiable Jews. The non-messianic Jewish community is not yet concerned about Isaiah 53. Rather, their felt concern is the continued existence of the Jewish community. Will we continue as an identifiable people? This must be our concern as well.

Sadly, believers have dismissed this concern in many ways. The victory of Messiah over sin and death was often pictured as the church over the synagogue. The lack of Jewish identity in the faith was thus seen as purity of faith in Messiah; our Jewish identity was described as our "mark of Cain."[29]

I've witnessed the residual effects of this anti-Jewish posture throughout my ministry. Back when using the label "Hebrew Christian" was suspect, a great expositor and president of my bible college looked me in the eye and said to me, "I *hate* hyphenated Christians." As the movement grew, some Christians even accused Messianic congregations of diluting the biblical message with Jewishness to "Lure Jews to Christianity."[30] We could have responded, "So you're expressing your faith using a Gentile culture to lure in ignorant Gentiles?" The president of a Christian university was aghast that our sanctuary didn't display a cross. He concluded that not displaying the cross denies it! The truth is that many identify their faith by their cultural expression. For them a change in cultural expression is a change in the actual faith as well.

Moreover, it is assumed that *Am Yisrael Chai* is irrelevant. Salvation as a concern always trumps Jewish identity. Like our sins, Jewish identity was made past tense by whatever church we joined. As a young believer I was taught, "Jews won't come to faith in any great numbers now; those that do are no longer Jews but are Christians." I was taught this in the most pro-Jewish group I could find!

The loss of Jewish identity means the loss of the identifiable Jewish community. This loss was one of the great threats of our messianic faith to the non-messianic Jewish community. The testimony of one lone brilliant Hebrew Christian is less effective to the larger Jewish community than most impressed churches understand. It may actually reinforce the Jewish community's fears, as they see another Jew lost to the Jewish community. The messianic congregation must share that concern. For this problem didn't go away with Jewish revivals of the '70s and the '90s; success only made the loss more obvious. Now what was an occasional issue was seen as a growing threat. The response in major Jewish communities was no longer "ignore it, and hope it goes away." With the exception of a few noted rabbis,[31] for the most part the greater Jewish community circled the wagons, developed strategies, and became alert to missionary presence in their midst.

I must assert that I am *not* primarily driven to express my faith via my culture by the desire of being a more effective witness to the greater Jewish community. If every Jewish person were already a believer, I'd still be determined to establish messianic synagogues. The importance of our Jewish community's visible existence is the importance of God's faithfulness to His word. God started with one man, and said, "I will make of you a people." Starting with a couple unable to naturally have a child He produced a people as proof of His faithfulness and power. His testimony of faithfulness to His promise is seen in a community of Jews. For the One who came to "confirm the promises to the fathers" therefore came to keep this people as His testimony, admittedly as a remnant, but as an identifiable remnant. God's testimony through Israel is His testimony through a people, a community.[32] So Yeshua said that "upon this rock" He'd build His community. [33]

The Jewish community's concern to survive is not just our Jewish concern; it is also the God of Israel's concern![34] The Body of Yeshua in general and the messianic congregation in particular are established by HaShem to represent to the world His faithfulness in Messiah to the Jew first. The messianic congregation shares and speaks to this divine concern testifying of Messiah's faithfulness to Israel as an identifiable Jewish community. As that part of the Body of Yeshua within the Jewish community, the messianic synagogue has the dual responsibility for being a witness to Israel, and a witness of Israel. Therefore, this should be every believer's concern and stewardship, whether Jewish or Gentile. Let us consider how the messianic congregation demonstrates the testimony of both groups:

1) *A Jew in the present tense.* First, the messianic congregation is the best testimony for the present tense Jewish believer. If in the Good News of Yeshua, God is supposed to be seen as presently faithful to Israel, then the Good News must manifest Jewish believers living as present tense Jews. The messianic synagogue is the best means to maintain the present tense community of Jewish believers.

Our desire, prayer and goal is for "all Israel to be saved,"[35] that is, for every Jewish person to come to personal faith in Messiah Yeshua. I see not only the difficulty of realizing this lofty goal but a more serious dilemma if this prophetic objective were actually realized any time soon! If every Jewish person came to faith in Yeshua today, where would these millions of new Jewish believers go for fellowship and discipleship? For even if they went to genuinely good churches (doctrinally sound, even pro-Israel), within two generations it's unlikely that there would remain an identifiable Jewish community! God's commitment is to preserve Israel as an identifiable people. Some might say, "Well isn't keeping the Jewish people as an identifiable people God's sovereign business?" Certainly, it is His sovereign business, and therefore as His servants it is also our stewardship responsibility.

Some Christians do not realize that there are Jews who are unlearned about their heritage. In any Jewish community there are some unlearned Jews, but they're not expected to represent the entire community. But by being part of their community their existence is itself a meaningful testimony. So also, the messianic community has all sorts of Jews. Each person's existence as part of community contributes to the communal testimony, without placing undue expectations on any individual.

In Romans 11:1-10, the Jewish remnant according to grace is Paul's first evidence of God's faithfulness to Israel. Paul views himself

(11:1), along with the testimony of Elijah (11:2-4) and all the Jewish believers at "this present time" (11:5-6), as one proof of God's faithfulness, that HaShem has not rejected His people. Paul says, "I *am* an Israelite" even as he had said, "I *am* a Jew."[36] For Paul, God's present tense faithfulness to the Jewish people is seen in the present tense Jewish testimony of a Jewish believer.

A Jewish believer saying "I *was* an Israelite," or his child saying, "My dad was a Jew but now he's a Christian," becomes an ineffectual testimony of God's faithfulness. It reinforces the canard that faith in Yeshua ends Israel's existence. This inadequate witness develops from a lack of proper discipleship. In light of the messianic Jewish remnant's existence, Israel's national unbelief is only *partial* (11:1-10); the Jewish remnant is the guarantee, as it were, of the future national revival that all Israel will be saved.

2) *And also to the Gentile!* Since Messiah is God's faithfulness to Israel, it is present-tense Gentile believers who as Gentiles make Israel jealous for Messiah, that effectively communicate the Good News. Thus, the messianic congregation is also the best testimony for the present tense Gentile believer.

The status of Gentiles in Messianic Congregations is a controversial issue for many. Because this is so controversial, I want to take a deeper look at this issue. I suggest that the inclusion of the properly taught Gentile believer in the messianic congregation enhances the testimony of the messianic Jewish community. Such a Gentile believer represents the testimony of God's faithfulness to Abraham, Isaac and Jacob.

God said to the Fathers: "In your seed all the nations of the earth will be blessed."[37] From the beginning, HaShem's ministry to "the Jew first" inseparably assumed "and also to the Gentile."[38] This inseparability is actually highlighted in the prophetic testimony of the Messiah, the greater Seed of the Fathers. It was directly stated that to be the Redeemer of Israel, He must also be the Savior of the world.[39] To Shiloh would come "the obedience of the peoples."[40] The root of Jesse would be "a standard for the peoples" to whom "the nations would resort."[41] The "King upon Zion" installed by HaShem has the "nations as an inheritance."[42] This credential, so vital in the *Tanakh* and the rabbinical writings, is that the Jewish Messiah has a sovereign impact on the nations for Israel's good.[43] The messianic congregation's testimony pictures restored Israel with the Nations in the commonwealth of Israel.[44]

I believe this is why Paul writes that the faithfulness of God in Messiah is further evidenced by the Gentile believers' calling to make Israel jealous.[45] How were Gentiles to make us jealous? It is by the same mercy they received.[46] On the other hand, if their faith were expressed in arrogance, then it would bring about Christianity's anti-Jewish posture, as Paul feared.[47] Ironically, the same history that has obscured the testimony of Yeshua to our people has also obscured the Gentile believers' calling.

Paul writes, "I am writing to you who *are Gentiles*."[48] Just as Jews that believe in Yeshua are still present tense Jews, so Gentiles who believe in Messiah are still present tense Gentiles. Paul wanted Gentile believers to reach out to the Jewish people *as Gentiles*.[49] Paul's apostolic calling was to show Israel that the Abrahamic Covenant was fulfilled in Yeshua, the greater seed of Abraham.[50] Gentiles' love and mercy to the Jewish people is God's spiritual proof to Israel of the fulfillment of the Abrahamic Covenant in Yeshua; and so, Yeshua is truly Israel's Messiah.[51] The messianic congregation testifies that the same God who by grace keeps a Jewish remnant also calls the Gentiles to love Israel. In Yeshua, God proves He's faithful to Israel in this dual-witness testimony.[52]

Messianic discipleship is the key to Gentiles understanding how to make our people jealous, because one is jealous over something that rightfully belonged to him. Since we are *His* people, going after other gods makes the Lord Himself "jealous".[53] You kiss your spouse, fine; you kiss my spouse, not so fine! Christmas trees and Easter eggs may even evoke envy from some Jews, but they do not arouse the proper jealousy that God is talking about. According to Paul, seeing the Jewish relevance of faith in Messiah will bring about this sort of "zeal for righteousness according to knowledge" that is to say, faith in Yeshua.[54]

The messianic congregation is the Jewish Olive Tree through which the present tense Jew and Gentile proclaim the Good News that in Messiah: God is faithful to Israel! *Am Yisrael chai b'Yeshua haMashiach!* The people of Israel live in Yeshua the Messiah! I believe the messianic congregation is the most advantageous spiritual home for Gentile believers who desire to demonstrate God's faithfulness to Israel and identify with the visible remnant of Israel.

Yeshua commanded us to make disciples, not merely decisions.[55] As we are convinced of His Lordship, we are to be committed to His discipleship. Discipleship may start with identifying with Messiah through immersion, but it's a lifetime of following and growing in Messiah that reveals the faithful character of God.[56] We are created to relate to God so we can represent Him. We reveal Him best as we lovingly relate in community. God's faithfulness is seen in a well-taught believer. Just as in the Good News of Messiah, God is committed to keep an identifiable Israel, so all His disciples must have this same Good News commitment to Israel.

It is the messianic congregation that must assume leadership in the Body of Yeshua to effectively proclaim the Good News to our people and all people, and to make mature messianic disciples. So for the sake of HaShem's testimony of faithfulness, I'm praying for many more evangelistic and disciple-making messianic congregations to be established worldwide.

MY PRACTICE OF PROCLAIMING THE GOOD NEWS THROUGH THE MESSIANIC CONGREGATION

All of what I've said thus far amounts to nothing if we do not put these things into practice. Our congregation may easily become the best-kept secret to our greater Jewish community.

The early messianic believers who did all they could for our people encourage us. They may not have had printing presses, newspapers, or the Internet, but they reached the crowds as best they could. In Ephesus, Paul taught "both publicly and from house to house."[57] Sometimes, He "sat in the synagogue" and waited to be called upon to speak before saying anything.[58] Elsewhere, he initiated action, boldly preaching in the marketplaces "to anyone that happened to be present."[59] In general, Paul made himself to be as a "servant to all … that unto the Jews he became as a Jew, to those under the Law as under the Law … that he might be a partaker of the Good News."[60] If "Wisdom shouts in the street" and "lifts her voice in the square,"[61] should not those who are wise today do the same?

Our congregational leaders try to model the values that we teach and expect the congregation to follow. We use our opportunities and occasions for sharing Yeshua with our people each week. Our congregational responsibility is to cast a vision for outreach.

For our congregation, the Shabbat service is the chief vision-casting opportunity. I've found that if the *bema* isn't behind outreach, it doesn't go very far. Our sermons teach the responsibility to bring the

Good News to all people, especially to our people. Our congregational outreach is profiled, prayed for, and promoted.

Our congregation's intercessory prayer teams pray daily and then together for an hour before Shabbat School. We pray during weekly Shabbat services for Israel's coming to faith in the Prince of Peace. We pray once a month after the Shabbat service for the partners we support around the world.

About 15-18 leaders in the congregation go away for a planning weekend once a year. We work together on developing our witness and outreach. There is planning for developing materials for outreach training and discipleship as well as planning to communicate vision for the outreach and training. We plan on evangelistic outreach through various means: external, internal and personal. While we don't presume any method in particular to "work," we continue to try different things.

We have several outreaches a year, for campuses, parks or beaches and other events such as concerts, sporting events or at busy street corners, where Good News materials, books, and bibles may be distributed, and where contacts are made and followed up on. Teams may go to Israeli stores on Myrtle Beach, or speak to Israelis working the local malls. Others are involved in activities at the JCC, and in pro-Israel rallies. We have several *chavurot* (home meetings) each week that reach out to different neighborhoods. Some members volunteer at a mostly Jewish senior citizen center. For a time we had weekly studies and monthly music for the residents there. We also use the Internet, profiling the Good News through our website and blog. We have weekly ads in the local paper, which also gets us contacts and visitors. We likewise place ads for the various festival services.

We purposely reach out to local churches for them to learn about witnessing and also to invite their Jewish friends, neighbors, co-workers, etc., to our various meetings. We have a quarterly congregational newsletter to encourage them in this regard. We have Shabbat School classes, yearly Jewish evangelism seminars, and regular midweek evening classes for understanding the distinctives, developing the proper sensitivity by learning how to strengthen our relationships through asking and answering questions. Since Gentiles are called to make Israel jealous, our congregation purposely reaches out to churches encouraging them to witness and teach them to more effectively witness to and to disciple their Jewish friends.

We plan all our services to be visitor friendly, encourage members to invite family and friends and expect interested Jewish visitors from the various outreaches.

The Shalom team, which is our Greeters ministry, tries to connect members with visitors from their area. After each service, our *oneg* (after-service food) is designed for members to mingle and meet visitors. Our internal monthly newsletter and visitor packets further explain our congregation and Messiah. The packet contains a card that is filled out, put in the *pushke* as they leave. That information is recorded that day, and sent out for follow up within two weeks by phone, email, or personal visit. People further away are sent letters, their names being passed on to messianic congregations closer to them. All of our festival and special services are advertised in the papers, on the radio, and on the Internet, and we see it as opportunity to share Yeshua. There are congregational business cards and messianic Good News material in racks in the foyer; the material is in English, Russian and Spanish.

For our congregation, however, the personal approach is still the most effective. We encourage members that outreach starts in our personal worship,[62] is in our personal works,[63] and then is in our personal words.[64] In our various classes, we teach that personal spiritual maturity must include sharing Yeshua with others. The Body in general and the individual member in particular must be "other-oriented" to be spiritually healthy. Our personal discipleship includes "sharing Messiah with those around you" as normative for all maturing believers in all circumstances of life.

In considering membership individuals need to be aware that sharing your faith with Jewish people is a congregational value for all congregation members. Upon acceptance into membership each person becomes a part of our various service ministries and of the outreach of the congregation. Each member is expected to have a messianic expression of faith at the congregation or in all public congregational activities, as they represent the congregation calling to be a witness to Israel and of Israel.

The proclamation of the Good News within the greater Jewish community through a messianic congregation has permitted our whole membership to testify as a witness to Israel that Yeshua is the Messiah, and of Israel that the people of Israel live for God is faithful to Israel in Messiah! For the membership of Hope of Israel Congregation, the Good News has produced Tikkun Olam in a loving community of

Jewish and Gentile believers; the Good News has meant Kiddush HaShem as our faith honors and suffers for the Name that is above all others; and the Good News has created Am Yisrael Chai as a living hope for the promises found in Yeshua, who is the same yesterday, today and indeed forever.

BIBLIOGRAPHY

Augustine, *Contra Faustum*, Book 12, 318-322, in *The Master Christian Library*: *Version 8* on CD-ROM, Disc 2.

Bereishis: Genesis: A New Translation with a Commentary Anthologized from Talmudic, Midrashic, and Rabbinic Sources: Vol 1a. Brooklyn: Mesorah Publishers, 1986.

Bruce, F.F. *The Epistle of Paul to the Romans.* Grand Rapids: Eerdmans, 1975

Calvin, John. *Calvin's Commentaries: Vol. 19, Acts 14-28, Romans 1-16.* Grand Rapids: Baker, 1981

Clarke, Adam. *Clarke's Commentary, Vol. 4, Matthew—Revelation.* Nashville: Abingdon, 1832

Cranfield, C.E.B. *The International Critical Commentary: Romans*: *Vol 1: 1-8*. Edinburgh: T & T Clark, 1982.

Fruchtenbaum, Arnold *Israelology: The Missing Link in Systematic Theology*. Tustin: Ariel Ministries, 1993.

Goldberg, Louis, ed. *How Jewish Is Christianity? Two Views on the Messianic Movement*. Grand Rapids: Zondervan, 2003.

Haldane, Robert. *An Exposition of Romans*. McLean: MacDonald, 1958

Kasemann, Ernst. *Commentary on Romans*. Grand Rapids: Eerdmans, 1980.

All Talmud, Midrash Rabbah, and Zohar references are from Soncino Classics Collection, Davka Corporation, Judaica Press, on CD–ROM, 1991-1996

All biblical references are from NASV, 1995, unless otherwise noted.

ENDNOTES

1. For some "church," but this term is not used as its usage suggests a non-Jewish identity.
2. 1 Tim. 3:15; Acts 14:23; Deut. 21:1-9; Matt 18:15-17; 1 Cor. 5:1-6:8; Acts 2:42; Luke 4:16; Heb. 10:24-25; Isa. 56:7; 1 Tim. 2:1; Isa. 2:3; Mic. 4:2; 1 Tim. 4:6, 13.
3. There are many that share these simple definitions but may yet differ greatly on many other areas. This simpler definition provides a wide variance of application because of the liberty of expression in the Good News, as in 1 Cor. 9:19-23.
4. Admittedly, these three values broadly reflect Jewish thinking that is mainstream, rabbinic and Zionist.
5. Gen. 1:26.
6. Gen. 2:15.
7. Gen. 1:28. Translations are in NASB unless otherwise noted.
8. Ibid. Italics mine.
9. Gen. 3:15.
10. Gen. 12:1-3.
11. Gen. 22:18.
12. Gen. 12:8.
13. "All proselytes are considered 'children' of Abraham because it was his mission to draw all peoples toward the service of HaShem ... (R. David Cohen)." *Bereishis*, Vol 1(a) (Brooklyn: Mesorah, 1986), 432; Quoting *Rambam*, "Because Abraham is the *'father' of a multitude of nations*, all converts are considered as his descendants and a convert is therefore referred to as *son of Abraham*." ibid., 562 (italics in original).
14. Gen. 14:13-16.
15. Ezek. 33:1-11; Isa 6.
16. Gal. 3:8, John 8:58, Matt. 13:17; Heb. 11:13, 39-40.
17. Like Abraham, He also left his Father's house for the promise of world redemption, Gen. 12:1; John 16:27-28; like Isaac, who never left the promised land, Yeshua went only to the lost sheep of the house of Israel; Gen. 26:2; Matt. 10:5; but as Jacob had many sons, so "He will see His seed" and "lead many sons to glory," Gen. 35:23-25 and Isa. 53:10, Heb. 2:10.
18. Rom. 1:2; 1 Tim. 1:9; Heb. 1:1-3; 6:18.
19. This is especially emphasized in John 5:43; 10:25; 12:13, 28; 17:6, 11-12, 26; Rev. 15:3-4; 19:12-13, 16.
20. Rom. 1:16-17. This is the normative view held by most commentators, e.g., Robert Haldane, *An Exposition of Romans* (McLean: MacDonald, 1958), 55; C.E.B. Cranfield, *The International Critical Commentary: Romans*: *Vol 1: 1-8* (Edinburgh: T & T Clark, 1982), 89; Ernst Kasemann, *Commentary on Romans* (Grand Rapids: Eerdmans, 1980), 21; and F.F. Bruce, *The Epistle of Paul to the Romans* (Grand Rapids: Eerdmans, 1975), 77.
21. Lev. 19:2; Isa 64:6; Ezek. 3, 18, 33; Ps. 15, etc.
22. "The Lord our righteousness" (Jer. 23:6), this has always been our only hope in all Tenach (Gen. 15:6; Isa. 45:24; Jer. 33:16; Ps. 32:1-2). And so therefore Paul in Rom. 3:21-26; 2 Cor. 5:21; and 1 John 2:1-2.

23. Just as the present tense of "unashamed" and "it *is* the power" refers back to the Good News, so the present tense of "believe" refers back to the Good News in order to have God's righteousness.
24. In Isa. 53:1, the prophet assumes that Messiah's atonement is applied to believers only, and that not all will believe it. The partial acceptance is restated in 53:11, "to the many" (לָרַבִּים); and see Rom. 5:15, 19.
25. Gen. 15:6; Rom. 3:21-22; 4:16-25.
26. As *proton* is used in Rom. 2:9, 10; 3:2.
27. Some have taught that Rom. 9-11 is written to justify God's rejection of the Jews. Adam Clarke, *Clarke's Commentary, Vol. 4, Matthew—Revelation* (Nashville: Abingdon, 1832), 107; Calvin notes that through this passage the Jews "were at last cut off from the covenant John Calvin, *Calvin's Commentaries: Vol. 19, Acts 14-28, Romans 1-16* (Grand Rapids: Baker, 1981), 409. Calvin sees "all Israel" Israel as "the Church" including all Jews and Gentiles, leaving no hope for the Jewish people as Israel, Ibid. 437.
28. For even as the New Covenant is made with the same people He brought out of Egypt, so the actual inauguration of the New Covenant by Messiah at the Passover commemoration of the Exodus also simultaneously "confirmed the promises to the fathers." Jer. 31:31-34; Luke 22:20; Rom. 15:8, here Paul's summarizes Yeshua's work as a ministry to the Jewish people to confirm the Abrahamic Covenant promises.
29. Augustine, *Contra Faustum*, Book 12, 318-322, in *The Master Christian Library*: *Version 8* on CD-ROM, disc 2.
30. From a letter from Grace Community Church, dated Feb. 1985, titled "The American Messianic Synagogue Movement: Deficiencies, Mistakes, and Errors in Light of the Scriptures," quoted in Arnold Fruchtenbaum, *Israelology: The Missing Link in Systematic Theology* (Tustin: Ariel Ministries, 1993), 929.
31. As noted by John Fischer in *How Jewish Is Christianity?: Two Views on the Messianic Movement*, Louis Goldberg, (Grand Rapids: Zondervan, 2003), 50-51.
32. Gen. 12:3, "I will make of you a people." "The LORD did not set His love on you nor choose you because you were more in number than any of the peoples, for you were the fewest of all peoples, but because the LORD loved you and kept the oath which He swore to your forefathers," Deut. 7:7-8; cf. Exod. 32:13, etc.
33. Matt. 16:18; Ps. 138:4.
34. Jer. 31:35-37. This also seems to be the intent of Gen. 17:4-13, 19 as understood by the psalmist, "He has remembered His covenant forever, the word which He commanded to a thousand generations, which He made with Abraham, and His oath to Isaac. Then He confirmed it to Jacob for a statute, to Israel as an everlasting covenant" (Ps. 105:9-10). It was also seen as an eternal commitment through His covenant promise by the New Covenant writers, Luke 1:55, Acts 7:5; Rom. 9:3-5; 11:28-29; 15:8.
35. Rom. 10:1; 11:26.
36. As Paul declared in various settings, e.g. Acts 21:39; 22:3.
37. Gen. 12:3; 18:22; 18:18; 26:4; 28:25. This recognized relationship between Israel's calling and the well being of the nations was at times overstated in Rabbinical tradition, e.g., Numbers Rabbah 2:13, "Israel is indispensable for the existence of the world as it is written 'in your seed all the nations of the earth will be blessed.'"

38. And it was so assumed in Song Rabbah 7:11, "this is the Messiah who will guide all humanity in the way of repentance before the Holy One, blessed be He."
39. Gen Rabbah 44:23, "But in the days of the Messiah they shall once again belong to Israel, in order to fulfill God's promise [to Abraham's seed]."
40. Gen. 49:10, Genesis Rabbah 97 905-906; 98:8; Zohar Bereshit, 1:143a; 1:237b-240a.
41. Isa. 11:10; Genesis Rabbah 97: 900; 98:9; Zohar 2:172b.
42. Ps. 2:7-8; Sukkah 52a. See also Gen. 9:27.
43. We might easily add that as HaShem's Servant, it is by being "cut off from the land of the living for the transgression of my people to whom the stroke was due" that His atonement would "sprinkle many nations" and therefore "bring justice to the nations" (Isa. 52:15; 53:8; 42:1). And so as the Zion's humble King "endowed with salvation" He therefore "will speak peace to the nations" (Zech. 9:9-10).
44. Eph. 2:12, 19, as pictured in Gen. 17:4-7, 16; 35:11.
45. Rom. 11:11-32.
46. Rom. 11:30-31.
47. Ibid., vv. 17-18, 25.
48. Ibid., vv. 13.
49. As Gentiles, that is, *not* by calling themselves Jews or by becoming Jews.
50. So Paul understood from the beginning, Acts 9:16, 20; 13:46; 24:14-15, 17; 26:6, 20, 23; 28:20.
51. This may also explain why Paul risked his life, let alone his freedom, to bring the Shavuot love gift from the Gentiles to Jerusalem (see 1 Cor. 16:3; Rom. 15:25-27; Acts 21:11-13). To Paul, this gift would be the first fruits of what God had promised in the prophets, as Isaiah says, "The wealth of the nations will come to you" (Isa. 60:5). Thus Yeshua is the seed of Abraham, for in Him all the nations are blessed, and blessing Israel (Isa. 2:3; 60:1-6; 66:19-21).
52. Deut. 19:15; Matt. 18:16. The apostolic mission also reflected this purpose. Paul saw himself as representative redeemed Israel in bringing the Messiah, the seed of Abraham to the nations (Gen. 12:3; Matt. 28:19), but not to the neglect of Israel. Ministry to the Jewish people is Paul's ministry as well as Peter's, for all believers are called "to the Jew first."
53. Num. 34:14.
54. Rom. 10:2-4
55. Matt. 28:18-20.
56. The reality of God's faithfulness is always reflected in those that follow Him, for we're to be "holy as He is holy" (Lev. 19:2; 1 Pet. 1:15).
57. Acts 20:20.
58. Acts 13:14-15.
59. Acts 17:17.
60. 1 Cor. 9:19-23.
61. Prov. 1:20.
62. Ps. 122:6; Matt. 9:28, Rom. 10:1; Col. 4:2-4.
63. Prov. 11:30; Matt. 5:16; Col. 4:5.
64. Prov. 14:25; Dan. 12:3; Col. 4:6; James 5:20.

PRESENTING THE GOSPEL TO THE JEWISH PEOPLE—AN ASSESSMENT OF WHAT IS AND A PLEA FOR THE FUTURE

Susan Perlman
Communications Director and
Associate Executive Director, Jews For Jesus

I want to tell you about three people and how they came to faith. The first is Marilyn. Marilyn came to a church in Sacramento, California where I was speaking on he topic of the Fall Feasts just a few weeks ago. She approached me at the book table afterwards. "I'm Jewish," said this woman in her late thirties, "and I came to know the Lord over ten years ago when someone like you came to this Baptist church to speak. I was invited by a friend who had been witnessing to my husband and me. Meeting another Jewish person who could articulate her faith in Jesus was what I needed. That meeting was the final step that brought me into the kingdom." Marilyn then went on to tell me about how our missionary met with her regularly for several years in a discipleship role. She appreciated talking with someone who was somewhat like her. Marilyn told me how grateful she was for the many visits from our staff missionary where the word of God was opened up and she grew her faith and her connection with this local congregation, which is still her home congregation.

The second person is Cynthia. Cynthia called me about a month ago and told me her story. She is a Jewish believer who has known the Lord for about a year. She had some questions of a spiritual nature and she thought about where she could get some answers. She reasoned that searching on Google was a good place to start looking for answers. So she went and found Jews for Judaism. She assumed they would be the place to get information. She read through a lot of the material on their web pages including proof text materials as well as their warnings about the missionary groups. Since Jews for Judaism made many references to Jews for Jesus, she became curious and decided to check out our website. She surfed our site and landed in the apologetics section. Cynthia found the answers challenging. She told me of how she would go back and forth between the two sites to see what each had to say on issues like the resurrection, the virgin birth, atonement and particularly the Messiah. She eventually concluded that the case for Y'shua's messiahship on our website was much more compelling than the case that Jews for Judaism made that Messiah has yet to appear.

Interestingly, she didn't get in touch with our mission agency but instead went to a local church in her area and it was there that she professed her faith in the Messiah. Only now is she beginning to connect with the larger community of Jewish believers in her part of the country. But she searched for the Lord on the Google search engine.

The third person is Andrew. Andrew is the son of a Holocaust survivor. He called us as a brand new believer. He prayed the prayer to receive the Lord on the tag at the end of the film, Survivor Stories. This was five years ago. For some reason, his therapist, an unbeliever, had given him the DVD. He called us with questions and concerns, and was very cagey about meeting with other Jewish believers. Anyway, Ruth Rosen was the one to talk to him back then so when he called our office recently, he asked for her. Andrew had been reading the Bible and sounds like his five-year old faith is solid. He has reached the point of wanting to feel more connected to his Jewish background and to Jewish believers.

Now you might be thinking, Susan, you've missed some other approaches, some methods that have anecdotes of their own. Oh you mean approaches like:

Knocking on the doors of Jewish homes or apartments? Calling Jewish people by surname from the phone book? Sending out evangelical mailings to Jewish homes? Handing out gospel literature? Setting up a book table on local university campuses with significant Jewish enrollments? Walking around those campuses with surveys that have questions tailored for Jewish students? Leasing kiosks in malls in Jewish areas where you can engage with Jewish shoppers? Holding up evangelistic banners on roads and at intersections where Jewish motorists can read them? Mailing evangelistic journals by subscription to Jewish seekers? (I think I know of one called ISSUES.)

Evangelistic books and DVDs that are offered to seekers in a variety of ways? Public Bible studies on Jewish oriented themes? Personal one-on-one bible studies in homes? Evangelistic campaigns that employ many of these methods while focusing on a particular community for a short period of time? Public debates between apologetically savvy Jewish believers and traditional rabbis or Jewish community spokespeople? Full-page evangelistic print and broadcast ads with a Jewish theme in major secular media? Eye-catching billboards with slogans to capture the attention of seeking Jews? Letters to the editor in secular publications that raise the issue of Jews and Jesus? Invitations to holiday event sponsored by the local messianic congregation or mission agency?

The weekly messianic congregational services as a place of proclamation? Utilizing stories of Jewish believers from different walks of life in a wide variety of ways? Booths and Chai shops at New Age festivals? Making New Testaments available to Jewish seekers in their mother tongue? Apologetics material on the web? Praying for the salvation of individuals? Delivering holiday baskets to Jewish homes? Chatrooms on the web? Utilizing social networks like MySpace and Facebook? Getting viral with a Jewish gospel message on YouTube? Messianic music concerts? Dramatic presentations? Use of Messianic prophecy to make the case? The use of end times prophecy to make the case? DVDs shown in private homes that tell the Y'shua story? Lectures by Jewish professionals (doctors, lawyers, etc.) that draw out other Jewish professionals? Humanitarian efforts? Living in community with Jews who do not believe and developing meaningful relationships that lead to decisions for Y'shua? Providing special interfaith programs for Jewish/Gentile couples with an evangelistic edge? Gentile Christians who share their faith with their Jewish friends, college roommates, co-workers, neighbors and acquaintances? Direct revelation from God? Meeting one-on-one at Starbucks? Radio programs? Television programs? Doing interviews with the press where you strategically look for ways to present the gospel to the listening or viewing audience? Dance ministry? Nursing Home ministry? Messianic chalk drawing on the street?

Now I'm sure each of you could offer an anecdote off one of the approaches on the list I just rattled off or from another list you might come up with that could easily use up all our time this morning. But what do these stories really say about effective evangelism among our Jewish people? If we took a vote among us and came up with the three top approaches to use, would we be accurate? I think not.

Our stories are true, but they are anecdotes. And we all have wonderful, encouraging, inspiring anecdotes that illustrate how some Jewish people have come to faith. There is nothing wrong with anecdotes, but they don't help us to quantify the best or most effective approaches, nor do they provide a magic bullet for effective Jewish evangelism.

I am convinced that in our hearts most of us believe we think we know the most effective ways to make Messiah known to our Jewish people. In the same way, we tend to conclude that other methods are not as effective. But to be honest, all that data out there is mostly old and not anything close to comprehensive. Perhaps the largest study done was over twenty years ago by Jews for Jesus (Mitch Glaser and Beverly Jamison put it together) in which the first 1,014 responses were used as the sample. The most common initial attraction to the gospel cited by Jewish believers was through individuals and the most common agent directly influencing spiritual decision was individual as well.

The break down of the figures is in the paper:

INITIAL ATTRACTION TO THE GOSPEL

Persons	468	47%
Search/Quest/Truth	109	11%
Bible	76	8%
Book/Lit.	60	6%
Supernatural Intervention	62	6%
Group	48	5%
Conviction/Holy Spirit	37	4%
Life Crisis	35	3%
Radio/TV/Movies	25	2%
Curiosity	20	2%
Afterlife/Fear	12	1%
Ideals/Condition of the World	13	1%
No answer	49	4%
	1014	

AGENT THAT HELPED

Persons	620	62%
Group	180	18%
Conviction/Holy Spirit	30	3%
Book/Lit.	31	3%
Bible	27	3%
Radio/TV/Movies	28	3%
Supernatural Intervention	29	3%
Search/Quest/Truth	11	1%
Life Changes	9	1%
No answer	49	3%
	1014	

Michael Schiffman's 1987 survey of Messianic Congregations noted that of 52 congregations that responded to the question on what activities have been most successful in making new contacts and in sharing their faith, more than half of the congregations responded with "friendship" or "holiday celebrations". Again, the full chart appears in the paper.

Activities that have been the most successful in making new contacts and in sharing their faith

Friendships	16	53%
Holiday Celebrations	13	44%
Special Activities	9	30%
Advertising	6	20%
Musical Presentations	6	20%
Literature Distribution	2	7%

Outreach methods which the congregation is most comfortable with:

Friendships	17	57%
Holiday celebrations	16	53%
Special Activities	9	30%
Advertising	8	27%
Musical Presentations	6	20%
Literature Distribution	1	3%

Our most recent study was tabulated in 2003 and had the question of "Who most influenced you in coming to faith in Jesus?" Only 660 of the 1183 used in the survey responded to that question. They answered as follows: 290 said they were influenced by a believing Gentile friend and 42 by a believing Jewish friend. 48 by a parent, 10 by a sibling, 16 by one of their children, 33 by agency and 221 checked off other. More than fifty percent were influenced by a friend and mostly by non-Jewish Christian friends.

I would love to know about other surveys that have been conducted in other countries or among subsets of our people, like Hassidic Jews or post-moderns, or interfaith couples, etc. But I suspect that our market research is just not adequate to draw hard and fast conclusions. I don't think that our agencies or congregations are putting a substantial line item in our budgets for market research, but then would we even know the right questions to ask if we did make this a priority? Apart from comprehensive studies, what are we doing to track our own efforts? What congregations are tracking over time those Jewish visitors who are coming to services and becoming believers? What are the responses to direct mailings into Jewish homes, not just the filling out of coupons or calling an 800 number, but actual decisions that result? How many viable contacts can you get through "cold-calling?" Is it different from neighborhood to neighborhood, city to city, country to country? When a debate is held and there is a significant unsaved Jewish attendance, what follow up apparatus is in place to track the attendees and are we being effective? How effective are surveys? Coffee houses? Certain web sites? And how do we measure what makes these or any other methods effective or not. Some among this group might even say that the questions formulated by the planning committee as a guide in this discussion might not be the right ones to ask.

But let's just say that we could figure out the scientific way to let us know which methods are most effective. And then we could perfect those methods of sharing the gospel. What would that mean to you? What if the particular way that proved "most effective" was outside your skill set, or something that just really goes against the grain of your personality to do? Does that mean that if you want to be effective, you need to fit yourself into the mold required by that method or approach?

While none of us wants to waste our time and resources, as long as our message is Y'shua, I'm not sure that anything we do to tell people about Him could be a waste. Well, maybe if we spend all our time stuffing tracts into various trashcans, hoping that there are Jewish garbage men who will see them, that could literally be considered a waste.

Yet Y'shua said, "But I, when I am lifted up from the earth, will draw all men to myself" (John 12:32). In context, we see the Y'shua of the crucifixion, the scandalized Y'shua.

We can talk about Y'shua the Rabbi, Y'shua the Righteous One, Y'shua the Redeemer, but we must not forget that His name is one of scandal. He is commonly known in Israel as Yeshu, the acronym for *yemach shemo vezichro*, "May his name and memory be obliterated." We must not shy away from the scandalized Y'shua. Our methods can vary, our materials can be nuanced, but our message must be Y'shua. We can give food to the poor and medical services to sick among our people, but if it's not done in Y'shua's name, we've done a good thing, but we haven't lifted Him up. We can beautifully celebrate the Sabbath but in doing so it will only have its full meaning when we lift Him up as Lord of the Sabbath. We can produce the most clever arguments or eloquent words to answer a point of theological minutia, but if He is not lifted up, we have just drawn the attention to ourselves and our abilities.

We not only need to be Y'shua centered in our message, but sometimes we get too sophisticated for our own good. David Brickner put it this way in a recent newsletter,

"We make things more complicated than they need to be. It is easy to become enamored with our apologetics and our fancy methodologies and forget the power of God. People need to know what the gospel is, not necessarily all the reasons why they should believe it. It is the work of the Holy Spirit to convict the world of sin, of righteousness and judgment. It is the simple good news of Y'shua's death, burial and resurrection that is the power of God that changes the hearts of those who believe."

Let's stop fooling ourselves into thinking that it is our methods and our strength that convince our Jewish people of the truth of the gospel.

You might think it a mystery how God could use me to win people to Himself, and I might be having the same thoughts about you. And we'd both be right. It is a mystery how God uses any of us to win people's hearts to Himself. But one thing I've noticed. God seems to like courage and he seems to like humility, and those aren't methods, they are character traits. I'm not sure any of us ought to be satisfied that we've got enough courage or humility, much less both. I know I don't. It took courage and humility for Y'shua to allow himself to be lifted up on that cross, or tree and it still takes courage and humility for us to lift Him up, to talk about our sin, his sacrifice and the narrow road he asks his disciples to follow.

So, whatever our approach, are we willing to take the risk of lifting Y'shua up? I don't mean to ask whether each of us is ready to tell others to take risks that we believe are appropriate, but to ask whether, each of us is willing before God to humbly accept whatever risks He may ask of us (not the person sitting next to us) in order that our people might be drawn to Jesus? Do we have enough courage ourselves to be able to pass on some boldness and enthusiasm to others? Do we have enough humility to encourage others when they don't do things the way we would?

Will we encourage one another to lift Him up in diverse ways that various ones are suited for according to our diverse gifts, personalities and opportunities? Or will we dismiss one another's approach as too old (passé) or too new (if it isn't broke don't fix it) and discourage anyone who doesn't do things the way we think they ought to be done?

Will we be humble enough to see that God reaches hearts in many different ways, and will we be sensitive to His leading? Or will we fool ourselves into thinking it is our methods and our strengths that win people's hearts?

Will we recognize that God is calling people to Himself and He has not dictated to us the way in which we can be used in His plans to reach our people? Or will we be tempted to call people to ourselves and our own way of doing things?

Maybe the best way for us to be effective is to be committed to encouraging each other to keep a wide variety of approaches but stick to the unvarying message that "if we confess with our mouth that Y'shua is Lord and believe in our heart that God raised him from the dead, we will be saved."

Conclusion

What can we do to enhance cooperation between mission agencies and messianic congregations when it comes to outreach? We need to begin by believing in the best of one another when it comes to wanting to see our people saved. It means strengthening one another in the equipping and training of believers for the task. It means providing cutting-edge materials that we can share. It means financially supporting the work of evangelism locally and abroad. It means that congregations will send out congregants to the mission field with joy and mission agencies will rejoice to see Jewish people who come to faith in Y'shua grow in local congregations. It means brainstorming on ways we can do joint outreaches.

And what do we have to offer the next generation when it comes to a vision for reaching out to the lost sheep of the house of Israel? Hopefully we have ourselves as an example. We need to be passionate about reaching the lost. We need to see the urgency of the task. We need to be courageous in proclaiming the Good News. We need to be committed to encouraging one another. We need to rejoice in one another's victories and be saddened at our failures. We need to be ready to see the value of using a wide variety of approaches, remembering that if the truth could be spoken by Balaam's ass, God can even use us. If the next generation sees that in us, we will have done well.

PRESENTING THE GOSPEL TO THE JEWISH PEOPLE: COMMUNICATIONAL PERSPECTIVE

Vladimir Pikman, Th.M.
Executive Directive of Beit Sar Shalom, Berlin, Germany
Th.M. Dallas Seminary

Introduction

This is the second time in the last two months when I am to deliver a paper to the people most of whom are more experienced in theology and ministry than I am and all of whom have a settled opinion about my subject. And it is the second time I am going to approach the subject not from theological but primarily from communicational point of view for two reasons: (1) I think that this subject is extremely important, while not sufficiently considered in contemporary Jewish outreach, and (2) I learned to appreciate it by my life circumstances (in my comparatively short life I have immigrated five times and resided in four different countries/cultures).

Approaching this subject from communicational standpoint, I am assuming that I am addressing an audience that consists of the people who believe in the Messiah Yeshua, know how good it is to live with him, rely on the future promises concerning all believers in him, and want our Jewish people to experience peace, joy, blessing, and the new eternal life that Yeshua gives to those who believe in him.[1] All this normally produces strong desire to communicate it to others (cf. Act 2-7).[2]

With this assumption in mind, I want to propose and discuss in the paper the following exhortation for Jewish outreach, namely, "*Beginning with appreciation of Yeshua, by the power of the Holy Spirit genuinely reach out to the Jewish people through word and deeds with maximum life involvement possible in unity!*" Now, we will talk about this exhortation one phrase at the time.

"Beginning with Appreciation of Yeshua … "

It seems that some Jewish believers suffer from inferiority complex, trying to be accepted by the majority of the Jewish people on any expense and through any compromise. But what we need is healthy pride and overflowing joy of being "messianic"—people who belong to the Messiah of Israel, the King of all Kings.

Importance of Worship

It is possible to be distracted from God in trying to serve God. The most crucial issue in evangelism is the centrality of God in our life. Where passion for God is weak, zeal for outreach will be weak. Congregations or individuals that are not centered on the exaltation of the majesty and beauty of God will unlikely desire to "declare his glory among the nations" (Ps. 96:3).[3]

God is most glorified in us when we are most satisfied in him.[4] Our delight in him reflects his glory the most. It is also clearly God's desire that our message and worship concentrates on Yeshua (John 5:22-27; Eph. 1:20-23; Phil. 2:9-11; 1 Pet. 3:22). The one who does not appreciate the magnificence of the Messiah will not be able to be effective in the outreach to the Jewish people. Passion for God and his Messiah in personal and communal worship prepares the offer of God in preaching.

Importance of Emotion

Our appreciation of Yeshua, our understanding of how good it is to be with him, our joyful commitment to him, being evidently expressed in our life and our words, will provoke others to jealousy and will motivate them to consider getting what we have. And our appreciation cannot be separated from our emotions.

Although much attention is given to the rational content of communication, in fact emotion is the largest part of all human communication.[5] When changes are sought at the deeper levels, communication should be primarily emotive.[6] Therefore it is important to pay attention to what our emotions represent and how they do it.

Importance of Suffering

Suffering with joy for the sake of the great cause and heavenly reward demonstrate importance of our faith. Acceptance by Yeshua is more important that acceptance by our own people, friends, and family (e.g. Matt. 10:37-39; Mark 8:35; 10:29-30; Luke 8:29-30).

The supremacy of God's and the Messiah's glory shines most brightly when the satisfaction that we have in them endures in spite of suffering and pain in the ministry of love.[7] Thus, we need to be ready to suffer in our outreach to our Jewish people, following the example of Yeshua, his apostles, and his faithful disciples of all ages (cf. Matt. 5:10-12; 10:16-19; Luke 21:12-17; John 15:20-21; 1 Cor. 4:12; 2 Cor. 11:23-26; Gal. 5:11). God, Yeshua and our people are worthy of it.

" ... By the Power of the Holy Spirit ... "

The Holy Spirit plays a crucial role for success of Jewish outreach (cf. Matt. 10:19-20; John 16:4; 1 Cor. 12:3). We can often get very busy with different strategies and methods, but forget about the biblical fact that without God's Spirit successful communication of the spiritual truth will never take place. Remembering it will help us to more rely on God and to use the necessary power of prayer more often.[8]

" ... Genuinely Reach out to the Jewish People ... "

This phrase itself looks familiar and banal. But the word "genuinely," being uncommon in this phrase, is something what I want to discuss.

Importance of Orientation on Receptor

The message that we send is not necessary the message that will be received. Significant part of the message will be filtered by the sender and then by the receiver. Communication can be psychologically characterized as "important is not what you say but what I hear/feel you say." To love communicatively is to put yourself, following God's example, to whatever inconvenience necessary to make sure that the receptors understand ("receptor-oriented communication").[9]

An evangelistic question that is usually asked is "How are we going to present the Gospel to our Jewish people?" Such question has "we" in the center. In order to be oriented toward other Jewish people we should rephrase the question—"How are our Jewish people going to hear the Gospel?" It makes a big change in the perspective, helping us to get less selfish. In this case we start to better appreciate ministries of others and stop thinking in terms of only "our" programs and projects. It frees us for partnership with others.[10] It is also important to keep in mind that people have to be reached not for "us" (our congregation, ministry, etc.) but for the Messiah.

Importance of Genuineness

Authenticity and integrity are needed especially today. Postmodern people will first test our sincerity before they listen to our message. They discover first attractive things in our life, then join our environment and afterwards come to believe in Yeshua.[11]

Anti-missionaries often accuse those involved in the Jewish evangelism or the messianic movement that we use Jewish symbols, terminology and etc. in order to allure the Jewish people. And they seem to be right in many cases. Many training programs in Jewish evangelism are evidences of it (e.g. terminology as a nice-looking "wrapping" of the message, holidays as means of evangelism, etc.). It reminds me sales-agents' training, though "clients" here are different and the motives are godly.

We are accused of hypocrisy and we are giving reasons for this accusation by lack of sincerity and consistency in what we are doing. It strongly damages our testimony and harms our cause. Identification with any nation is not "playing" traditions but living the life of the people. Especially it is important for the so much sensitive Jewish people.

I believe that sincerity of our lifestyle strengthens our testimony and advances our Jewish outreach. The "messianic" life-style, in my opinion, should not be practiced in order to "attract" Jewish people, but simply because the "messianics" consider it to be the right life-style for them. If somebody lives like a "Christian," what is the reason for him to wear a "mask" and "play" Jewish?[12] We have to live according to the way we identify ourselves in the culture we minister in. E.g., if you call yourself a "Jew" you got to live like one in the given culture.

Acceptance depends first of all on honesty and mutuality of an evangelist.[13] Trust is the fundament of a good relationship. It is based on the deep conviction in truthfulness, integrity and reliability of another person. Trustworthiness is the foundation of credibility of any relationship and words.[14] To be a person of integrity who humbly tries to understand, love and accept others is a worthy goal.

Importance of Respect

Very common Jewish stereotype is that most Christians are anti-Jewish. The Jews can be suspicious even to those Christians who do good things to them ("they simply want to convert us"). There is an assumption that Christians want to destroy Jewish people if not by force then by assimilation.

Any effective outreach requires respect for the culture of the people ministered to. It is also very true for Jewish evangelism. It is also important to consider that the Jewish culture is primarily linked to the Law that was given by God to the people. Even in case of a liberal Jew, the Torah is always important for the Jewish identity. Any offence against the Torah can be easily understood as anti-Semitic or anti-Jewish, leading to rejection of the entire message.[15] Therefore, even if somebody considers himself "free" from keeping the Law and does not see advantages of keeping it, he is still under obligation to respect the Law and those who keep it (this idea is biblically relevant; cf. Rom. 2:9-16; 9:1-5).

It assumes adequate reaction to the Law in speech, absence of sarcasm and jokes regarding the Law and its keepers. It concerns not only Gentiles, whose comments about the Law can be easily interpreted by the Jews as anti-Semitic, but also Jewish believers in Yeshua, who are often considered by the Jews not to be part of the Jewish nation any more.

Importance of Identification

In Romans 9:1-5 Paul fully identifies himself with his Jewish people. He calls all Jews (even those who do not believe in Yeshua and even his opponents) "my brothers." Unfortunately, in evangelistic zeal, many Jewish believers often divide the Jews in "us" and "them," setting a border between "us," the ones who believe in Yeshua, and the rest of the Jews. But for Paul all the Jews were his "brothers." In the whole book of Acts we can see Paul as an evidently Jewish leader, who was considered Jewish by all Jews and Gentiles around him. He was not only not ashamed to be Jewish in his lifestyle but also was always ready to demonstrate it (e.g. Acts 21:20-26; 23:1-6; 25:8). It is remarkable that even ministering among the Gentiles, Paul was evidently identified as a Jew (cf. Acts 16:19-21). And at the end Paul still calls even Jews who do not believe in Yeshua his "brothers" and insists that he has always lived according to the Law and traditions of the fathers (cf. Acts 28:17). From Paul's example we cannot drive a commandment to do the same but I think that Paul is a good example to follow, especially due to the recognized fact that identification always greatly helps in communication.

" … Through Word and Deeds … "

The gospel became uncomfortable in the post-modern society. It is especially true in regard to the Jewish people, while the natural human tendency is to avoid any opposition and to be in peace with others, being accepted and recognized.[16] It naturally pushes us to retreat from open evangelistic work toward "humanitarian efforts" and "social work" that are well accepted by others. However, it does not bring desirable results.[17]

Although social actions are biblically encouraged and important, they are in no way a substitute for proclaiming the King Yeshua. Evangelism and disciple making is not a social action, although charity may be well involved.[18] In "social work" situations, nothing ever happens for God until somebody presents the gospel.[19] The apostles did not turn the world upside-down by social work, but they did it by proclaiming the King Yeshua and the Word of God (Act 6:3-4; 20:20-21; 1 Cor. 1:17-21; 9:16). Thus, while social work is important, it is not a substitute for the proclaiming of the King Yeshua. However, there is nothing quite so crippling to both evangelism and social action as to confuse them in definition or to separate them in practice.[20] It is recognized today by most those involved in outreach that balance is needed.[21] But we need more than balance—we need a partnership between the two, while the leading partner is evangelism.[22] This is not to exalt the proclamation at the expense of our actions. They belong together. But it does insist that, while without the accompanying deeds the good news is scarcely credible, without the word the news is not even comprehensible! Besides, the real good news is not what we in our benevolence do for others, but what God has done for us all in the Messiah.[23]

" … With Maximum Life Involvement Possible … "

After discussing Jewish outreach through word and deeds, we will discuss some communicational considerations.

Some "Myths"

We will start with some "myths" concerning communication of the gospel.[24]

Myth 1: Hearing the gospel with one's ears is equivalent to "being reached" with the gospel.

But hearing and intelligent understanding are quite distinct kinds of activity. And unless the hearers are already positive toward the message, deep-level understanding requires persuasion, a kind of communication not easily accomplished via superficial outreaches like preaching, "street-evangelism," superficial uses of mass media, etc. They can be effective when the receptors already feel a great need for the message that is presented. Otherwise, there is the need for person-to-person, long-term communication of the gospel message.

Myth 2: The words of the Bible are powerful in themselves.

But though God sometimes works through his Word alone, his primary vehicle is still people who in word and deed interpret that Word. (cf. Acts 8:26-39)

Myth 3: Preaching is God's ordained means of communicating the gospel and initiating life-change.

But it is helpful to remember that today, similar to the apostolic times, the message of the gospel itself remains "foolishness" to the majority of people (cf. 1 Cor. 1:18-25). Biblical and contemporary Jewish way of teaching is not a monologue. Yeshua himself much preferred personal, interactional communication that encourages immediate feedback and, if necessary, adjustment of the message to assure greater relevance. A monologue approach is appropriate in case of presenting a body of cognitive information in a fairly short period of time for the purpose of increasing knowledge in a giving area. But this approach is very poorly suited to either changing people's opinion or leading to significant life-changes.

Myth 4: There is one best way to communicate the gospel.

But it is commonly recognized that people and situations are so different that no single style is going to be appropriate for all people in all situations. Adaptability is what is needed.

Myth 5: The precise formulation of the message is the key to effective communication.

> But it is the receptor who has the final say concerning what is communicated.[25] It is important to use ordinary, highly communicative language to convey spiritual truth. In message construction personal factors are more important than impersonal, structural, and linguistic factors. It is also important to remember that a given word can have different meanings for different people and that the nature of the medium modifies the total impact.[26]

Myth 6: What people really need to believe in Yeshua is more information.

> We can tend to think that, e.g., if we will explain the messianic prophesy or qualitatively answer all "Jewish objections," people will immediately believe in Yeshua. But the reality is that many "informed" people do not believe or even abandon their faith. The crucial problem mostly is motivation, not lack of knowledge. We are to stimulate people to respond to the God they probably already have enough information about.

Myth 7: The Holy Spirit will make up for all mistakes if we are sincere, spiritual, and prayerful enough.

> He definitely can. But it does not give us a mandate for mistakes or passivity.

Myth 8: Contemporary Mass Medias are "magic" opportunity to reach all people.

> Indeed, the mass media can multiply an effective message or messenger in interpersonal communication. However, it is able to use fewer of the signal systems than do "face to face" interpersonal relationship. It leads to the loss of information. Also it appears impersonal and reduces desire of involvement, while reaching only those who have commonality with the sender.[27] It works better in strengthening existing belief than leading

somebody to Yeshua. There is definitely no magic in media.[28] We need to watch for the media outreaches not to become a substitute for personal participation, because adequate gospel communication strategy must use both interpersonal and media methods, supplementing each other.

Importance of "Life Involvement"

It is recognized that a monologue approach is appropriate for public communication to sizable groups. With small groups a dialogue or discussion approach is usually the most satisfactory. As a means of influencing the total behavior of receptors, however, there is no substitute for life involvement. This method takes much more time to cover a given amount of information, but it is covered at a deeper level of understanding and application. Although Yeshua had to turn to monologue having something to say to larger groups (cf. Matt 5-7; 23), life involvement was his preferred method and the monologue was a last resort.[29]

Communication is a relationship. The closer the relationship, the better the communication. Indeed, without constantly increasing commonality in interests and experience, there cannot be an increase in understanding. When we know the recipients' needs, we can find ways to communicate to them that Yeshua is the answer to their particular needs. And vice versa, no matter how valuable the message is, no matter how much it is needed, it will not even be "heard" if the message does not seem to meet any felt needs.[30] Close relationship happens through life involvement. To separate an act of "communication" from a continuing involvement between equal participants is to reduce communication to babble of symbols with uncertain meaning. Effective communication that leads to deep comprehension and response occurs only through involvement in each other's life and interests. Thus, without involvement, the most skilled use of media and techniques may be only an imitation of communication.[31]

Communication is a process. A particular conversation, sermon, song, or drama never stands by itself. There is no solitary act of communication. It is a process without clear beginning or ending. Effective communication requires awareness of the past, present, and future dimensions for all involved in communicating.[32] That is possible through involvement.

Usually, the communicator chooses both content and communicative style based on his or her ideas about the audience. Thus, a step in improving communication is to gain a more accurate understanding of the audience. Good communication requires the ability to hear as well as the ability to speak. That is the best possible through life involvement.

Humans are social beings. Change in an individual produces reaction in his social group. It opens for us an opportunity to reach the whole group by reaching just one individual. And vice versa, the group can be the channel for changing the individual. In order to use these opportunities, talking to an individual, we need to keep in mind his group, sending the appropriate message to it. In any case, the group must be involved if an effective communication strategy is to be developed. Jewish people are traditionally the people of community and tend to live in "networks." Entering these networks, with the possibilities of give-and-take that shape the form of the message, enables us to be effective participating "evangelists." That works the best through life involvement.

Thus, no techniques, no standard methods can substitute real life involvement with the Jewish people. It is the most difficult and slow, but the most genuine, godly, biblical, human, and effective way of outreach. By the way, home and small groups can also help here.[33]

Importance of the Christian Friends

Some messianic leaders underestimate the importance of Christians in Jewish outreach. But, interestingly, I know more orthodox and liberal Jews who came to Yeshua through the testimony of their Christian friends and in the Christian churches than through the Jewish missions and the messianic congregations. Christians indeed can play a crucial role in reaching Jewish people for Yeshua if they will properly use their life involvement with their Jewish friends, colleagues, neighbors, etc. They can do it with great effectiveness of friends—an opportunity that we could never have otherwise. And we need to motivate and train them to do that.[34] It means that we should go to churches and Christians not primarily to raise support of any kind, but with the primer goal to raise proper life involvement "evangelists."[35]

" … In Unity!"

The last but not least: according to Yeshua, unity of the believers is a necessary condition for the successful outreach (cf. John 17:21-23). Therefore it is essential for all of us to cross the boundaries of our personal convictions and put aside all possible disagreements in order to make our outreach to the Jewish people more effective. It is important internally for organizations and congregations and for the external relationship between them. Regardless of our attitude to the Law, Jewish life-style, preferred types of outreach, etc., we should remember that the commandments about love and unity have always been the most important (cf. Rom. 12:5; 1 Cor. 1:10; 12:12, 25-27; 13:1-3; 1 Pet. 4:8; Phil. 1:27; 2:1-4).[36] Are you not tired of conflicts? I believe God is. We got to stop harming our testimony by public conflicts and offensive disagreements.

Additionally, Jewish audience does not notice the variety of messianic movement and Jewish missions. They consider us all to be one and the same. Therefore, in outreach, we are responsible for each other. If one of us commits a mistake, we all will be blamed. Thus, we have to think in terms of "each other."

Conclusion

You can disagree with some of my ideas in this paper or consider them banal but please do not stop learning and changing.[37] Especially if you are involved in the outreach for many years, you are in danger of being caught in the traditional ways that used to work for you and others in the past, but are not effective or improper for the present. Do not be afraid to change your ministry strategy or paradigm. Usually, the longer a ministry or a congregation remains unchanged, the more difficult it is to accept any change and the higher the probability of "dying."

Somebody can ask why I have not mentioned messianic congregations. The reason is simple: while believing in necessity of messianic congregations and being involved in five congregational plantings in the last 14 years, I do not see them as a "way" of Jewish outreach but as the biblical and functional form and expression of messianic communal life. Biblical congregations are not an "outreach" themselves but they do outreach as communities of people who highly appreciate Yeshua, whose life is a good genuine testimony and who can clearly testify their faith in their words.

At the very end of this paper I want to repeat my key exhortation for Jewish outreach that I stated at the beginning and that was discussed one phrase at the time, namely, "*Beginning with appreciation of Yeshua, by the power of the Holy Spirit genuinely reach out to the Jewish people through word and deeds with maximum life involvement possible in unity!*"

BIBLIOGRAPHY

"Jewish Identity." *Encyclopaedia Judaica*. Jerusalem: Encyclopaedia Judaica, 1972.

"Judaism." *Encyclopaedia Judaica*. Jerusalem: Encyclopaedia Judaica, 1972.

Hiebert, Paul G. "Cultural Differences and the Communication of the Gospel." In *Perspectives on the World Christian Movement: a Reader*, ed. Ralph D. Winter and Steven C. Hawthorne. Pasadena, CA: William Carey Library, 1999.

Kraft, Charles H. *Communication Theory for Christian Witness*. Rev. ed. Maryknoll, NY: Orbis Books, 1991.

Lingenfelter, Sherwood G., and Marvin Keene Mayers. *Ministering Cross-Culturally: an Incarnational Model for Personal Relationships*. 2nd ed. Grand Rapids, MI: Baker Academic, 2003.

Moffett, Samuel Hugh. "Culture, Worldview and Contextualization." In *Perspectives on the world Christian movement: a Reader*, ed. Ralph D. Winter and Steven C. Hawthorne. Pasadena, CA: William Carey Library, 1999.

Piper, John. *Let the Nations be Glad! The Supremacy of God in Missions*. Grand Rapids, MI: Baker Books, 1993.

Roembke, Lianne. *Multikulturelle Teams*. Giessen: Campus fuer Christus, 2000.

Schoenheit, Swen. *Unter Offennem Himmel Bauen*. Hamburg: CGE, 2006.

Samovar, Larry A., and Richard E. Porter. *Communication between Cultures*. 4th ed. Belmont, CA: Wadsworth/Thomson Learning, 2001.

Smith, Donald K. *Creating Understanding: a Handbook for Christian Communication across Cultural Landscapes*. Grand Rapids, MI: Zondervan, 1992.

Yohannan, K. P. *Come, Let's Reach the World: Partnership in Church Planting among the Most Unreached*. Carrollton, TX: GFA Books, 2004.

ENDNOTES

1. Compassion for those who do not believe in Yeshua is a high and beautiful motive for outreach.
2. If it all is not about you, you can just disregard this paper but please talk to those who appreciate Yeshua about their reasons.
3. Even outsiders feel the disparity between the boldness of our claim upon the nations and the blandness of our engagement with God. Cf. John Piper, *Let the Nations be Glad! The Supremacy of God in Missions* (Grand Rapids, MI: Baker Books, 1993), 12.
4. Ibid., 26.
5. Approximately 80 percent of the information load in typical communication is carried through emotion, and 20 percent or less by reason. Both elements are present at the same time in all human communication, in varying degrees in each situation.
6. Donald K. Smith, *Creating Understanding: a Handbook for Christian Communication across Cultural Landscapes* (Grand Rapids, MI: Zondervan, 1992), 300-301.
7. Piper, *Let the Nations be Glad!* 112.
8. It is important to remember that we are at the spiritual war. It requires our alertness, readiness, persistence and much prayer. It should not be only "domestic" (for the personal problems or the problems of the own community, congregation, family, etc.). Cf. Ibid, 43, 45.
9. God shows respect toward his receptors and toward the context in which he finds us. He is receptor-oriented, seeking to reach his receptors by entering their frame of reference and by participating in their life, in order to be maximally intelligible to them. Cf. Charles H. Kraft, *Communication Theory for Christian Witness*, Rev. ed. (Maryknoll, NY: Orbis Books, 1991), 15.
10. Congregations can be too much centered on "we," emphasizing the programs, strategies and what works the best in/for the congregation, instead of focusing on "them," the people who are still in the need of Yeshua.
11. This principle is usually called "belonging before believing." Cf. Swen Schoenheit, *Unter Offennem Himmel Bauen* (Hamburg: CGE, 2006), 68.
12. I think it is not less glorious to be "Christian" than to be "messianic." What was wrong with the term "Hebrew-Christian" that indicated a Christian with Jewish background? In most of the cases the mission to the Jews has been designed so that the Jewish people would abandon the essential elements of the Jewish life. Indeed the new Jewish believers will be told that Shabbat is not necessary and kosher makes life more difficult. And if you do so, it would be right to tell to the Jews, "Yes, we want you to live like Christians" and honestly explain them why you think it is better for them. I have a friend who is 100% ethnically Jewish but considers himself to be a Christian. We enjoy arguing with each other whether it is right for him to act this way or not. But regardless of our disagreement I highly respect him for his consistency in life. And, believe it or not, Jewish people respect him and listen to him.

13. Cf. Lianne Roembke, *Multikulturelle Teams* (Giessen: Campus fuer Christus, 2000), 96.
14. Ibid., 37.
15. Torah is considered to be one of the core Jewish beliefs. Challenging core beliefs directly brings rejection of the message and often of the messenger as well.
16. It becomes more frequent to see messianic believers rejoice by the fact that Jewish, primarily Israeli, leaders show favor to them due to the social or similar programs. I can also feel joy in such cases. But the problem is that in many such cases the favor is shown on expense of compromising our public testimony of the King Yeshua.
17. The experience of "social gospel" tendencies worldwide indicates that such attempts bring desirable result neither evangelistically nor socially. It also usually does not grant the expected acceptance and recognition. Cf. K. P. Yohannan, *Come, Let's Reach the World: Partnership in Church Planting among the Most Unreached* (Carrollton, TX: GFA Books, 2004), 60-61.
18. Although evangelism is not to be confused with social service and protest against the world's injustices, in the context of the kingdom, however, the evangelistic proclamation was never so narrow that it became isolated from the immediate pressing needs of the poor, the imprisoned, the blind and the oppressed. But if there is anything worse than taking the text out of the context, it is taking the context without the text. In Yeshua's and the apostolic ministry it was always combined. Cf. Samuel Hugh Moffett, "Culture, Worldview and Contextualization," in *Perspectives on the world Christian movement: a Reader*, ed. Ralph D. Winter and Steven C. Hawthorne (Pasadena, CA: William Carey Library, 1999), 575.
19. In every type of outreach a believer must have freedom and time to present the Word of God clearly and openly. Cf. Yohannan, *Come, Let's Reach the World*, 68.
20. Moffett, "Culture, Worldview and Contextualization," 576.
21. Evangelism is the best motivated by zeal for the glory of God together with a servant spirit and a heart of mercy of those involved. Otherwise it is either humanism or hypocrisy. Piper, *Let the Nations be Glad!* , 30.
22. Here the leading partner has definitely to be our "vertical" relationship to God and the Messiah because it makes our ministry different from all others. Our "horizontal" relationship to our neighbor is indispensable, but is still the second.
23. Moffett, "Culture, Worldview and Contextualization," 576.
24. The first seven "Myths" presented in this paper are adopted from the bigger list in Kraft, *Communication Theory for Christian Witness*, 24-37.
25. We need to be constantly conscious of and oriented toward the impression our messages make on their receptors. We should study the Bible from a communicational point of view because sometimes we tend to be overformal in our communication of the gospel.
26. Message received = Content + Medium. Cf. Smith, *Creating Understanding*, 103.
27. The larger is the audience, the greater is the diversity of interest and cultural patterns existing within that audience. Communication effectiveness normally decreases with increasing size of the audience. Therefore, mass communication

(e.g. far-reaching media), while speaking to many people, in reality reaches only those who have commonality with the sender. In many cases "localized" media, being directed to a particular group, can be far more effective, reaching many more people.

28. Smith, *Creating Understanding*, 179.
29. For further discussion see Kraft, *Communication Theory for Christian Witness*, 60-66.
30. Smith, *Creating Understanding*, 276.
31. Ibid., 39-40.
32. Ibid., 49.
33. Home and small groups are good in providing life-involvement atmosphere. They are also effective and time-proofed outreach opportunities. They can provide us with all possible ways of outreach and the community that are working today. It is better though for the groups not to stay alone but to be joined in a network of an existing congregation. For further discussion see Schoenheit, *Unter Offennem Himmel Bauen*, 70-77.
34. It surely includes the necessity to teach "messianics" to do the same, giving the proper teaching of outreach.
35. Unfortunately, in my view, although we are usually glad to come to speak to the Christians, the message that is spoken is primarily to edify the believers through the recognition of their Jewish roots. It is very suitable for making Christians exited and to raise necessary ministry support, but it is not what should be our first priority if we care about our Jewish people.
36. Meanwhile, some Jewish believers still consider Torah-observant believers as misguided and talk lightly about them, while the same is often also true vice versa.
37. I would recommend learning more about intercultural communication and methods of communication, attending some classes or courses in communication, using the information you are learning to examine and critique all methods and ways you have tried to communicate the gospel before.

DREAMING OF THE DAY: A PROPHETIC PORTRAIT OF REVIVAL

Rabbi Jason P. Sobel, M.A.
Director of Fusion,
Leader of Ruach LA Messianic Community
Associate Director for under-40 intiatives with
Union of Messianic Jewish Congregations (UMJC)

Introduction

For the last couple of decades, many Jewish leaders have been terribly concerned with the relatively small percentage of Jews who are committed to practicing Judaism. This lack of commitment has contributed to a high degree of assimilation among our people. As a result, the number of Jews in the US will dwindle by one to two million within the next two generations. This has led many community leaders to speak out about the need for Jewish survival. Our leaders are asking what can be done to help save the Jewish people from further demographic and spiritual decline. Similarly, over the years many Messianic Jewish leaders have wondered if this will be a one generational movement. They have asked what can be done to save our congregations as well as the Messianic Jewish movement as a whole.

To ask ourselves what we need to do to survive is to ask the wrong question. If survival remains our focus, we will never spiritually flourish. The issue is not survival; rather it is personal and communal revival. What the Messianic movement needs is another Shavuot experience like our ancestors experienced both at Sinai and in the Book of Acts. That is why I am pleased to share this address entitled "Dreaming of the Day: A Prophetic Portrait of Revival."

There are many different perspectives on what authentic revival looks like. The Messianic movement ought not to pattern its vision of revival after our memories of past ones, but rather after the promises of God outlined in the Hebrew Scriptures and *Brit Hadasha*. In this presentation, I will share the four key signs of revival. When these signs are missing, authentic revival does not occur, and we miss out on the fullness of God's blessing.

A Commitment to Greater Unity

The first sign of true renewal is increased unity among God's people. Greater unity helps to foster revival and is its natural outcome. God works most powerfully among his people when they are unified. This is demonstrated by two important biblical events that occurred on Shavuot.

Fifty days after our ancestors left Egypt, God descended upon Sinai and spoke to over two million of them. Rashi states that Israel camped "In a state of total unity, as if they were one person with one heart." His comments are based on the fact that Exodus 19:2 uses both the singular and plural forms of the Hebrew verb "to camp" to describe Israel's encampment at Sinai. As the Torah states, "They encamped [plural] in the desert. Israel encamped [singular] there towards the mountain." This reading of the text underscores the fact that God's manifest presence and power are inextricably tied to the unity of God's people.

Israel's spiritual state at Sinai stands in stark contrast to the disunity that characterized their Egyptian exile. Stephen highlights this state of disunity and its serious consequences:

> When Moses was forty years old, he decided to visit his fellow Israelites. He saw one of them being mistreated by an Egyptian, so he went to his defense and avenged him by killing the Egyptian. Moses thought that his own people would realize that God was using him to rescue them, but they did not. The next day Moses came upon two Israelites who were fighting. He tried to reconcile them by saying, 'Men, you are brothers; why do you want to hurt each other?' But the man who was mistreating the other pushed Moses aside and said, 'Who made you ruler and judge over us? Do you want to kill me as you killed the Egyptian yesterday?' When Moses heard this, he fled to Midian, where he settled as a foreigner and had two sons. (Acts 7:23-29)

Their utter disunity and lack of love for one another made them oblivious to the work of God in their midst and even seems to have delayed their redemption by forty years. This same sort of *sinat hinam*, baseless hatred, which also characterized the Jewish Community in first century Judea, culminated in the death of our Messiah and the destruction of the Second Temple (Yoma 9b). In the same way, we must be careful that our disunity and lack of love do not hinder the work that the Lord wants to accomplish through the Messianic Jewish Movement.

The Book of Acts uses similar language as Rashi to describe the love and unity among the first followers of Yeshua:

> When the Day of Shavuot [Pentecost] had fully come, they were all with one accord in one place. (Acts 2:1)

> All the believers were *one in heart* and mind. No one claimed that any of his possessions was his own, but they shared everything they had. (Acts 4:32)

> The apostles worked many signs and miracles among the people. *One in heart*, they all used to meet in the Portico of Solomon. (Acts 5:12)

From these two Shavuot experiences, we learn that loving other people and striving to cultivate unity among God's people helps to foster the fullness of His power, presence, and revelation among us. In fact, Yeshua himself specifically prayed for our unity:

> I pray also for those who will believe in me through their message, that all of them may be one, Father, just as you are in me and I am in you … I have given them the glory that you gave me, that they may be one as we are one: I in them and you in me. May they be brought to complete unity to let the world know that you sent me and have loved them even as you have loved me. (John 17:20-23)

When God's people put aside their differences to build the Kingdom, awesome things occur. Unity is one of the chief desires and greatest values of our younger people. They cannot understand why some leaders do not get along and why they do not want to partner in expanding the Kingdom of Heaven. Many think, and I believe rightly so, that we will not experience true renewal in our movement until we cultivate love for one another that leads to better relationships. The younger people's desire for unity is evident in both the formal and informal gatherings that are already taking place. Examples of this include the Young Messianic Jewish Scholars Conference and the Young Messianic Leaders Shabbaton, which are organized by the Yachad Network with sponsors and attendees representing diverse sectors of the Messianic world. Recently, there have also been informal gatherings of MJAA and UMJC young people for the purpose of fostering greater unity. This Symposium has the potential to set a great example for the next generation.

Unity does not mean uniformity. Unity does not mean we all have to come to a theological consensus, or that we have to express our Messianic and Jewish commitments in the same way. It does mean that we share basic core commitments like the ones outlined for this event. It is also predicated upon the belief that our success as a Jewish people movement for Messiah Yeshua rises or falls on our success as an entire community. No matter what our differences, every individual present at this forum is invaluable to the development of our movement. We all have something unique to contribute and therefore we need to respect, appreciate, build relationships with, and learn from one another, even those with whom we might disagree. If this Symposium helps to move us a little further in this direction it will have been a great success.

Loving Others through Social Justice: *Tikkun Olam*

A second evidence of revival is a greater commitment to helping the needy and fighting injustice through charity (*tzedakah*) and social action (*tikkun olam*). Engaging in *tikkun olam* involves partnering with God in healing and redeeming the world from the forces of oppression. When our community lacks sensitivity and commitment to social issues, we have missed the heart of God and are far from experiencing authentic renewal.

The early Yeshua community demonstrated their commitment to helping the poor and disenfranchised through both word and deed:

> Now the multitude of those who believed were of one heart and one soul; neither did anyone say that any of the things he possessed was his own, but they had all things in common. And with **great power** the apostles gave witness to the resurrection of the Lord *Yeshua*. And great grace was upon them all. Nor was there anyone among them who lacked; for all who were

> possessors of lands or houses sold them, and brought the proceeds of the things that were sold, and laid *them* at the apostles' feet; and they distributed to each as anyone had need. (Acts 4:32-35)

And Ya'aqov, the brother of Yeshua states:

> Religion that God our Father accepts as pure and faultless is this: to look after orphans and widows in their distress and to keep oneself from being polluted by the world. (James 1:26-27)

If our communities were as socially conscious and as radically committed to helping the needy, I believe we would experience a great work of revival in our midst.

A key prophetic text that also ties renewal to social justice is the *haftarah* for Yom Kippur, Isaiah 58:

> 'Why have we fasted,' they say, 'and you have not seen it? Why have we humbled ourselves, and you have not noticed?' Yet on the day of your fasting, you do as you please and exploit all your workers. Your fasting ends in quarreling and strife, and in striking each other with wicked fists. You cannot fast as you do today and expect your voice to be heard on high.

> Is this the kind of fast I have chosen, only a day for a man to humble himself? … Is not this the kind of fasting I have chosen: to loose the chains of injustice and untie the cords of the yoke, to set the oppressed free and break every yoke? Is it not to share your food with the hungry and to provide the poor wanderer with shelter—when you see the naked, to clothe him, and not to turn away from your own flesh and blood?

> Then your light will break forth like the dawn, and your healing will quickly appear; then your righteousness will go before you, and the glory of the LORD will be your rear guard … You will be like a well-watered garden, like a spring whose waters never fail. Your people will rebuild the ancient ruins and will

> raise up the age-old foundations; you will be called Repairer of Broken Walls, Restorer of Streets with Dwellings. (Isa. 58:1-12)

A radical corporate commitment to treating each other with kindness, helping the oppressed, and taking care of the poor is one concrete sign of, and condition for, authentic renewal.

Furthermore, if we are going to impact younger people and the Jewish community for Messiah, we must not underestimate the importance of engaging in *tikkun olam*. When a 1988 LA Times poll asked what was most essential to Jewish identity, only 17% said religious observance, but 59% said a commitment to social justice.[1] This is corroborated by the 2002 "Eight Up" study in which 58% of the one thousand college students surveyed said that making the world a better place was very important to them and their identity as Jews.[2] If we want to be attractive, relevant, and engaging to younger Jewish people and develop a better reputation and testimony in the wider Jewish world, we must find ways to participate in social action.

Conversely, if we fail to help the needy, do not fight against racism and discrimination, and show little concern for environmental issues, we run the risk of disenfranchising the younger people in our communities. This is precisely what happened to Monique, a human rights lawyer, who shared the following with me:

> I grew up in the Messianic movement and have always considered it my spiritual home. As a child I always envisioned taking a leadership role within the movement. I loved God, loved living as a Jew, and wanted to help other people, so I thought about pursuing full time spiritual work. But it soon became clear that vocational ministry wasn't for me. And as I abandoned my plans for ministry, my eyes were opened to the presence of systemic injustice in the world. Violence against women, genocide, slavery, torture, poverty, disease … I'm a Jew, so I had to do something about it, of course.
>
> My consciousness and commitment to pursue justice grew as I came into my 20s, but I was surprised by the negative response that I encountered by some Messianic leaders to my musings. It should be no

> surprise that this response to my call to seek justice was one reason that I left the movement (temporarily, at least) as a young adult.
>
> In the end, what drew me back was a series of fortuitous meetings with Messianic leaders and young people who actually care about repairing the world and fulfilling the Torah's mandate to seek justice. They articulated interests in alleviating poverty, assisting immigrants and refugees, preventing torture, ending slavery and genocide, and combating violence against women. Their very existence and passion to do something has drawn me back into my spiritual home. It's here more than anywhere else that I feel called to pursue God's call to seek justice. I'm hoping now that in addition to being called, I'll be able.

All of us, like Monique, have a God given responsibility and mandate to bring healing and hope to this world through engaging in *tikkun olam*.

Historically, Messianic Jewish organizations like the International Messianic Jewish Alliance and Chosen People Ministries were heavily involved in social ministry. Today, this same sort of social commitment is being demonstrated by Messianic organizations like Chevra International and the Messianic Jewish Alliance of America, which have invested a great amount of time and resources to meet the material needs of our people both in Eastern Europe and Israel. By cultivating this sort of social commitment we bring honor to God (Matt. 5:16), inspire younger generations, and bring hope to Israel and the nations.

Returning to Torah

True biblical revival is always marked by a return to Torah. The third sign of biblical renewal is an increased commitment to observing God's commandments. The portrait that the prophets paint for us is very clear:

> When all these things befall you—the blessing and the curse that I have set before you—and you take them to heart amidst the various nations to which the LORD your God has banished you, and you return to the

> LORD your God, and you and your children heed His command with all your heart and soul, just as I enjoin upon you this day, then the LORD your God will restore your fortunes and take you back in love … You, however, will again heed the LORD and obey all His commandments that I enjoin upon you this day. And the LORD your God will grant you abounding prosperity … since you will be heeding the LORD your God and keeping His commandments and laws that are recorded in this book of the Teaching/Torah. (Deut. 30:1-10)

> This is the covenant I will make with the house of Israel after that time," declares the LORD. "I will put my law/*Torah* in their minds and write it on their hearts. I will be their God, and they will be my people. (Jer. 31:33)

> In the last days the mountain of the LORD's temple will be established as chief among the mountains … Many nations will come and say, "Come, let us go up to the mountain of the LORD, to the house of the God of Jacob. He will teach us his ways, so that we may walk in his paths." The law/Torah will go out from Zion, the word of the LORD from Jerusalem. … They will beat their swords into plowshares. … Every man will sit under his own vine and under his own fig tree. (Mic. 4:1-8; Is 2:3)

The first Servant Song of Isaiah, which describes the Messiah's mission on the earth, also calls for a return to Torah:

> A bruised reed he will not break, and a smoldering wick he will not snuff out. In faithfulness he will bring forth justice; he will not falter or be discouraged till he establishes justice on earth. In his law/Torah the islands will put their hope. (Isa. 42:3-4)

The *Brit Hadasha* also sees a return to Torah as evidence of revival. In the Book of Acts, Ya'aqov the brother of Yeshua relates to Paul that many priests had believed in Yeshua and were zealous for the Torah. Why did Ya'aqov feel the need to make this statement? He mentions God's work among the priests in relation to Torah to underscore that what was happening in Jerusalem was authentic revival in the prophetic sense. The Messiah, as the prophets clearly foretold, would lead Israel back to Torah and not away from it.

As a Jewish movement for Yeshua, we cannot fulfill the Great Commission if we do not bring Jews closer to Torah. We must be vigilant to guard against the mistake of making generic followers of Messiah, which is the natural outcome of neglecting Torah. For if we fail to make better Jews out of Jewish believers, we fail both our people and our Messiah. By not placing emphasis on Yeshua and Torah, our Messianic young people will likely assimilate into the larger Gentile *Ekkleisia,* thereby losing their Jewish identity, or reintegrate into the wider Jewish community apart from faith in Yeshua. Both paths detract from the growth of our Messianic Jewish community and the health of the wider Jewish community.

In addition, if we fail to return to Torah as a movement, we will never have any credibility in the eyes of the Jewish community. Guarding our credibility in relation to Torah observance was a task of the first Messianic leaders in Jerusalem. They sought to quell the rumor that Paul was teaching that Jews should *not* keep the Torah.

> Then they said to Paul: "You see, brother, how many thousands of Jews have believed, and all of them are zealous for the law. *They have been informed that you teach all the Jews who live among the Gentiles to turn away from Moses*, telling them not to circumcise their children or live according to our customs. What shall we do? They will certainly hear that you have come, so do what we tell you … *Then everybody will know there is no truth in these reports about you, but that you yourself are living in obedience to the law.* (Acts 21:20b-24; emphasis added)

Without a return to Torah, we are not truly experiencing the type of renewal promised by the Prophets, but something other. For centuries, the Jewish community has perceived a disregard for Torah among Jewish followers of Yeshua. The contemporary Jewish community also continues to see us as a key factor in their continued spiritual decline. This perception is reinforced by the negative testimony of the many Jews who to come to faith in a Gentile context and as a result lose their Jewish identity and commitment to live as

Jews. When the Jewish community sees a Jewish believer who does not possess the Torah, our message sounds hollow and communicates that belief in Yeshua undermines living as a covenantally faithful Jew. No matter how we slice it, if this is the message we send, than the mainstream community will not view us as Jewish or as an authentic revival. We must therefore be diligent and intentional about making *talmidim* who are passionate and committed to Messiah Yeshua and God's Torah, which a sign of revival according to Torah, the Prophets, and the Brit Hadasha.

Today, Messiah *Yeshua* is guiding many Jewish believers into the path of *Torah* like the priests in the book of Acts. Many Jews, myself included, have returned to the *Torah* on account of our *Yeshua* faith. Our embracing of *Torah* has fueled our zeal for *Yeshua* as well as our passion for Israel. The story of my friend Ben is but one example of a Jewish believer who has found a greater connection to Yeshua and personal renewal through returning to Torah.

> When I was a boy, the words of Yeshua, then known to me as Jesus, comforted me, challenged me, and held me in awe. By the time I had reached middle school, I "learned" that even though I had a rich Jewish heritage, I could not "believe in Jesus, and be Jewish." This lie affected me so deeply that I could not even bring myself to continue believing in Yeshua until I was in my senior year of high school. At that time I vowed to dedicate my life to God and his Son.
>
> During my first two years of college, things became increasingly difficult for me spiritually. My faith was a budding flower that had not been planted in the proper soil. There was no Christian community that I felt called to, and I was, for all intents and purposes, a nominally practicing "believer." Then, I finally decided to try a Messianic Synagogue, Ruach Israel, and after a Yachad sponsored Shabbaton during Shavuot, I received the Torah of God, the Torah of Sinai, the Torah of our people, and it illuminated the Living Torah within me, Yeshua; the one whom I had received, but had not understood. If Yeshua had not brought me back home to Torah I would have lost him altogether. It is my love for Yeshua that brought me to

> his Father. And it is his love for me, that he has brought me to the soil where I can grow and flourish … the Torah.

This return to Torah is not a matter of personal preference but rather the leading of Yeshua who is drawing us back through his Spirit. When we see tens of thousands of Messianic Jews like Ben who are zealously striving to fulfill the Torah on account of their faith in Yeshua, it will be clear to all that God is working in our midst. We cannot truly fulfill our destiny as the Messianic remnant of Israel nor experience the End Times revival spoken of by Scripture if our faith in Yeshua does not lead us back to greater covenant faithfulness. Each of us must become a Messianic Jewish disciple who lives out Yeshua's words: "If you continue in My word, then you are truly disciples of Mine" (John 8:31). By returning to Torah we powerfully testify to the reality and power of Yeshua, the one who will ultimately bring about large-scale prophetic renewal in and through our movement.

Hoping for the Messianic Redemption: *Tzipita L'yeshua*

The fourth sign of revival is an increased hope and longing for the Messianic redemption—*tzipita l'yeshua*. The purpose of prophecy and prophetic events is to transform us in the present and prepare us for the Messiah's coming. Prophecy and prophetic events are meant to foster our transformation to prepare us for Messiah's return. God's vision for the future is our blue print for life in the present. If we desire to be biblical, our view of revival must focus upon both personal and global change, not on End Times prophetic events. As Peter states, "You ought to live holy and godly lives, waiting for and hastening the coming day of God" (2 Pet. 3:11-12). By focusing upon End Times scenarios and by marrying prophecy to current events, we miss the transforming power of *tzipita l'yeshua* and prophetic renewal.

The opening chapter of Acts highlights this connection for us:

> When they had come together, they asked him [Yeshua] saying, "Will you restore the kingdom to Israel at this time?" He answered and said, "It is not for you to know the time or seasons which the Father has put in His own authority. But you shall receive power when the Holy Spirit comes upon you; and you

> shall be witness to Me in Jerusalem, and in Judea, and Samaria, and to the ends of the earth." (Acts 1:6-8)

Yeshua draws his disciples' attention away from speculation about Israel's prophetic fulfillment. Instead, He calls his *talmidim* to work on building the Kingdom of God in the here and now. This passage also clearly associates their longing for the Messianic redemption with Yeshua's promise of God's empowering Spirit. When we labor in the present we begin to experience the prophetic renewal of the Kingdom now.

Luke 2:25-28 further underscores the connection between longing for the Messianic redemption and the work of God's renewing Spirit:

> Now there was a man in Jerusalem called Simeon, who was righteous and devout. He was waiting for the consolation of Israel, and the Holy Spirit was upon him. It had been revealed to him by the Holy Spirit that he would not die before he had seen the Lord's Messiah. Moved by the Spirit, he went into the temple courts. When the parents brought in the child *Yeshua* to do for him what the custom of the Law required, Simeon took him in his arms and praised God.

True biblical renewal is always accompanied by a heightened love for Messiah and a desire for the consummation of all things. By corporately longing for the Messianic redemption, like Simeon and the early Messianic community, we will not only experience a greater work of the Spirit in our midst, but also provide clear evidence that authentic renewal is occurring among us.

By cultivating this type of longing for Messiah and the final redemption, we will transform and inspire a younger generation to sacrificially serve *Yeshua*. Our Movement should always be marked by a contagious zeal for the Messianic redemption. When we celebrate Shabbat in our home, we often sing a *niggun*, a wordless melody, to which we add the following lyrics, "We want Mashiach, send us Mashiach, we want Yeshua right now!" When Messiah comes He will bring the fullness of revival. In the mean time, however, we must strive to make this prophetic vision of the future a present reality in accordance with the expectation of the Prophets.

Conclusion

Would you please take a moment to dream with me? Imagine the day when thousands of young Messianic Jewish leaders are faithfully serving Messiah as they longingly await the Messianic redemption. Imagine the day when we will be of one heart and one mind in Messiah. Imagine the day when Messianic Jews of various stripes will stand together in Jerusalem and raise their collective voices in prayerful thanks to the Lord. Imagine the day when we will unite in order to build something beautiful for future generations. Imagine of the day all Israel will recognize that the Messianic Jewish movement is the result of a prophetic move of the Spirit of God. Imagine the day when all Israel will recognize that *Yeshua* is *Melech HaMashiach*

If we as a body of leaders commit to living out these biblical signs of the End Time renewal promised by the Prophets, it will change the very course of our future. God's revelation in Scripture ends with a prayer; let it be our prayer as well, "*Bo na Ha-Adon Yeshua*! Come Lord Yeshua!" (Rev. 22:20).

ENDNOTES

1. Elliott Abrams, *Faith or Fear* (New York: Free Press, 1997), 128.
2. Ariela Keysar and Barry Kosmin, "*Researching Findings on the Impact of Camp Ramah*" (New York: The Jewish Theological Seminary, 2004),. 20.

Printed in the United States
by Baker & Taylor Publisher Services